MAKING A DIFFERENCE IN URBAN SCHOOLS

Ideas, Politics, and Pedagogy

Making a Difference in Urban Schools looks at the efforts of educational reformers in two Canadian cities, Toronto and Winnipeg, over the past fifty years. While different demographics, institutional structures, cultures, and politics in the respective cities resulted in different approaches, reformers in both cities faced common issues and dilemmas in their attempts to improve educational outcomes. The reformers, who included elected trustees, administrators in district leadership roles, teachers, and community activists, were concerned about low student achievement in disadvantaged urban schools and about poverty concentrated in urban areas. Individually and collectively they worked to address the implications of high inequality and diversity by changing school operations, curriculum, pedagogical methods, and school-community relationships.

Jane Gaskell and Ben Levin focus on the political contexts that initiate, sustain, block, and change efforts for school reform. After presenting an overview of urban education in Canada and internationally, the authors provide historical accounts of developments in Winnipeg and Toronto, and introduce some of the key actors and events through a series of case studies and interviews. Later chapters look at the role of ideas and research and the politics around education reform in both districts. The book concludes with an examination of ways in which reformers have tried to affect teaching and learning in classrooms, with an eye to determining which factors ultimately make a difference to students, and advocates for new strategies and policy reforms that will help educators and policy makers promote greater equity within urban school districts.

JANE GASKELL is a professor in the Department of Theory and Policy Studies in Education and former dean of the Ontario Institute for Studies in Education, University of Toronto.

BEN LEVIN is Canada Research Chair in Education Leadership and Policy and a professor in the Department of Theory and Policy Studies in Education at the Ontario Institute for Studies in Education, University of Toronto.

Making a Difference in Urban Schools

Ideas, Politics, and Pedagogy

JANE GASKELL AND BEN LEVIN

UNIVERSITY OF TORONTO PRESS
Toronto Buffalo London

ISBN 978-0-8020-9872-6 (cloth)
ISBN 978-0-8020-9581-7 (paper)

Library and Archives Canada Cataloguing in Publication

Gaskell, Jane S. (Jane Stobo)
Making a difference in urban schools : ideas, politics and pedagogy / Jane
Gaskell and Ben Levin.

Includes bibliographical references and index.
ISBN 978-0-8020-9872-6 (bound). ISBN 978-0-8020-9581-7 (pbk.)

1. Education, Urban – Canada – Case studies.   2. Poor children –
Education – Canada – Case studies.   3. Children with social disabilities –
Education – Canada – Case studies.   I. Levin, Ben   II. Title.

LC5134.G38 2012   370.9173′2   C2012-901582-2

University of Toronto Press acknowledges the financial assistance to its
publishing program of the Canada Council for the Arts and the Ontario
Arts Council.

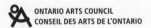

University of Toronto Press acknowledges the financial support of the
Government of Canada through the Canada Book Fund for its publishing
activities.

To all those who have worked for better education for
children and families in Canada.

Contents

MAKING A DIFFERENCE IN URBAN SCHOOLS

Ideas, Politics, and Pedagogy

Introduction

A campaign to improve education in Canada's poorest urban areas began towards the end of the 1960s. Reformers, who included elected trustees, administrators in district leadership roles, teachers, and community activists, were responding to the fact that student achievement was and remains significantly lower in urban schools with high levels of disadvantage and that poverty was and remains largely concentrated in urban areas. They worked to address the educational implications of increasing levels of inequality and diversity by changing what was taught, how it was taught, and how the school system related to the broader community. *Making a Difference in Urban Schools: Ideas, Politics, and Pedagogy* focuses on the efforts of these reformers in two Canadian cities: Toronto and Winnipeg. While different demographics, institutional structures, cultures, and politics in each city resulted in different approaches, reformers in both faced common issues and dilemmas as they attempted to transform education for the better.

More than thirty years later, the achievement gaps between poor urban schools and provincial or national averages remain large nearly everywhere. In late 2008, Ontario's Commission on the Roots of Youth Violence (McMurtry & Curling, 2008) reported on the challenges involved in improving poor urban schools and noted the lack of progress over time. Contemporary Canadian policy ideas around inner-city education are remarkably similar to the ideas – and in many cases the programs and practices – of three decades ago. Once again there are calls for revised curricula, more effective teaching, greater parent engagement, family centres, social services integrated in schools, youth workers, and outreach to various communities. Which raises the question of what, if anything, has been accomplished in the last several decades. Why do the problems of urban schools seem so unchanged despite so much effort? What can be done to improve the situation? In recounting and analysing the reform efforts in Winnipeg and Toronto, we hope to shed light on the problems of urban education, particularly in Canada, but also around the world.

We started this research with the intent of studying how urban school districts in Canada have addressed issues of poverty over the last thirty years. Having spent our careers in education in large urban centres, we were both aware of the effect of poverty on educational outcomes, and of the challenges faced by urban school districts trying to provide effective and engaging education. We wanted to examine these efforts in two districts, Vancouver (where Gaskell was living) and Winnipeg (where Levin was living), through analysing documents and interviews with key participants. In 2003, we received a research grant from the Social Sciences and Humanities Research Council of Canada for the study. We thank the Council for its support, without which this project would never have happened.

A research project is always a journey, and usually one that has some unexpected turns. This study changed course for a number of reasons, related both to our careers and to the findings emerging from the data. Within months of receiving the grant, Gaskell was appointed dean of the Ontario Institute for Studies in Education (OISE) and moved to Toronto, so we switched the Vancouver case study to Toronto, which also has a long and rich history of urban education and poverty. Then Levin accepted a Canada Research Chair at OISE, to start in 2005. Before that appointment began, he received a leave of absence to serve as the deputy minister of education in Ontario. By that time most, but not all, of the Winnipeg research, interviews, and document analysis had been completed.

Having both investigators holding major administrative roles delayed the progress of the research substantially. However, when Levin took up his academic post at OISE in early 2007, the data gathering was substantially completed. We then began the process of data analysis, working with several graduate students – Amanda-Mae Cooper, Kelly Gallagher-Mackay, Kalyan Horner, Laura-Lee Kearns, Jennifer Lawson, Antum Panjwani, Katina Pollock, and Sobia Shaikh – to review the fifty interviews and thousands of pages of documents we had put together. This book has taken longer to complete than we had hoped; we thank the University of Toronto Press for its patience.

One of the challenges in any social science research is to look honestly at the extent to which the data support the researchers' initial ideas. Although we started with a focus on the way these urban school districts had addressed poverty, as we worked through our data, we realized that we had to tell a broader story. First, efforts to address poverty in the late 1960s and early 1970s were only one part of a broader effort to change schools and school systems, led by reformers who had a radical agenda for public education. The reformers were trying to reshape schools broadly, changing not only how they responded to poverty but also how they were organized and governed. The schools' failure to ensure the success of children from poor homes was connected to curriculum, governance, financing, and political relationships. Focusing our analysis narrowly on poverty would not give a full picture of what was happening, and would ignore the data we had gathered on the connections among different kinds of reform efforts.

Second, during much of this period, school boards were in their heyday, reflecting Canada's strong commitment to local governance and community activism. The Winnipeg and Toronto boards each had a high degree of autonomy to shape policy, budget, and teaching. That is why reformers were largely concerned with the school district as the locus of reform, especially in Ontario. The initial burst of effort occurred in an era when education policy was focused on realizing the potential of students in their local communities, rather than on ensuring Canada's competitive advantage in a global economy. It was before international testing and the ranking of student achievement across systems. Looking at system reform helped us focus on the role of school boards, which is how we framed our study.

We also realized that the dynamics of each district were affected by demographic changes that went well beyond variations in income levels. The increase in visible minority immigrants in Toronto and Aboriginal students in Winnipeg shaped the way that education reformers in each city thought about their roles. Some immigrant groups, especially certain visible minorities, were experiencing worse outcomes than in previous generations. Education outcomes for Aboriginal students lagged badly behind those of non-Aboriginal students. There is a strong connection between visible minority or Aboriginal status and poverty, but issues of identity, language, and racism have their own dynamics and are not fully subsumed by a focus on poverty.

We decided, therefore, to recast our analysis and this book more broadly. Instead of focusing on the response to poverty, we discuss reform efforts in Winnipeg and Toronto from the late-1960s to the mid-1990s, with a particular interest in how the school boards tried to address students who were perceived to be disadvantaged and underachieving. In Toronto, the demise of the former Toronto Board of Education, with its amalgamation into the Toronto District School Board in 1997, marks an end point. There is no similar demarcation in Winnipeg, so that story continues a little further.

We have both been interested in this story for many years, and have devoted much of our careers to studying and working on issues of equity and disadvantage. This interest is driven by our shared concern about the negative effects of inequality on Canadian society. We believe that everyone in Canada ought to participate in the many benefits that living in this country confers, and that it is a violation of human rights for children to grow up without them. We believe that high levels of inequality in education and income – and in related areas such as employment, housing, and health – are inconsistent with the kind of country most Canadians want to have. We are convinced by the evidence we discuss in chapter 1 that links greater equity with better economic and social outcomes. Many people believe that education is one of the key paths to reducing inequality. Education is not the only way to address inequalities; if anything, its role may be overestimated in contrast with factors such as employment, taxation, and housing policies. Still, better educational outcomes are clearly associated with better individual and societal outcomes, and so improved schooling must be one part of the efforts towards greater equity.

These commitments have marked our careers and biographies. We are both children of the 1960s, a period of great optimism and energy. In Winnipeg, Levin was an active participant in some of the events described in this book as a high school student 'radical,' as a very young elected school trustee, and later as a senior civil servant working on education policy. He knew many of the people interviewed for this book, watched many of the events unfold, and participated in some of them.

Although Gaskell grew up in Toronto, she spent most of her career in Vancouver and observed events in the Toronto Board of Education from a distance. But her scholarship has been marked by engagement with social movements and activism around equity. As a graduate student in education, she was introduced to debates about equality through heated discussion of the Coleman report (Coleman, 1966). Her scholarship has continued in this vein, examining the way feminism, multiculturalism, local community politics, and economic opportunities affect schooling.

Although we began this project out of social and political conviction, we have tried to conduct the research and write this book in an analytic and balanced way. Gaskell is a sociologist by training and inclination; Levin's first degree was in history. Our disciplinary backgrounds help us explore the diverse but deeply held views people bring to public issues such as education, as well as the limits of any perspective and the constraints involved in dealing with complex contemporary social problems. In our view, the study of social history should deepen our understanding of our work, increase our desire for improvement, and generate ideas about how to achieve that improvement.

This book explores two districts in a way that we hope is accessible to a broad audience and of interest to a wide variety of people engaged in educational arguments. The technical methodological details are in our appendix. Debates about education can benefit from evidence from well-contextualized stories about school reform. People often draw their views from another single person's experience, such as that of a child in school, or a friend or partner who is a teacher. Local policy and practice are often shaped by the personal experience of a principal or a superintendent or a trustee. Statistical or research-based evidence can play an important role, as it did in Toronto and Winnipeg. But research has an impact only when it connects to a narrative about what it means – what former Ontario education minister Gerard Kennedy calls a 'storyline.'

The Canadian debate is often influenced by the United States, even though the educational contexts in question are very different. In education, as in many areas, it is important for Canadians to know their own stories. We believe that the histories of these two districts can contribute to that understanding, though readers may disagree about the lessons that should be derived from them.

As we studied the efforts to reform and improve education in the two cities, and particularly as we reviewed the documents and interviews, we were struck by the passion and commitment of our subjects. The people we interviewed, whether they were elected to office or career educators or community activists, contributed a great deal to public education, including seemingly endless amounts of time and energy, often for small recompense. Their work was never as successful as they wanted and, given the grand scope of their ambitions, probably never could be.

Clarence Stone and colleagues (1998, 2001) point out that multiple factors have to come together and stay together for a city to make progress in education. Such progress is extraordinarily difficult work. Our respondents discussed the contradictions, challenges, tensions, and compromises that are necessarily part of public policy and public institutions, along with the idealism, energy, and optimism.

Although larger social, economic, and political trends and forces shaped what happened in these two cities, so did particular people and circumstances. In any setting, the impersonal forces of history, sociology, and economics are expressed by particular individuals with specific biographies. The ideas, preferences, styles, and choices of those individuals can have important impacts on their organizations. The collision of particular people with larger circumstances is one of the fascinating elements of these stories.

In this book, we intend to have those voices come through, which is why we give so much room to the words of our respondents. Accounts of research necessarily impose an order on what was found but, to the extent that any researcher can, we want to display the debates and decisions in their complexity. We illustrate the ways the reformers thought, the actions they took, and the reasons behind those actions as well as the constraints they faced.

Of course, our approach has its limitations. Although we talked to some fifty people, they were a small sample from the hundreds who played important roles in these events, and the thousands who were participants in one way or another. Our interviews, which lasted one to two hours, were mainly with people involved in the reform agenda, and we do not represent all views equally. We also spoke to people many years after some of the events in question, and thus rely on memories that may be faulty or incomplete. While we do not claim to provide a complete history, we do provide a picture of events and approaches – one we hope will stimulate more work on urban educational politics in Canada.

If we have been successful, the reader will have some of the same impressions we had when doing this research: respect and admiration for the efforts of so many people, recognition that there are multiple legitimate perspectives on the problems of urban education, and an understanding that improving education in Canada's cities is possible, but requires a combination of sustained effort and the right circumstances. We hope that these stories inspire the next generation of advocates for better urban education.

   The book is organized as follows. Chapter 1 discusses urban education and its challenges in Canada and internationally; sets the context in which these events unfolded; and reviews the literature on urban educational reform in other jurisdictions. The following two chapters are chronological accounts of major events and developments in each city – Winnipeg in chapter 2, and Toronto in chapter 3. They introduce some of the key actors and recount some of the most salient events, providing the historical scaffolding on which later chapters build. The next three chapters take up the central themes in our analysis: ideas, politics, and pedagogy. Chapter 4 looks at the role of ideas and research, and explores how ideas about education were important in motivating and sustaining change and how research was organized to provide evidence and inform public opinion. Chapter 5 examines the politics around education reform in both districts, looking at school boards as political sites in which elections, institutional traditions, and public servants shape what can be achieved. Chapter 6 looks at the ways that reformers tried to affect teaching and learning in classrooms – the factors that ultimately make a difference to students. Chapter 7 provides a conclusion and suggestions for what might happen next to improve education in Canada's cities.

   Finally, a word about language. In equity discussions, there is considerable debate around the terms people are called or call themselves. We have tried to respect current conventions on terminology, but in the interests of readability have also used somewhat colloquial language. We use a number of terms interchangeably, such as 'poverty' and 'disadvantage.' We also use urban education and inner-city education as substitutes throughout the book, although in Toronto today disadvantage is concentrated outside of the city's core.

1 Setting the Stage: Poverty, Diversity, and Urban Education

The events that took place in Toronto and Winnipeg schools in the last thirty years of the twentieth century were part of, and deeply influenced by, changes in the larger social, economic, and political environment. In this chapter, we contextualize these events by discussing the challenges of poverty and diversity for urban education broadly, both nationally and internationally, and by reviewing some of the academic literature that has influenced our thinking.

High poverty levels and increasing demographic diversity create challenges for all large urban school districts, and these challenges became more acute between the late 1960s and mid-1990s. Both poverty and diversity increased in Toronto and Winnipeg, and reviewing these trends reveals the ways in which they are linked to unequal educational opportunities.

Ideas about equity in education also changed over the period we are discussing. In the 1950s, it was accepted that only a small number of students would succeed in university or even high school, but we now expect higher results for many more students. This has made it more pressing for educators to address the links between poverty, diversity, and educational outcomes. It has also produced a rethinking of what equal educational opportunity means, and has led to attempts in many parts of the world to create policies to increase equal opportunities for students.

In this context, there has been a growing amount of literature on strategies to improve urban education in selected countries around the world. Despite the large quantity of literature, particularly in the United States, most research focuses on practices in individual schools or achievements in particular programs. Although, as we argue later, improving teaching and learning is a vital and underappreciated issue, we make limited reference to work that discusses the effectiveness of specific teaching and learning practices or tells the story of particular programs, people, schools, or initiatives. Instead, we focus on how urban education systems over time have understood and responded to the challenges they face.

While the literature from other countries is important, contextual, cultural, and institutional frameworks limit its applicability to specific places, including Canada. There is not enough history, analysis, and story-telling about Canadian schools; the U.S. literature tends to dominate the educational reading lists of both universities and politicians, and today U.S. educational policy is moving in directions that are quite different from Canada's. While other cases can highlight important themes and discussions, Canadian schools are funded, governed, and discussed in distinctive ways that require their own analysis and can inform other jurisdictions.

Demographic Challenge and Change

The literature on the two main challenges for urban education – poverty and ethnic diversity – is enormous. Both poverty and ethnic diversity have increased in urban settings over the past fifty years, and both correlate to educational outcomes in different ways. If the increasing numbers of children from disadvantaged families and non-dominant cultures are going to succeed in school, educational systems must take account of their environment and change to meet their needs.

A substantial academic literature documents many ways in which poverty and diversity complicate the work of schools (Thrupp, 1999; Raffo et al., 2009). Children who live in poverty and do not share the dominant culture and language may attend school with fewer of the skills, behaviours, or understandings that teachers expect them to have. They may have more health problems and less access to material supports such as books or study space. They are more likely to move, and thus change schools more often. Their parents may be less able to help them or to advocate effectively on their behalf. Poverty and diversity also affect how schools, teachers, and administrators work. Teachers may hold lower expectations for students' achievement, and offer less challenging instruction as a result. They may struggle to provide engaging learning experiences, and may stream students into separate groups in order to teach them more easily. Timetables and curriculum may change to respond to the perceived needs and destinations of students. The time spent on behaviour, counselling, and community liaison may increase, while instructional time decreases. None of this happens in all schools or families; the data, however, make it clear that all of these processes take place, with the result that schools are less effective at educating students who come from disadvantaged and ethnically diverse backgrounds.

Poverty

Socio-economic status (SES) is the single most powerful factor correlated with educational and other life outcomes, as has been found in virtually every important study of these issues, over time, in every country where such studies have been conducted. The power of this association is repeated in many different reports, books, and articles, as the following quotations and paraphrasing illustrate. But the meaning and causes of this association can be interpreted in many different ways, as these quotations also illustrate.

> Parental income is positively correlated with virtually every dimension of child well-being that social scientists measure, and this is true in every country for which we have data. The children of rich parents are healthier, better behaved, happier and better educated during their childhood and wealthier when they have grown up. (Mayer, 2002, p. 30)

> For over 50 years, findings on the relationship between income and academic competence has accumulated ... data have continued to mount linking poverty with lower levels of school achievement ... There is substantial evidence that poverty is associated with less optimal outcomes in every area of functioning. (Bradley & Whiteside-Mansell, 1997, pp. 21–2)

> In most [Organization for Economic Cooperation and Development (OECD)] countries children from poorer homes are between three and four times more likely to be in the lowest scoring group in mathematics at age 15. (OECD, 2007b, p. 11)

> On the PIRLS [international literacy study], United States schools with less than 10% of the students eligible for free school meals [a poverty indicator] scored on average a full standard deviation higher than schools with 75% or more of students eligible. (Bracey, 2003, p. 795)

Deprivation can have a large and pervasive impact on educational attain-ment . . . on average, even those children from lower socio-economic groups performing well initially (at 22 months) were overtaken by others by the time they started primary school. These early differences were . . . found to be strongly associated with inequalities in educational outcomes in later life . . . Low income has an independent effect on children's educational outcomes after controlling for measures of family background and child ability. (Department of Children, Schools, and Families, 2009, p. 6)

There is clearly a relationship between SES and a wide range of social out-comes, which are evident at birth and persist throughout the life cycle. On average, across 23 Canadian communities . . . a child of low SES . . . would have an expected score [in receptive vocabulary] that was about 9 points lower than a high SES child . . . This is a large difference . . . that could have a substantial effect on children's skills upon entry to school. (Willms, 2003, p. 29)

The conclusions – regarding a strong relationship between family SES, particularly parental education and family status and young adults' edu-cational attainments – are remarkably robust. (Curtis, 2007, p. 42)

SES is a very important determinant of a wide range of social and psycho-logical functioning. These data are consistent with the possibility that SES may affect school achievement regardless of what families do to modify the conditions of learning within the home. In fact, the effects of SES are pervasive. (Ryan & Adams, 1999)

Poverty is not easy to measure. Osberg (2008) notes the many differ-ent views that have been argued in the Canadian discussion about how to measure poverty, while Bradley and Whiteside-Mansell (1997) pro-vide a thorough discussion from a child development perspective in an international context. Different measures of poverty reflect different assumptions, and each results in a different statistic that can be used to support or attack particular policy positions or proposals (OECD, 2006). The most widely adopted poverty measures in wealthier countries are relative rather than absolute, which reflects the view that poverty is a relational concept, measuring the ability to participate in a particular society at a particular time (UNICEF, 2007).

While the proportions of a population or of children living below a defined poverty line are most often reported, other dimensions of poverty are also important. These include the level of poverty (under any definition some people have less than others who are also considered poor), its duration (many families are poor for a relatively short time but others are poor for many years and over generations), and its geographical concentration (when entire neighbourhoods are poor, there are implications for the available services, including schools). Today, about one in eight Canadian children lives in a family below the low-income cut off after social transfers (Campaign 2000, 2009). These families have inadequate income, no wealth, and very little social or cultural capital. They often experience food shortages. They have low levels of formal education and about two-thirds of them have been poor for a long time and have little prospect of improving the situation (Phipps & Lethbridge, 2006). Children in families facing long-term poverty often have 'much worse outcomes than other children' (p. 22).

The increase in income inequality in Canada in recent years has contributed to the high poverty rate. The Gini coefficient, a standard measure of income inequality, increased from .38 in 1980 to .42 in 2005, where 0 is perfect equality and 1 is complete inequality. Osberg (2008) shows that the proportion of total income received by the bottom 20 per cent of Canadians peaked at 4.6 per cent in 1981 and has declined since, while the proportion taken by the top 20 per cent has grown from 41.6 per cent in 1981 to 46.9 per cent in 2005. Almost all the gain in incomes since 1996 has been among high-income individuals and families. In particular, 'incomes at the very top of the Canadian income distribution have risen dramatically' (Osberg, 2008, p. 8). Inequality in Canada between 1995 and 2005 rose more rapidly than in any other country in the OECD except Germany. This differs from the pattern prior to 1980, in which real incomes rose among all segments of the Canadian population.

In 2004, 17.7 per cent of Canadian children were in low-income families – compared to 15.1 per cent in 1989, the year Parliament pledged to end child poverty. Canada-wide statistics are similar to those in cities. In 2004, Winnipeg reported a child poverty rate of 17.5 per cent and Toronto reported 16.6 per cent (Canadian Council for Social Development, n.d.). Food bank use has increased, reaching more than 700,000 people in 2008 (Food Banks Canada, 2009). Moreover, the new poverty is concentrated in families with young children, whereas seniors, who used to be poor in large numbers, now have reduced poverty levels. Data reviewed more fully in later chapters show that poverty became deeper and more concentrated in both cities between the late 1960s and late 1990s. Osberg's (1981) metaphor of income distribution is helpful: if the world's population were a parade one hour long with people's height proportionate to their income and everyone in ascending order by height, it would take nearly fifty minutes before people of average height appeared, but the last few people in the parade would be hundreds or thousands of feet tall.

Wealth is distributed even more unequally than income. The top 20 per cent of Canadians in 1984 owned nearly 70 per cent of all assets (such as housing, stocks, and bonds), while the middle 60 per cent owned about 6 per cent of all assets, and the bottom 20 per cent had negative wealth as their debts were greater than their assets (Stanford, 2001). Osberg (2008) estimates that the Gini index for wealth increased from .69 in 1984 to .75 in 2005. During that period, the wealth of the bottom 40 per cent of Canadian families decreased, while the median worth of the top 10 per cent grew to nearly $1.25 million.

Family income remains the most common measure of poverty and socio-economic status, but it has long been recognized that income is not the only measure of hardship faced by individuals and families, and is not necessarily the best prediction of educational or health outcomes (Mayer, 1997). Poverty can be not just economic, but cultural, intellectual, physical, and emotional. The effects of poverty are mediated by factors such as parental education and attitudes, neighbourhood status, support networks, or family structure (Bradley & Mansell-Whiteside, 1997; Sirin, 2005). That is why some analysts argue that family income is a less important measure than parental education or parenting practices (Willms, 2002). In its Program for International Student Assessment (PISA) studies, the OECD uses measures of 'cultural capital,' including the presence of certain material possessions in the home, such as books of poetry, dictionaries, an Internet connection, and number of televisions or cars, to measure socioeconomic status (OECD, 2007a).

International evidence shows that poverty levels are amenable to policy measures in areas such as income supports, housing, childcare, and other government policies (Micklewright, 2003). In a recent OECD comparison, Canada ranked eighteenth in income inequality among thirty countries – less unequal than the United Kingdom and the United States but more than most of Western Europe, Australia, and South Korea (OECD, 2008). International inequality has worsened in recent years, in part because of reductions in social programs. The main policies reducing inequality are transfer payments such as pensions, child benefits, and unemployment insurance, along with reasonable wage rates. Wages are especially important because poverty is not primarily the result of unemployment; most poor families have at least one full-time, year-round wage earner.

Over the last twenty years, the welfare state has been under attack; cutbacks in government programs have increased inequality in Canada and exacerbated the extent and depth of poverty (Osberg, 2008). The decline in the Canadian social safety net in the 1990s involved falling real welfare rates, decline in the real value of the minimum wage, cuts in employment insurance, and the virtual disappearance of social housing, among other changes. This increased inequality, especially in earned incomes; incomes are less unequal after taking the effect of taxes and social transfers such as pensions or employment insurance into account (National Council of Welfare, 2006).

Inequalities in education are generally smaller than overall inequalities in society, which suggests that school systems have some positive effect on equality of outcomes (Levin, 2003). Evidence from PISA (OECD, 2007a) shows that the link between inequality and educational outcomes varies across countries, and that steps can be taken to lessen this relationship. Some countries, Canada among them, are able to maintain both relatively high levels of educational attainment and relatively small levels of inequality; there is no necessary trade-off between equity and excellence in education.

Although poverty remains a powerful predictor of life outcomes, it is not an absolute determinant. Growing up poor vastly increases the chance of having negative life circumstances, but a large proportion of children who grow up in poverty are able to construct successful lives for themselves. Social scientists have been interested in what factors might account for these variable outcomes, and a large literature has emerged in social psychology around 'resilience,' or the capacity of individuals to overcome highly adverse circumstances (Masten, 2001; Ungar, 2007), and in sociology around 'social capital,' or the networks that allow communities to work together to respond productively to the challenges they face (Jenson, 1998; Woolcock, 1998; Putnam, 2000; Policy Research Initiative, 2005). Schools can promote resilience and social capital, and can also change the teaching and learning conditions in classrooms to be more effective for students from low-income families. How the Toronto and Winnipeg school systems managed to move in these directions is the subject of our inquiry.

Diversity

The second key demographic factor affecting urban education in Canada is the increasing number of visible minorities, linguistic groups, and Aboriginal people in cities. The connection between population diversity, poverty, and school success is more complex than that between poverty and school success, but there are clear patterns of failure for some groups of students with Aboriginal and recent immigrant heritage. Schools have been challenged with successfully educating students with diverse cultural, linguistic, and racial backgrounds.

Immigrant and Aboriginal status is linked to poverty. There is a strong connection between ethnic identity and poverty, with some groups, including Aboriginal people, much more likely to live in poverty than the Canadian mainstream. Rothman (2007) notes that 40 per cent of Aboriginal children and nearly half of the children of recent immigrants are in the low-income category. Ornstein, reviewing the status of immigrants in Toronto from 1971 to 2001, concluded that 'the experience of extreme disadvantage is highly racialized. Every one of the twenty poorest ethnoracial groups is non-European' (2006, p. 80). The same factors that lead to deficient school outcomes, including overt and covert discrimination, also lead to less adequate employment, lower incomes, and other negative consequences. Each can have an independent negative effect on outcomes, but the conflation of poverty and diversity creates a double jeopardy for many young people.

There is also a link between immigrant or Aboriginal status and school achievement, although on the whole, Canadian immigrants have relatively good educational outcomes. In the OECD's PISA studies, Canada and Australia are the only two countries that show equal outcomes for students who are recent immigrants compared with those who are native born (OECD, 2007b). In most of Europe, immigrant students perform substantially less well than native-born students. The differences at least partly reflect differences in immigration policies: Canada gives preference to those to who are well-educated, while other jurisdictions give preference to labour market needs in less skilled areas.

However, the overall success story in Canada disguises some serious problems. Immigrants to Canada are often highly educated, which would suggest that their children should do well in school. But children from some immigrant groups consistently have poorer school outcomes than other groups, even though there are no discernable differences in their parents' education levels or the length of time they have lived in Canada. Those who do less well tend to be 'racialized,' i.e., identified by others by their race. For example, black youth tend to be suspended more, held back more, and are more likely to be placed in special education, and less likely to graduate compared to others with similar backgrounds (Ontario Human Rights Commission, 2004). Not all visible minority populations experience the same problems; some, such as people of Chinese or Korean descent, have had more success in obtaining both education and income. Among some immigrant groups who are not visibly minorities, such as the Portuguese, economic disadvantage and worse educational outcomes extend to children born in Canada and even to a third generation. The Ontario Commission on the Roots of Youth Violence (McMurtry & Curling, 2008) discussed such differences, based on the thorough review of research it commissioned:

> The worst impacts are being felt in neighbourhoods that are often already isolated from the rest of the community because of the circumstances of poverty. What is particularly disturbing is that many of these communities are largely composed of members of racialized groups ... racism and other barriers have concentrated poverty in these groups, and ... the housing market has then driven them into concentrations of those who suffer from high levels of poverty.

When poverty is racialized and concentrated geographically, the potential for stigmatizing specific groups is high. That stigmatization can, in turn, further reduce opportunities for those groups. If these trends and impacts continue to grow and the conditions that give rise to them are not addressed, the prognosis for the neighbourhoods and for the future of Ontario could be grim (2008, p. 4).

Many Canadians, including many members of minority groups, believe that discrimination based on ethnicity seldom occurs in Canada. Yet the evidence strongly suggests otherwise. Poorer outcomes in education and the labour market persist for black male and Aboriginal youth, even when studies control for prior achievement and other factors. This is why, in 2005, the Supreme Court of Canada stated that 'racial prejudice against visible minorities is ... notorious and indisputable ... [it is] a social fact not capable of reasonable dispute' (R. v. Spence, 2005).

Canada has been populated by waves of immigrants from different countries of origin. Aboriginal inhabitants were subjugated and outnumbered by European immigrants in the seventeenth century. Today, the proportion of Aboriginal Canadians is about 4 per cent, while the proportion of Canada's population that is foreign-born has reached more than 18 per cent, its highest level in seventy years. From the seventeenth century until the 1960s, most immigrants to Canada were white Europeans. After Canada's immigration policy changed in the 1960s to emphasize education, skill, and family ties, the immigrant population became mostly visible minorities from Asia, Africa, Latin America, and the Caribbean. In 1971, more than 70 per cent of Canadian immigrants were from Europe or the United States. In 2001, nearly 80 per cent were from Asia, Africa, Latin America, and the Caribbean, with nearly 60 per cent from Asia.

Immigrants have always struggled to find a place in Canada. Generations of immigrants have taken on relatively low-paid work, lived in substandard housing, but gradually made their way into the mainstream. Newer immigrants to Canada, despite their higher educational levels, are less successful in achieving good jobs and incomes than previous immigrant groups (Galabuzi 2005; Omidvar & Richmond 2005). According to Galabuzi,

> as the flow of immigration has shifted from European sources to Asian, African, Middle Eastern, Latin American and Caribbean sources, the normal processes of integration have began to falter for too many immigrants. National data show that immigrants arriving since 1980, are disproportionately stuck at the bottom of the economic ladder, in terms of income, employment, access to high-paying sectors and jobs and employment status. (2005, p. 53)

Aboriginal Canadians, including Indians, Métis, and Inuit, continue to have worse education, health, employment, and other life outcomes than do other Canadians. They have lower levels of income and education, which are compounded by the history of government- and church-run residential schools with assimilationist goals. The single parent population is much higher among Aboriginal people and the population is significantly younger. The proportion of Aboriginal youth aged fifteen to twenty-four who are not attending school is also higher.

Unlike poverty, diversity is centred in urban areas. The bulk of Canada's immigrants settle in cities, especially Toronto, Montreal, Vancouver, and their metropolitan regions. According to the 2001 census, Toronto's foreign-born population was 44 per cent and rising rapidly. Winnipeg's population was about 16 per cent foreign-born in 2001, a slight decline from 1991. Aboriginal Canadians have also increasingly moved to cities from the reserves, a trend that is particularly significant in major cities in Western Canada. Winnipeg has the highest number of people reporting Aboriginal ethnic origin in the 2001 census, at more than 62,000 or 10 per cent of the total population (very similar to Saskatoon and Regina). In Toronto, that proportion is lower than 1 per cent (Jantzen, 2004).

Urban cultural, linguistic, and racial diversity can produce global awareness, economic prosperity, and social vitality. Schools have a critical role in such outcomes, and in reducing the possibility of misunderstandings, discrimination, and violence. Our study took place as diversity increased in Toronto and Winnipeg, and our focus is on what we can learn about how they responded to these new challenges.

The Changing Meaning of Equity

Ideas influence the way people approach social issues, whether they define them as problems, as inevitable or as the way things should be. Whether connections between social position and school success are a problem or not, and how strongly educational policy should address those connections, has been a matter of much debate. Discussions of inequality are deeply shaped by beliefs and ideological orientations. Those who see poverty as a result of poor choices (substance abuse, dropping out of school, or failing to work hard) will be sympathetic to one possible set of solutions; those who see it as the result of circumstances (job loss, marital breakdown, or disability) beyond individual control will be sympathetic to another. Those who see income inequality as an inevitable consequence of the economic and political organization of society will define it as less of a problem than those who see it as the result of deliberate economic and political choices. Those who perceive immigration and diversity as a cultural and economic asset will emphasize immigration services more heavily than those who perceive it as producing lower levels of social cohesion and higher social costs. Ideas about the causes and consequences of poverty and immigration are closely related to the kinds of social and educational policies that people will support.

As a result, the form and impact of social policies designed to reduce the impact of poverty and diversity continue to be debated vigorously, in Canada and elsewhere. Proposals range from efforts to get individuals to change their behaviour to taxation or benefit programs that try to change economic conditions. While research plays a role in shaping ideas about policy and social organization, it is rarely the most influential factor. O'Connor's (2001) conclusion about the impact of poverty research in the United States also applies to Canada:

> However impressive its data or sophisticated its models, poverty knowledge has proved unable to provide an analysis or, equally important, a convincing narrative to counter the powerful, albeit simplistic story of welfare state failure and moral decline – a narrative that, with the help of well-organized conservative analysts, has come to inform policy discourse. (p. 5)

In his discussion of research and intellectual history, O'Connor goes on to discuss the ways in which the research enterprise itself contributed to poor policy choices through its reflection of dominant ideologies and its reluctance to question the existing organization of social class, inequality, race, and gender.

In Canada, debates about poverty and diversity reflect ideological perspectives on the nature of Canadian society (Marchak, 1975). The salience of and discourse around these issues has evolved over time. It is unwise to generalize about intellectual trends over time, but the 1960s were a period of relative optimism, when it was widely believed that poverty could and should be alleviated or eliminated through government action. Governments in many countries took steps to try to reduce poverty rates (for example, Silver & Silver, 1991). In Canada, Medicare, the Canada Pension Plan, the Canada Assistance Plan, and more generous unemployment insurance were introduced in the 1960s. In 1971, the Senate issued an important report on poverty that recommended a national guaranteed minimum income, which was debated but never implemented.

The long-standing belief that immigrants and Aboriginals should be assimilated was also challenged in this period by a new appreciation of the value of diversity and difference. In 1970, the Royal Commission on the Status of Women reported that the government should take active steps to create more opportunities for women. In 1971, Prime Minister Pierre Trudeau declared Canada a multicultural country. In contrast to earlier practices, minority groups were encouraged to celebrate their heritage and maintain their language. Aboriginal cultures were slowly recognized as having their own integrity, legitimacy, and rights. When the Constitution was repatriated and reshaped in 1982, it included guarantees for the equality rights of disadvantaged groups and recognition of Aboriginal rights, which further entrenched these ideas.

There was always political tension around equity and social policies, and in the 1980s, more conservative views gained prominence. They were fuelled in part by changing economic circumstances and pressure on government finances, and in part by recognition that the grand ambitions of the 1960s were not going to be easily realized. Public spending was cut, and so was taxation, which made it difficult to restore the programs of the 1960s (Levin, 2001). Many of the anti-poverty efforts of the late 1960s and early 1970s were dismantled; minimum wages fell in real terms and social services were curtailed. Equity concerns largely disappeared from state policy agendas in many countries. In countries including the United States, Canada, and England, income inequality and child poverty grew worse, with bad results for schools as well as for society (Micklewright, 2003).

Even in these times, discussions of poverty and diversity remained lively. In 1989, the Canadian Parliament unanimously resolved to end child poverty by the year 2000, reflecting growing attention to the plight of children in poor families, and skilful lobbying by those committed to reducing it. A number of education groups, such as the Canadian Teachers' Federation (1989) and the Canadian School Boards' Association (2001), took on projects related to poverty in schools. These discussions emphasized, in particular, the status of very young children, and in 2000 Canada's federal and provincial government signed an accord committing to greater investment to assist very young children, although it was not realized.

In recent years, several groups have tried to influence the debate by providing more arguments and evidence. The National Council of Welfare, the National Anti-Poverty Organization, the Canadian Centre for Policy Analysis, and Campaign 2000, supported by academic researchers who provide much of the material on which these groups draw, have argued for more publicly-supported programs to reduce and alleviate the effects of poverty. Academic analyses have pointed to the need for action (Ungerleider, 2003; Gallagher, 2007; Gerin-Lajoie, 2008). Labour organizations, teacher unions (such as the Canadian Teachers' Federation, the British Columbia Teachers' Federation, and the Elementary Teachers' Federation of Ontario), school board organizations, and similar groups have supported these efforts. On the other hand, more conservative social policy organizations, such as C.D. Howe, the Fraser Institute, and others, have supported market-oriented policies that rely more on incentives to reduce bad choices by individuals than on publicly supported programs.

The arguments around equity today are different than they were forty years ago. They are often less centred around concerns about fundamental justice, and more connected to the requirements of successful modern economies and societies driven by growing concern about international economic competitiveness. Ideas about the importance of human capital for that competitiveness have also been changing. There is growing recognition that inequality is linked to reduced social cohesion, which is in turn linked to poorer economic growth and less ability to attract investors (Osberg, 1995; Lloyd-Ellis, 2003; Green, Preston, & Janmaat, 2006). There is evidence that countries with less inequality tend to have better economic and social outcomes (Wilkinson & Pickett, 2009), bringing together the seemingly disparate economic and social arguments for reduced inequity. But these arguments are unlikely to supplant beliefs about the importance of competition, individualism, and the dangers of big government in countries where public provision is suspect.

There is also growing international interest in globalization, as migration increases and countries look for new ways to reach minority and immigrant populations. Many countries are coping for the first time with significant populations who do not speak the national language, while other countries that have long had immigrant populations are more interested in enhancing their educational success (Joshee, 2004).

The issues that the OECD studies often serve as a barometer of changing interests in the international education policy world. In 1996, the OECD produced *Lifelong Learning for All* (OECD, 1996), a sophisticated statement about the importance of improved and more equitable educational outcomes. Over the last ten years, the OECD has given substantial attention to equity in its education policy work, including in early childhood (OECD, 2001b), adult education (OECD, 2003), and school-to-work transitions (OECD, 2000). The analysis of the results of PISA has also given prominence to equity, with countries being assessed as much on the size of their achievement gap as on their overall standing (OECD, 2001a; Sahlberg, 2006). In several countries, such as Germany and Hungary, the equity gaps identified in PISA have led to fundamentally rethinking education policies. One of the most recent contributions is the OECD report, *No More Failures* (Field, Kuczera, & Pont, 2007), which is part of a succession of analyses on improving the results of education.

Whatever the reason, there is once again recognition that large educational inequalities based on socio-economic status, language, gender, ethnicity, or immigration status are undesirable and need to be addressed. Highly educating as many people as possible has become a broadly accepted policy goal. Many human rights advocates remain uncomfortable with the economic rationale, but welcome the attention to equity issues.

Fifty years ago, only small minorities completed secondary school in most countries – smaller than the proportion now completing tertiary education. Some countries have shown very rapid increases in both secondary and tertiary completion recently. For example, Korea's secondary completion rate rose from twenty-third in the OECD to first over a twenty-year period, while post-secondary participation in Mexico has gone from 1 per cent to 26 per cent in just a few decades (OECD, 2009). Given global competition for jobs and skilled workers, many national governments and international organizations have been discussing the need to improve participation and success rates at all levels of education.

Many countries around the world have also been paying more attention to efforts to decrease inequities in educational outcomes (sometimes prioritizing them over related issues such as employment, social benefits, or housing). In U.S. education literature, there are numerous studies and reports that look at the achievement gap and assess the many different attempted strategies to reduce it. The measures used may be contentious – for example, extensive testing to demonstrate accountability has many critics – but the intent of reducing outcome disparities is generally supported.

The same focus exists in many other countries. The strategy statement for the Irish Department of Education and Science lists equity and inclusion as a priority goal. New Zealand has produced some important analyses of the power of socio-economic status (Mayer, 2002), and the country's attention to greater success for the Maori people is one of the strongest efforts in the world to respond to the educational needs of indigenous peoples, who are almost universally less successful in mainstream education systems than are majority populations. The European Union has recently issued a major report on the need for greater equity in education across its member states (European Commission, 2006).

In Australia, which has no school boards and a federal structure with more state/federal cooperation around education than in Canada, the Disadvantaged School Program was in place from 1973 to 1996. It was replaced by the Commonwealth Literacy Program, which continued to provide funding to the same schools identified by census/welfare data as having significant concentrations of low-income students, but at a lower level and with a narrower focus.

The Disadvantaged Schools Program focused on schools, rather than on children, as the unit of change (Connell, White, & Johnston, 1991; Thomson, 2007). It provided funding to the bottom tier of Australia's school-age population, regardless of school sector or location, with the goal of changing the way schools operated and improving school-community relationships. It embodied ideas of teacher research and community participation. As Thomson (2002) put it, the DSP also tried to compensate by having schools provide what families could not afford; to innovate; to provide equal opportunity; and to change outcomes dramatically. The tension – between compensation and emancipation; between changing society or achieving a better distribution of credentials; and between teacher professional development, school reform, and better infrastructure – rippled through the program throughout its lifetime, during which inequities in Australian society grew.

Equity in urban education has also been an important subject of study and policy in Britain, where poverty and minority status are also concentrated in urban areas (Barber & Dann, 1996). The English experience has not had as much impact on Canadian policy as that of the United States, and school districts (called local educational authorities, or LEAs) have not been as important in Britain as they have in the United States and Canada. In the 1980s and 1990s, individual schools were given much more autonomy at the expense of LEAs, which became relatively unimportant in the education system. Tony Blair's New Labour government was elected in 1997 with a strong commitment to improving education outcomes, especially for children in high poverty communities, and legislated England-wide approaches to reform. Seventy-three 'education action zones,' funded 75 per cent by the central government, were created between 1998 and 2000 in an attempt to integrate education with other social services addressing poor outcomes for children. The action zones eventually included approximately a third of the most disadvantaged schools in England. However, evaluations suggested that the zones did not work effectively (OfSTED, 2001, 2003a; Halpin et al., 2004) and the program was cancelled after a few years. The government then developed Excellence in Cities, a program which concentrated on smaller clusters of schools. The model was simpler, and emphasized direct provisions for students. It included elements such as investment in trained mentors; development of support for gifted and talented students in disadvantaged areas; funding for inter-school coopera- tion; and development of learning support units in secondary schools. Evaluations tended to show that the mentorship aspects of the program were the best-received and best-supported, and that the learning sup- port units were the least so (OfSTED, 2003b).

In the last few years, England has been rediscovering the importance of districts, especially in high-poverty urban areas. External inspections defined a number of LEAs as 'failing,' leading the government to invoke a 'ladder of sanctions' (Audit Commission, 2002) including government support for improving LEAs' internal capacity, partnership arrange- ments that combine internal improvement with external support, and outsourcing arrangements in which a contractor takes over the LEAs' direct responsibility for specific functions for a specified period of time (Campbell et al., 2004). The affected districts included a number of the most difficult urban areas in the country, such as Liverpool, Bristol, Leicester, and Bradford, as well as some parts of London.

The education partnership boards that were set up in a number of LEAs brought a form of co-management that included local community leaders as well as school leaders. The boards also often led to significant changes in senior management, organization of authority, relationships with schools, and approaches to improvement. They usually resulted in improvement in the follow-up inspection, although creating lasting improvement in student outcomes was, not surprisingly, more chal- lenging (Campbell et al., 2004).

In 2003, the English government set up the London Challenge to bring central leadership to the improvement of education outcomes across London's thirty-three local authorities, and especially in its most challenging areas. (Prior to 1990, the inner-London boroughs had a common education authority, but this was abolished by the Thatcher government, leaving education in the hands of each separate borough.) In 2008, the 'challenge' approach was extended to Manchester and to an area around Wolverhampton known as 'the black country.' The main goals for the challenge program in all three areas are: to decrease the number of underperforming schools, particularly in English and math; more outstanding schools; and significant improvements in educational outcomes for disadvantaged children. The challenge pro- grams also altered existing governance patterns by bringing many authorities together, by networking schools that were often otherwise autonomous, and by making access to additional resources contingent on the adoption of particular improvement strategies. The London Challenge has been considerably successful, but recent evidence from the government shows that gaps in achievement based on socio-economic status are still very large (Department for Children, Families and Schools, 2009).

These latest efforts around the world to improve equity of outcomes from education are important, but their effectiveness depends on a careful consideration of knowledge and strategy. Just focusing on an issue does not lead to success; discussing an achievement gap is not the same as acting to reduce that gap. Inequities have resisted previous educational efforts, in large part because inequity is produced in society as a whole, not only in schools (Anyon, 1997; Mortimore & Whitty, 2000; Willms, 2002; Rothstein, 2004). Efforts to address inequities have also used a sporadic and limited range of strategies. If one considers the possible options – ranging from support services in schools to early childhood development to changed instructional practice to community outreach to community economic and political development – the history of the last thirty-five years shows only limited efforts in many domains, with little evaluation of impact (Payne, 2008; Darling-Hammond, 2010; Ravitch, 2010). There are no easy solutions, but many stories of school reform, and so we must examine these stories carefully and try to learn what we can from them.

The Literature on Urban Educational Systems

In education policy and discourse, attention to equity as a vital goal must be combined with knowledge about what strategies are effective and how they can be implemented. The many attempts already being made in schools and communities to improve the educational opportunities of the least well-off can demonstrate what strategies may be most effective and how these approaches can be used more widely. There is a growing literature on policy initiatives to improve urban schooling for the disadvantaged in many jurisdictions. The following section explores the educational policy landscape and academic literature on urban school reform, with particular emphasis on the United States, where the studies are multiple and influential, but need to be understood within the context of U.S. politics.

Public and policy thinking about urban education in Canada has been shaped largely by experiences in the United States as reported in scholarly literature and mass media. In the 1960s, Canadian educators were galvanized by president John Kennedy's war on poverty, the New York decentralization debates, and the struggle to desegregate large US school systems. For years, Canadians have read or watched the political struggles over governance, testing, ethnic integration, and the quality of instruction in large U.S. school systems.

The U.S. literature on urban school reform is a helpful and interesting one. A study conducted in the 1990s by Clarence Stone and colleagues (Stone, 1998, 2001; Henig, Hula, Orr, & Pedescleaux, 1999; Portz, Stein, & Jones, 1999; Stone, Henig, Jones, & Pierannunzi, 2001) provides a compelling discussion of urban literature. The authors studied education reform in eleven U.S. cities from a political science perspective and with attention to the entire political system, not just to the education system. The study, as others have, argues that the fate of urban schools is strongly linked to larger social developments, such as the growth of minority populations, the departure of businesses for the suburbs, and infrastructure changes. But it also points to the importance of creating the necessary political support for lasting reform:

> Many would-be reformers skip this intermediate, political step and go directly to the question of whether various initiatives improve test scores and enhance the academic performance of children from poverty backgrounds ... but first it must be established that reform initiatives can be put into place and kept there – not just in name but in reality. It is this issue that makes the political context of reform a matter of central concern. Talk about reform ... is not the same as a politically secured program of action. (Stone, 1998, p. x)

Stone and colleagues' research also concluded that education reform was strongly linked to general civic capacity and was influenced by political structures such as ward systems, electoral practices, board size, and the degree of involvement of elites in education politics. In U.S. urban education, the degree to which cities have attempted to address segregation and minority issues affects school politics in important ways (Portz, Stein, & Jones, 1999).

The Stone team's analysis points to the need for sustained efforts over time to improve urban education, something that requires careful planning and ongoing attention, both of which, they find, tend to be lacking in the United States urban political systems they studied:

> The civic challenge is to replace the individual interests of business leaders, politicians, educators, community activities, and others with

collective interests that include support for school reform. A problem definition must be crafted that encourages broad participation to address the
key challenges and obstacles to improving public education. (Portz, Stein, &
Jones, 1999, p. 158)

Creating this political support and commitment is difficult. Stone et al.
describe education as a 'high reverberation' policy system that involves
'frequent reshuffling of mobilized stakeholders, multiple strong competing value and belief systems, interests from both educators and parents, and ambiguous boundaries, making the prospects for establishing
a new equilibrium more problematic' (Stone et al., 2001, p. 50).

Stone et al. also conclude that neither school boards nor superintendents can make improvements alone, and that the ability of an education system to create lasting change fundamentally depends on factors
in the larger political world. In one of the final chapters, Danielson and
Hochschild write, 'We are sorry to conclude, therefore, that the most
powerful message emerging from these studies is that given the con-
figuration of local political forces, there are no clear rules about how to
create, sustain or motivate either educational reform from below or the
pursuit of national goals from above' (Stone et al., 1998, p. 294).

The academic accounts of the experience of school districts in large
U.S. cities bear out this analysis. Overall, the story is one of very poor
results and ongoing crisis. For many years, there have been regular
reports not only of dismal levels of academic achievement, but of lack of
funds, bitter labour relations, rapid turnover of superintendents, state
takeovers of city schools, and replacement of elected school boards by
mayor-appointed boards (Cuban & Usdan, 2003; Henig & Rich, 2004).

There are some key historical accounts of school district reform before
the past couple of decades, including books on New York (Podair, 2002;
Ravitch, 2000; Rogers, 1968), Detroit (Mirel, 1999), and Chicago (Shipps,
2006). These histories point to the connection between business interests, demographics, politics, and educational decision-making. In New
York, there were conflicts in the late 1960s between community control activists and teachers' unions in the predominantly black district
of Ocean Hill Brownsville, as well as the ongoing bureaucratic politics
of a very large district. Jeffrey Mirel's (1999) study of Detroit from 1901
to 1981 shows how the growing African-American population, coupled
with 'white flight' out of the city, led to political and financial struggles
for schools and steadily deteriorating situations and outcomes. Finally,
Shipps (2006) shows how business interests have shaped school reform
in Chicago since 1880. It is easier to see the impact of large political and

social changes in the early twentieth century than in more recent times, when the particular political and economic conditions are taken for granted and the focus tends to be more on the adequacy of the reform strategies themselves.

Despite these problems, there are some excellent studies of recent attempts to reform United States school districts, connecting school reform to the larger politics of cities and the nation. Among them, Jean Anyon's (1997) study of Newark, New Jersey, shows in detail the multitude of factors that impact urban poverty and therefore urban schools. The fate of the Newark schools was dramatically, and negatively, affected by decisions about housing policy, placement of highways, access to public transportation, availability of childcare, tax rates that caused employers to relocate, and the availability of public services such as recreation, the lack of which increased crime.

Gerald Grant's (2009) examination of the experience in school districts in Raleigh, North Carolina, and Syracuse, New York, also links city-planning policies directly to the fate of school district reform. The growing segregation in Syracuse has been reflected in the growing disparity in the quality of its schools; the merging of suburban and inner-city Raleigh into a single school district has allowed that school system to do much better.

The text of Larry Cuban's (2010) study of Austin, Texas, reflects the context of the American South: desegregation initiatives which make their way slowly through the court system; state testing and accountability systems which are introduced, subverted, and changed; budget fluctuations which test the district's capacity to plan; micromanaging school boards which prevent coherence and consistency; and philanthropic investments from the Bill & Melinda Gates foundation, among others, which shape the district's agenda and priorities. Social inequalities remain the intractable problem and the tensions they produce can only be managed, not solved, by creative and hard-working educators.

Chicago has received more recent attention from educational researchers than any other U.S. city. Few accounts of the lives of children in any city in a rich country are more chilling that Alex Kotlowicz's *There are No Children Here* (1992). Significantly, schools do not appear in this book as a significant factor in children's lives. The Chicago Consortium for School Research has produced reports for many years on the struggle to improve schools, starting with the decentralization initiative of the mid-1980s and tracing its transformation into more central control and charter schools. Lipman (2004), like Shipps (2006), draws attention to the impact business has had on the reform agenda, while Bryk et al. (1998, 2010) discuss the importance of social capital and community support in school reform. Hess (1995), like Payne (2008), concludes that Chicago has shown signs of improvement over the last two decades, but still faces significant challenges.

The urban school literature in the United States includes many studies looking at the effects of changes in governance. There have been some highly visible examples of cities where mayors replace school boards and appoint powerful superintendents who, with support from urban elites, engage in 'top down' reforms to bring about change. In Boston, Thomas Payzant was appointed by the mayor, Tom Menino, as superintendent of schools between 1995 and 2006; his experience is recounted in Reville (2007). Despite large investments by the Annenberg Foundation and a major policy push, the conclusion is that 'no miracles happened' (p. 3). In San Diego, another powerful superintendent, Alan Bersin, tried to change schools in the late 1990s by mandating professional development, requiring forms of 'balanced literacy,' and firing teachers and principals who failed to show their support (Hess, 2005; Hightower, 2002). While Hess's conclusions on the experience are measured, citing some improvements and some continuing problems, Ravitch (2010) provides a damning indictment of the very centralized control Bersin exercised, and the lack of political support that resulted in his ousting after three years: 'If a get-tough policy saps educators of their initiative, their craft, and their enthusiasm, then it is hard to believe that the results are worth having' (p. 67).

New York also turned to mayoral control of its schools in 2002 (Fruchter, 2008; Ravitch, 2010), arguing that the politics of the school board, where trustees represented diverse constituencies, prevented consensus and action on vital reform initiatives. Mayor Michael Bloomberg hired Joel Klein as superintendent, and he proceeded to reorganize the bureaucracy and provide extensive, centrally-designed professional development to teachers. Michelle Rhee was similarly appointed in Washington, DC, to bring about wholesale change in a district that was clearly failing (Hannaway & Usdan, 2008). She encouraged charter schools while emphasizing standardized testing, challenging unions, and championing innovation. Most analyses of these reforms suggest that top down strategies are not effective over time. While central leaders can spur reform efforts, without grassroots support from teachers and principals, they cannot implement any lasting change in a complex urban system, and the changes they do make have not reliably resulted in better outcomes for students.

There is also substantial literature on the impact of popular new policy approaches, particularly decision-making based on increased narrowly defined testing and accountability systems; changes to teacher and principal incentive plans; and the enhancement of private management, charter schools, and school choice. The literature on these reform strategies is large and often contested by those with different ideological perspectives. There is no consensus that such strategies have improved student achievement, especially for children who live in poverty or have English as a second or third language. Diane Ravitch, one of the leading proponents of increased school choice and new incentive plans, has concluded that the reforms she championed did not have the positive effects they promised (Ravitch, 2010). Linda Darling-Hammond, Obama's educational advisor in the 2008 election campaign, concludes that the opportunity-to-learn gaps faced by American students are growing, not decreasing, with the current reforms (Darling-Hammond, 2010).

Local control of schools, with increased school choice, charters, and testing is a particularly popular policy direction in U.S. cities in the current climate. Providing increased school choice as a solution moves in different directions from the top-down mandated professional development strategies discussed above, and encourages local parents and community activists to develop new models of education and take control of local schools. However, it takes a powerful political process to bring in these reforms, and the increased support for school choice in large cities has resulted from strong political leadership combined with dedicated research and advocacy. Some of the first initiatives took place in Chicago, with radical decentralization in the late 1980s. They were soon replaced by a return to centralization as the mismanagement and failure of some of these schools surfaced. In New York, the same process occurred. The widely-heralded success of New York's district two in creating small schools of choice was questioned, and replaced by more central directives. In Washington, DC, and Philadelphia, there have also been concerted efforts to outsource school management to private companies and to start charter schools that respond to a variety of communities. This remains a direction championed by the current secretary of education, Arne Duncan, who comes from Chicago, but it is not a direction that has proven its benefits.

In most cities, a number of new reforms are undertaken together, and it is hard to determine the effect of any one strategy. Most observers agree that there are no clear examples of policy measures that guarantee success, either at the program level or at the school district level. Cuban and Usdan (2003) describe the 'sorry state of urban school reform' after their review of the experience in several U.S. districts over a quarter century. Bill Boyd's (2008) edited collection on the transformation of public education in big cities concludes not that the achievement of students from poor families is getting better, or that the new reform strategies have been successful, but that school governance is moving from the local democratic politics and ideals of the progressive era to a more pluralistic, multi-level politics with a 'low-trt' logic and an emphasis on easily measured outcomes. Payne (2008) describes the persistent failure in urban schools, while allowing that there has been some progress on the standardized tests that are now mandated across the country: 'Some systems then, seem to be getting some grasp on some parts of the problem' (p. 4). This is not a promising assessment.

Canada's large cities do not experience the same educational challenges as those in the United States, and Canadian politics has sustained more commitment to robust public institutions than U.S. politics has (Gaskell, 2010). Canada certainly has issues of poverty, racism, intolerance, and urban segregation to overcome, but they have very different causes than their counterparts in the United States. Diversity in U.S. cities predominantly refers to relations among whites, African-Americans, and Hispanics; a legacy of both slavery and mass – and often illegal – immigration from Mexico. In contrast, Canadian cities are much more diverse, and no single ethnic group dominates across the country. Canadian urban municipal governance and financing are also different, and school district funding is much more equitable. Canadian provincial governments exercise more power in education than do most U.S. state governments. The Canadian federal government has almost no power over schooling, while the U.S. federal government exerts a significant steering effect through financing and policy directives. Canadian teachers' unions are stronger, and school districts do not have the same difficulties in finding qualified teachers for their urban schools. These differences partly explain why Canada's performance on international measures, such as PISA, is not only superior on average to that of the United States, but also has significantly less variation across districts (OECD, 2007a).

In Canada, every province has set goals to reduce inequities in outcomes and to recognize cultural diversity in its schools. However, there is very little Canadian literature on urban school reform. John Porter's landmark study of economic and cultural inequality in Canada, *The Vertical Mosaic* (1965), pointed to education as a key barrier to equal opportunity. Much of the Canadian analysis of education, poverty, and the experience of immigrant groups is, like Porter's, drawn from large statistical data bases, most recently from the Youth in Transition survey (e.g., Thiessen, 2007) and the National Longitudinal Study of Children and Youth (e.g., Willms, 2002). The federally funded 'exemplary schools study' provided portraits of schools that were deemed successful with students at risk of failing, but did not look closely at urban school politics (Gaskell, 1995). Hunter (2000) described efforts in a Winnipeg school to address broader community development as well as poverty. Maynes and Foster (2000) provide a survey of anti-poverty efforts in Canadian cities. The Canadian literature also includes provocative local glimpses of inner-city students, educators, and families. For example, Maynes (1993) concluded that many educators in Edmonton felt that the problems of poverty were intractable and demoralizing. Levin and Riffel (2000) analyse school system responses to poverty in several Manitoba districts. Works by teachers such as McLaren (1980), Solnicki (1992), and Gallagher (2007) reveal the classroom experience in diverse and disadvantaged Toronto schools.

However, there are no Canadian studies equivalent to the U.S. analyses of education policy in major cities. Taking a school district as the unit of analysis, placing it firmly in its context, and tracing its changes over time is the most useful way of understanding how reforms do (or do not) come about and how they make a difference. By looking at two very different cities, where poverty and diversity took different forms, provincial/municipal politics came together differently, and school board structures differed, we will present a grounded discussion of how boards go about the important work of making schools effective for vulnerable children.

Conclusions

Urban education in Canada is deeply shaped by issues of poverty, diversity, and inequity. These factors have powerful effects on student outcomes and understanding them is essential to any effort to improve urban education. Education outcomes are still worse in Canada for students growing up in poverty, for Aboriginal youth, and for members of some racialized and immigrant groups. The understanding of these issues has grown as a result of recent research, while changes in social and economic circumstances make them more pressing than ever.

Policy attention to these issues has fluctuated, but educational policy has not effectively addressed them. While the international literature can inform Canadian efforts, Canada's unique history and circumstances militate against borrowing policies or strategies from elsewhere. The next two chapters set out a brief history of two key Canadian school boards in Toronto and Winnipeg, illustrating the impact of demographic change; contextualizing the attempts to intervene at the school-board level; and providing a narrative of the people, events, and ideas that have been important in the Canadian educational experience.

2   Change in the Winnipeg School Division

Winnipeg is a city of about 650,000 people on the eastern edge of the Canadian prairies. It is the capital of, and only large urban centre in, the province of Manitoba, which has a population of about one million spread over 400,000 square kilometres. The nearest large city is Minneapolis, about 700 kilometres away, and the nearest large Canadian city is Calgary, more than 1,000 kilometres west. Winnipeg has a challenging climate, with long, cold winters and short, hot, and dry summers.

For the past fifty years, the city has grown slowly and has been surpassed in size by Calgary, Edmonton, and Ottawa. In Manitoba, like other areas of North America that were once centred on farming, the population has shifted from rural to urban areas, small rural communities have shrunk or disappeared, and the economy has diversified. The Winnipeg economy does not centre around any single key industry or engine, which means it tends to benefit less from economic booms, but also suffers less from downturns in particular industries or sectors.

Europeans settled in Winnipeg early in the nineteenth century, at the place where the Red and Assiniboine rivers converge. This place, now a popular park called the Forks, was a meeting and trading spot for Aboriginal people for thousands of years. The city grew rapidly in the late nineteenth and early twentieth centuries as Europeans settled in the Canadian West.

Winnipeg was built around its railroads. The north end of the city, around the Canadian Pacific Railway (CPR) station, became the area where successive waves of immigrants – initially from eastern Europe, then from central and southern Europe, and more recently from Asia and Latin America – arrived and settled. As immigrant groups gradually became more prosperous, they would move to wealthier parts of the city. The north end of Winnipeg is famous for producing talented children from immigrant families. The southern part of the city was, from the beginning, the preserve of the city's elite, which was for a long time primarily Anglo-Saxon. The gap between the two parts of the city, separated by the CPR rail yards, is portrayed in John Marlyn's novel, *Under the Ribs of Death* (1957). The north end has always been characterized by less adequate housing, higher unemployment, less infrastructure, and greater poverty.

This geographical segregation is reflected in Winnipeg's politics, with the north tending to vote for populist and left-wing parties while the south is more conservative. Winnipeg has had a very strong left-wing political element, including a substantial Communist presence in the years before the Second World War. In 1919, a general city-wide workers' strike pitted the two parts of the city against each other (Bumsted, 1994). As the suburbs grew, the inner city has become relatively smaller and less politically influential. The southern and western parts of the city also remain wealthier and more politically conservative than the north and east.

The geographical political divide characterizes the province as a whole. Manitoba elections typically divide along a line running from north-west to south-east, with northern areas voting for the social-democratic New Democratic Party and southern and western rural areas voting for the Conservative Party. The outcome of a provincial election depends on the vote in constituencies along that political fault line, and most Manitoba elections are quite close. Between 1969 and 1999, in nine provincial elections, the Conservatives won 235 seats and formed a government four times, while the NDP won a total of 233 seats and formed the government five times. Elections can be decided by a few hundred votes in a small number of swing ridings. The provincial government plays a very large role in influencing what happens in Winnipeg and has had important impacts on inner-city education.

Poverty in Winnipeg has historically been concentrated in what is known as 'the inner city,' an area that extends north from the city's central business district across the main CPR tracks into the north end. Although the specific boundaries of the inner city differ somewhat in different data collection exercises, the Social Planning Council of Winnipeg has created a demographic portrait of the area over time. These data show that the inner city has shrunk as a proportion of the whole city and grown relatively poorer. Urban poverty has been increasingly concentrated and increasingly severe.

Census data show that from 1966 to 2001, the population of Winnipeg's inner city decreased by from 145,000 to 105,000 people, while the population of the city as a whole increased by nearly 30 per cent. In 2000, the low-income incidence in the inner city for families was 33 per cent, contrasted with 16 per cent for the whole city, while for private households it was 40 per cent, contrasted with 20 per cent for the whole city. Only 3 per cent of inner-city families earned $100,000 or more in 2001, contrasted with 20 per cent for Winnipeg as a whole. From 1981 to 2000, average household incomes in the inner city fell from 60 per cent of the Winnipeg average to 55 per cent. Lower levels of education and employment also accompanied higher poverty levels. In 2001, 36 per cent of inner-city residents had completed less than a grade 12 education, contrasted with 28 per cent of the city as a whole. While education levels had increased, the gap with the city as a whole had also increased. Labour force participation is lower in the inner city, and unemployment has been much higher – typically nearly double – the rate for the city as a whole.

The demographic diversity in inner-city Winnipeg has changed in important ways over the last forty years. Visible minority immigrants from places such as the Philippines, the Caribbean, Vietnam, and China replaced immigrants from Central Europe. Canada's policy of accepting substantial numbers of refugees brought people from war-torn parts of the world, notably Africa and parts of eastern Europe. By 2001, visible minorities were 13 per cent of the city and 20 per cent of the inner city.

Winnipeg's Aboriginal population has dramatically increased as people moved away from rural and northern reservations. Aboriginal people now make up 10 per cent of the city's total population and 20 per cent of the inner-city population. Aboriginal people in Manitoba have lower than average levels of educational attainment and higher than average levels of poverty than other groups (Jantzen, 2004). The result of these changes is that whereas seventy or eighty years ago, many north-end Winnipeg schools were 80 per cent or more Ukrainian, Jewish, or German, and thirty years ago were heavily Portuguese or Italian, these same schools are now often 80 per cent or more Aboriginal.

The Aboriginal population is a diverse one. It includes a variety of First Nations people, a large number of non-status Indians and Métis, and a smaller number of Inuit. These groups have distinct views and separate political organizations and goals. There are more than sixty distinct and self-governing First Nations in Manitoba who frequently do not agree on priorities or strategy. Aboriginal issues are enmeshed in complicated constitutional, political, and institutional arrangements involving the federal government, provincial governments, First Nations, and other Aboriginal groups. In urban areas, jurisdiction and responsibility are particularly murky. Although more First Nations people live off reserves than on them, First Nations leaders are largely focused on the pressing issues on their reserves and do not have the means to represent urban Aboriginals. There are increasingly important new urban Aboriginal organizations in Winnipeg, though they do not have the same recognized political status as the chiefs or the provincial organizations.

From 1976 to 2001, while the total number of families in the inner city decreased by 35 per cent, the number of single-parent families increased by 42 per cent. The latter trend was mirrored in Winnipeg as a whole, but single parent families are about one sixth of all Winnipeg families, whereas they constitute nearly half of inner-city families. Although the number of families has declined, the number of children in the inner city has remained stable, while that same number has fallen in Winnipeg as a whole. Inner-city children now constitute a larger portion of the city's total population than they did in the 1970s.

Not surprisingly, education outcomes in inner-city schools in Winnipeg are generally much lower than those in wealthier neighbourhoods. Work by the Manitoba Centre for Health Policy (e.g., Roos et al., 2006; Brownell et al., 2004) has shown just how dramatic the socioeconomic gradients for success are in Winnipeg. Examining data that include all Manitoba children, not just those enrolled in school, shows very poor outcomes for inner-city children, especially those who grow up in poverty or who are born to very young mothers, compared to the child population of Winnipeg as a whole.

The Winnipeg School Division

The Winnipeg School Division (WSD) was created in 1890 when Manitoba established its unitary public system (in Manitoba, school districts are called 'divisions'). The WSD, which refers to itself as Division #1, was created from the former Winnipeg Protestant School Division #1, which had been founded shortly after the province was established (Chafe, 1967). As Winnipeg grew, new school divisions were created in suburban areas. When the City of Winnipeg became a single urban area in 1971, it contained the WSD and eight other school divisions. In 2001, as part of Manitoba's province-wide reduction in the number of school districts, the number of school divisions in Winnipeg was reduced from nine to six (Levin, 2005; Yeo, 2008). However, these changes did not affect the WSD, which has had the same boundaries since its inception.

The growth of the suburbs means that the WSD now serves only about a third of Winnipeg's population. Still, the WSD remains the largest school division in Manitoba by far. Over the last thirty years it has enrolled between 30,000 and 35,000 students and has operated about eighty schools, including about ten secondary schools. It has always viewed itself as separate from the rest of the Manitoba education system, due to both its size and its location in the centre of the province's only large city. This view, coupled with the need of the provincial government to be seen as influential in urban education, has created ongoing competition and tension between the WSD and the provincial Department of Education.

Financing education in Manitoba is the shared responsibility of districts and the provincial government, and there is constant debate about what the appropriate ratio should be. The province allocates annual funding from its budget based on its assessment of educational needs and costs. Local school divisions add to that funding by levying local property taxes. The Department of Education uses a funding formula that considers both the assessed needs of school divisions and their property wealth. School divisions that have higher needs or less local property wealth get more support from the province. In the early 1980s, the Nicholls commission on education finance proposed that the province should pay 80 per cent of education costs, with 20 per cent coming from local taxation. However, that ratio has rarely been achieved, in part because the province rarely increases funding at the rate desired by school districts, and in part because school districts have an incentive to raise local taxes since doing so puts pressure on the province to pay more. In 2007, local property taxes in Manitoba accounted for more than 40 per cent of all operating spending on education (the province pays all capital costs). The WSD has the richest local tax base in the province, and over the period of this study Winnipeg consistently spent more per pupil – typically about 10 per cent above the provincial average – and had one of the highest local tax rates.

From the late 1960s and late 1990s, the WSD was governed by an elected board of nine trustees, three from each of three wards that horizontally divide the district from north to south. The wards are large, and each contains approximately 70,000 residents. By comparison, an average Manitoba legislative constituency has about 20,000 residents. The large size of the wards has posed challenges for political participation in elections. The northern ward (ward 3) is the poorest and the southern ward (ward 1) is the wealthiest, although there are large variations in each. The elected board members have had the task of reconciling the divergent needs and interests of these communities. Sometimes board members have been primarily concerned with representing the interests of their own wards, but at other times they have taken a broader perspective. Inner-city issues have had support, and sometimes even critical leadership, from board members representing other parts of the WSD.

School board elections in Winnipeg are held every three years. Over the course of ten elections between 1970 and 2000, fifty different people served on the board, so the turnover in a typical election was about 50 per cent. Eleven people served more than two terms, and six served for four or more terms, so there was both substantial continuity and significant turnover.

Many of our interviewees noted that Winnipeg's school board was split politically over much of the time of this study. These splits were often, but not always, based on party affiliation. From the beginning, the board had members endorsed by the pre-cursor of the NDP, the Cooperative Commonwealth Federation, and the Communist Party. From the early 1970s, the NDP has typically held four or five of the nine seats, elected most often in wards 2 and 3, in the northern and poorer part of the district. However, NDP trustees did not always vote together and relations could be acrimonious. Quite frequently, disagreements were the result of personal animosities, sometimes among people who were ostensibly in the same political party. Don Reed, an NDP trustee from the early 1970s, noted in an interview that during his first term, the divisions were between incumbents and newcomers:

Of the five NDP members, four were elected for the first time with one member re-elected. While the NDP trustees had a majority on the board, control rested with the four newly elected NDP members and one newly elected independent trustee. The three independent trustees elected from the south end of the city and the re-elected NDP member were staunch defenders of the existing system ... Every major decision, consequently, was a five-four vote.

The debates could be quite difficult. Reed mentioned that during one intense debate,

> a trustee from the north-end ward asked the chair for the procedure to punch a south-end trustee in the nose. Since no such procedure existed, we went for a tea break. Reporters covering the board meeting indicated they would have to report the incident. The north-end trustee responded that where he came from, a headline that "north-end boy punches south-end boy" is worth 10,000 votes any day.

For much of the 1990s, the WSD board operated smoothly and effectively. Still, a five-four split among rival groups on the board was common throughout the period of this study, with different coalitions having majorities at various times. With a nine-person board, results were largely determined by the individual opinions of those in office. Anita Neville, a south-end trustee and board chair in the 1980s and early 1990s, described what happened when the dynamics were not working well:

> The board usually operated in a cooperative and collaborative way. However, there was a period on the board when there was what I would call an NDP cabal ... [that] formed a caucus and met and did all of the decision-making outside the boardroom. Before a board meeting, before a committee meeting, they would meet and decide what was going to be done and move their agenda forward. It was not a progressive agenda ... I went to board meetings, but it was not an easy time for me. It lasted for a few years.

With the board so often split, it was difficult to produce continuity in policy directions.

Several Winnipeg Leaders in Brief

Individual leadership matters in the context of competing party, jurisdictional, and personal relationships. The following trustees, educators, and community activists were some of the many leaders who were important to the development of education in Winnipeg.

The new 1969 NDP government hired Lionel Orlikow, a well-known teacher, writer, and controversial activist, to lead the Planning and Research Division of the Manitoba Department of Education. His division both worked and competed with the WSD in responding to urban education issues. Orlikow was appointed deputy minister of education in the mid-1970s, but fired by premier Sterling Lyon shortly after the Conservatives took office in 1977. Later, he headed the education program of the Winnipeg Education Centre, which trained inner-city residents as teachers, and in 1988 he was elected to the WSD, where he served until 1998. Orlikow was a committed left-winger who delighted in generating controversial ideas. He died in 2008.

In the early 1970s, Greg Selinger was a young social worker interested in community development in the inner city. He worked for Lionel Orlikow in the Department of Education as one of the first community school organizers in inner-city Winnipeg. Selinger became the first head of the Community Education and Development Alliance (CEDA), which had an often-difficult relationship with the WSD and whose funding was eventually terminated by the board. In the 1980s, he was head of the social work program at the Winnipeg Education Centre, which trained inner-city residents as social workers. Never a member of the WSD, Selinger is a prime example of the community advocates who work in the inner city and press the division on inner-city issues. In the early 1990s, he moved into electoral politics, first as a city councillor, and, in 1999, as an NDP MLA. Premier Gary Doer named him finance minister, a position he held for eleven years. In 2010, Selinger succeeded Doer as the premier of Manitoba.

Anita Neville started her career in education as a parent activist. She went on to be a volunteer coordinator for the WSD and joined the board of Rossbrook House, a centre for inner-city, mostly Aboriginal, youth. In the mid-1980s, she went to work for the Core Area Initiative (CAI), an inner-city regeneration project funded by three levels of government. When a long-serving school trustee retired in the mid-1980s, Neville was approached by friends to run for the position, as she had well-established political interests and strong connections to education in the WSD. She served on the board, including five years as chair, until her election as a Liberal member of parliament in 2000. Although Neville represented the richer south end of the WSD, she was always deeply interested in inner-city and equity issues and played a key role in brokering competing interests on the board. She was an important player in the creation of the Task Force on Race Relations and the subsequent implementation of its recommendations.

Pat Rowantree came to Canada in the early 1970s as a teacher with a strong interest in community development. She taught in inner-city schools and was one of the first community organizers, along with Selinger, hired by the WSD. She left Winnipeg when the policy climate changed in the mid-1970s and many projects ended, but returned in 1982 to head the training unit of the CAI for its first five years. In 1999, she was recruited as assistant deputy minister for training and adult education, and from 2002 to 2004 she was deputy minister both for education and for advanced education and training.

Mary Richard grew up in a large Métis family in rural Manitoba and learned to speak both Cree and Ojibway. After moving to Winnipeg, she became a lifelong advocate for Aboriginal people in the city, and held leadership positions in a wide range of Aboriginal organizations. Her career traces the development of Aboriginal political efforts and institutions in the city, from the 1960s when an Aboriginal leadership and political consciousness first took active shape through the gradual development of a whole range of institutions and organizations that gave expression to the needs of a rapidly growing and changing community. Education was always an important part of these endeavours, and Richard never stopped lobbying for better programs and services for Aboriginal students, including being an active proponent for a self-governing Aboriginal school system in the city.

Jack Smyth was a teacher and principal in the WSD. In 1980, he was appointed the superintendent of secondary schools after two chief superintendents were fired within a few years, reflecting turmoil in the WSD. In 1982, Smyth was appointed chief superintendent, a position he held for twenty years, providing considerable stability to the organization during a time of change. Laid-back and self-effacing, Smyth made many efforts to increase the attention the division was giving to Aboriginal education and inner-city education. He died shortly after his interview for this book.

Pauline Clarke's entire career in education has been with WSD, and almost all of it has been in or around inner-city schools. Her first two years at William Whyte School, she says, 'changed how I understood education. I have never lost that.' In 1980 she became assistant to Marcel Pelletier, the area superintendent in the north end of the city, and in 1982 she became executive assistant to Jack Smyth, the new chief superintendent. When the position of inner-city superintendent was created in 1987, Clarke was appointed and remained there until 2008, when she was appointed chief superintendent for the division. Her focus on teaching and learning practices in inner-city schools has been highly influential in the WSD.

The Development of Inner-City Approaches until 1975

Early in the twentieth century, settlement houses and other charities developed to assist immigrants and the poor in Winnipeg. Chafe's history of the Winnipeg schools (Chafe, 1967) has quite a bit of discussion of efforts to improve social conditions through the schools. Nursing, eyeglasses, and dental services were provided to needy students as early as 1915, and hearing screening took place in 1929. In the early 1930s, all new students received a medical exam, schools provided free milk, and nursing and dentistry were available in what one trustee described as an effort 'to give children of wrong-headed parents a chance to be healthy' (Chafe, 1967, p. 132).

By the 1960s, as completing high school began to be seen as a goal for all students instead of the preserve of a few, there was growing recognition that student success rates in urban schools were not satisfactory. By the late 1960s, there were active discussions about how to help children from disadvantaged homes be successful in school. Both the provincial Department of Education and the WSD were affected by this overall climate of intellectual and political ferment and innovation. Both organizations began to develop initiatives to address some of the problems of inner-city education.

In June 1969, the NDP won the Manitoba provincial election (albeit with a minority) for the first time. This was an era in which government revenues regularly ran ahead of expenditures and governments had annual surpluses. The new government made a number of efforts to improve the situation of the poor through higher minimum wages, better social assistance benefits, more public housing, and other initiatives. Frustrated by the conservative nature of the Department of Education, it created a new planning and research unit to introduce more innovation. The unit was headed by Lionel Orlikow and, under the direction of NDP education minister Saul Miller, immediately began to plan and implement a range of programs intended to address inner-city problems. The unit became the home to most of the new government's education priorities. Among these were initiatives to train inner-city residents as teachers, to strengthen parent involvement in schools, and to address some of the issues facing immigrant and Aboriginal children.

The WSD, meanwhile, was also trying to address inner-city education and poverty. In the fall of 1967, it hired Carmen Moir, who had a strong reputation as a progressive educator, as superintendent. In the fall of 1971, six new board members were elected, four of whom were members of the NDP. The new trustees found that there was not much that could be described as an inner-city strategy or approach. As trustee Don Reed put it:

> At that time, the Winnipeg system was quite closed. In general, the board had been very traditional and closely linked to the administration. It became clear that things had not changed for many years, and they were not about to change. The five newly elected trustees anxious to see significant change became impatient with the mounds of paper and motherhood statements about the wonderful system. The existing system had its merits rooted as it was firmly in the 1950s. However, there was no acknowledgement of the impending crises facing inner-city schools.

The combination of a new group of trustees and an activist provincial government produced the funding and political support for a variety of experimental and local initiatives. Some schools tossed out their previous curriculum and had teachers write new material. Some developed alternative programs. Some developed local community studies. Some looked at changes in staff or in the use of volunteers, such as hiring local residents as teacher aides and community workers. Reed commented that 'the idea that visible minorities from the community should work in schools was something new at the time. It is worth noting that two of those aides went into teaching and the others continued working in the school until their recent retirement.' Experimental initiatives were everywhere.

Most of these efforts were made by individual schools and depended on individual principals. These principals felt they had a lot of discretion in the actions in their schools. Marcel Pelletier, an inner-city principal in those days, recounted his school's efforts:

> I told [staff] to do whatever they thought necessary to help the children and not worry about the curriculum guidelines if they interfered ... They scrapped the whole-language program and spent the summer developing a new one. Instead of doing the language program we were doing, the children were asked to read and write every day. The children could go and read wherever they wanted, in the hallway or on the floor. Those children wrote every day, with considerable improvement as a result in their scores.

More systematic and institutionalized efforts were hard to sustain during this period, for the some of the reasons illustrated below.

Relations Between the WSD and
the Department of Education

The new NDP school trustees were close to the provincial government and spoke directly to provincial politicians, sometimes bypassing officials in both systems. Don Reed discussed how he worked with provincial politicians in the early 1970s to initiate programs:

> We were able to initiate the breakfast program, which had a somewhat turbulent start. The minister of education had at first said that there might not be sufficient funds for a breakfast program, so I went to the cabinet. Premier Schreyer asked me why I came to cabinet rather than speaking to the minister. I replied that I had seen the minister and that money was not available. Other ministers like Saul Miller said, 'this is the kind of program we got elected to support.' It was recommended that we receive the funding. They said that if the minister did not have the money in the budget they would find it.

There was often friction between the WSD and the Department of Education over who would control the initiatives they started. Staff in the division resented the degree to which the department intervened directly in its activities without consultation and agreement. Lionel Orlikow's planning and research branch was implementing many programs around inner-city education without going through the board. Greg Selinger, then a community worker in the WSD, remembered that 'the Winnipeg trustees really did not like Lionel Orlikow. They considered Lionel to be an annoyance from the Department of Education. These programs were part of his agenda. The division . . . has generally taken the attitude that it merely wanted the province to provide funding, and it would control its allocations.'

Entrepreneurial principals and staff who found resources and support externally did not always find the WSD supportive of their efforts. Carolyn Leoppky, a principal in the division, described it:

> There were a number of principals, including me, who were very aggressive [in the early 1980s] in soliciting ideas and money from outside the division. The division decided to institute a process whereby principals could no longer do that kind of entrepreneurship. They had to follow the process within the bureaucracy to get approval. For those principals who were aggressive and innovative, it discouraged them. Part of the reason

for such discouragement is that senior administration did not feel that there was equity anymore and that competition and jealousies were arising among schools.

These tensions persisted from the late 1960s to the early 1990s. Levin experienced them personally as a senior official in the Department of Education in the 1980s. Sometimes communications were stronger and program directions were more-easily agreed on because of close ties between NDP trustees and the NDP provincial government, but even that was not a guarantee of good relationships.

By 1973 or 1974, a number of programs and initiatives were underway in central Winnipeg in areas such as nutrition for children, parent involvement, early childhood programming, alternative programs for struggling students, and curriculum revisions. They included many of the approaches and strategies that continue to be advocated and sometimes enacted today. Those involved described it as a time of tremendous energy and excitement, with a sense of optimism that meaningful and lasting change in social relations could be created.

Two initiatives merit particular attention – the creation of the Winnipeg Education Centre to train inner-city and Aboriginal teachers, and the emergence of an inner-city community development agency, supported by the WSD.

Preparing Inner City and Aboriginal Teachers: The Winnipeg Education Centre

One of the enduring accomplishments of the early 1970s was the creation of the Winnipeg Education Centre (WEC) to prepare inner-city adults who were not qualified for normal university admission as teachers and social workers. The program was initiated and entirely funded by the province through Orlikow's branch but delivered by universities. At the time, there were very few Aboriginal teachers or other professionals in Manitoba or elsewhere in Canada. As several respondents told us, the WEC was intended to be a community-based teacher education model, where student teachers would do most of their practicum on a regular basis in community schools. While the focus of the WEC was on Aboriginal education, it also included non-Aboriginal inner-city residents.

There was initial resistance from the Winnipeg Teachers' Association and from universities, which were reluctant to admit students who did not meet their usual standards. Barry Hammond, a teacher and community activist, recalls that the University of Manitoba was 'not very interested in responding, so we approached Brandon University. Fortunately, Brandon University had some financial problems which we were able to solve and that gave them a reason to participate.' The WEC later moved from Brandon University to the University of Manitoba and, a decade ago, to the University of Winnipeg.

The WSD provided space for the WEC in an old school in the middle of the inner city, in a neighbourhood that was virtually completely Aboriginal. They recruited inner-city adults who, according to Barry, 'knew the social context. Everybody knew each other at WEC. We had only 120 students. Many of those who have passed through the program are leaders in their community.'

The WSD was at times ambivalent to the WEC. On the one hand, the division needed more Aboriginal teachers and was not getting them through regular teacher education programs. On the other hand, there were ongoing concerns about whether WEC students fit the model of a well-qualified new teacher – which many did not. Nevertheless, the WEC has survived for forty years. Throughout the 1970s and early 1980s, similar programs were created in nursing, law, and engineering (Levin & Alcorn, 2000). These 'access programs' have provided education and credentials to hundreds of people, mostly Aboriginal, who would otherwise not have qualified for admission into university (Sloane-Seale, Wallace, & Levin, 2004). Similar programs were created in Saskatchewan, northern Ontario, and British Columbia. They illustrate the contribution that even a fairly small initiative can make when sustained over time, since a substantial portion of Manitoba's current Aboriginal leadership is made up of graduates of this and other access programs. Greg Selinger, involved with the WEC social work program for many years, described the benefit of such programs this way:

WEC was a natural extension of the community-schools program because so many of the people who attended WEC, both in education and social work, were leaders of community development activities in the inner city, whether in the schools as teacher aides or in other community development projects. That leadership ability gave them the opportunity to meet the criteria for entering WEC. A ladder was created that took them back into their own neighbourhood with a stronger set of skills, better credentials, with more competence and more credibility. Once they returned to the neighbourhood schools after formal education, they could start building further ladders for other people. There are a host of inner-city people who became successful leaders in the inner city; they also got good jobs and a good education.

Community Development in the Schools: CEDA

A number of the Winnipeg reformers were deeply committed to the principles of social, political, and economic community development as a key part of improving inner-city education. Community development efforts were among the first initiatives of both the WSD board and the Department of Education in the early 1970s, with both organizations providing support and funding. Two inner-city schools, William Whyte and Shaughnessy Park, were the original focus of these efforts, which were later extended to other schools. As trustee Don Reed remarked, 'We did hire some of the best community development workers in the country. The community development workers ensured that parents were involved in the school in order to discuss relevant issues. There was a lot of excitement and positive dynamics in those schools.'

By 1975, these programs in different schools had been combined into a single initiative, with an emphasis on parental involvement and school governance. Active work by community organizers and a supportive board led to a short period in the 1970s when, according to Reed, 'we actually had parents involved in hiring principals and teachers, which was a very radical initiative at the time.' The schools offered adult education and attempted to coordinate among the various agencies providing service to the community. The staff members involved had a comprehensive view of their task, and recognized the vital role of staff and leadership in building strong connections with parents. Their stance is captured in this description from Greg Selinger, one of the leaders of this work in the early 1970s:

> Although we believed in volunteers, we also believed in creating jobs for inner-city people to work in the schools. We would hire people from the community to be community teacher aides. For instance, [one] school hired seven inner-city people to work in the classroom half-time and the community half-time mobilizing people to get involved in school and local issues; they were involved in everything from glue sniffing to housing to adult education. Since they were also in the classrooms helping teachers, it was a very effective model of bridging cultural differences and class differences.

To be successful, these initiatives needed support from principals, superintendents, and teachers. There was often tension, as the community workers would sometimes side with parents in disputes with the staff. Pat Rowantree, a teacher and community worker at William Whyte, helped lead parents in their efforts to change a board decision to tear down one of the school buildings. In other cases, teachers and community workers felt they had to challenge entrenched attitudes of professional colleagues. As Selinger put it:

> In the early years ... the teachers would complain about how horrible the parents were. They would write off the parents, and they would write off the children. In [this], for example, the basic attitude of the teachers was that the parents were the enemy. We had to have principals and teachers who perceived the community in a positive light and wanted to be a partner with it. That was a revolutionary change in the educational model, just to have teachers think differently about the community.

The new model called not only for the hiring of a committed community-school staff but also for a community-based curriculum. The staff started changing lesson plans in the schools to build on neighbourhood assets. They would do a study of a local street, bring Aboriginal elders into the school, and take students on trips to reserves in order to give value to Aboriginal culture and Aboriginal children.

Aboriginal Education

Aboriginal education was an area of ongoing concern. Even in the late 1960s, Winnipeg reformers were aware of the low employment, poor housing, and pressing educational needs of the rapidly growing Aboriginal population in the city. In 1970 the Aboriginal presence was smaller and much less politically potent than it would later become, and there was uncertainty as to what schools could or should do to respond to its needs.

The WSD as a whole did not have a policy or strategy addressing Aboriginal education at the time. Sporadic actions were taken. One of the first was the effort to train more Aboriginal teachers, through the Winnipeg Education Centre. A second was the creation of alternative or special programs for Aboriginal students. Quite a few such programs were created, often led by members of the local community, but while the alternative programs played an important role for some students, some reformers felt they allowed the mainstream system to resist becoming more flexible and responsive. A third was the integration of Aboriginal content and resources into regular schools – not only in the curriculum but in school activities. Much of this work was improvised in individual schools by principals or groups of staff. While some of it was quite extensive, it was not systematic.

Gerry Moore was a long-time principal in a school that had a large proportion of Aboriginal students. His account illustrates how rooted these efforts were in individual perceptions and motivation:

> I came to Canada in 1957 at the age of eighteen. Within three days of leaving Ireland I was working in the bush north of The Pas. While I was working there, a federal election was called and I was added to the voters' list compiled at the site. I was more than surprised that, as an Irish citizen, I could register to vote in a Canadian election. I had the right to vote, but ... an elderly Aboriginal man working beside me did not have that same right. [Note: Until 1960, Aboriginal people could only vote if they gave up their treaty status rights.] This experience of the denial of a basic right to Aboriginal people stayed with me as a lesson that helped to focus my career in years to come.
>
> [When I came to an inner-city school] in 1981 the Aboriginal population made up about 50 per cent of the student body. By 1984 it had risen to more than 75 per cent. Those were life-defining years. It was an experience that linked my past with the present in dramatic fashion. I found the urban Aboriginal community exhibiting many of the colonial characteristics that burdened my people, the Irish ... And here I was working in a community and witnessing the same pain and loss that was a holdover from the same form of repressive colonial rule ... I heard the familiar comments and judgments being around regularly in many settings – 'they can't raise children properly, they can't be trusted, they are drunkards and irresponsible, they are incapable of looking after their health needs, or of governing their reserves responsibly or serving on parent councils in their children's schools.' All are comments symptomatic of systemic racism.

The initiatives Moore undertook at the school illustrate the goodwill and effort involved, but also the absence of overall strategy that was characteristic of the time. He continued:

> The first parent event held the year I took over as principal was a school tea that was attended by fewer than thirty people, none of whom were Aboriginal. The following year we replaced the school tea with a traditional powwow. Over 450 people attended, most from the Aboriginal community. Staff development included participating in traditional sweats. Award ceremonies were replaced by honour ceremonies. The school had

its own drum built. We brought Aboriginal community members in as volunteers and then as staff. We team-taught to increase diversity of programming and reduce the frequency of discipline issues. We had teaching teams follow their student from grade 7 to grade 9 and then rotated back so they could get to know their students much better. We offered Cree as an option course. We hired community people to teach powwow dancing. We hired additional Aboriginal support staff. We brought in elders to preform pipe ceremonies. We undertook work on curriculum development with the assistance of the Division's language arts consultant.

On one occasion I had a meeting with the superintendent to present him with a motion of singular significance passed by the staff. It stated that any new staff hired at Aberdeen School should be of Aboriginal background whenever possible. The motion also expressed a willingness on the part of teachers to transfer to other schools if necessary to open up positions to teachers of Aboriginal background. The motion, a remarkable statement of principle, was never acknowledged by the board office administration. I'm sure they just didn't know what to do with it. The teaching staff worked well together and remained together for a period of eight years with few changes. The school had a keen sense of purpose and direction.

Despite the efforts taking place in individual schools, success at a system level was limited. An increasingly vocal Aboriginal community felt substantially alienated, as Aboriginal community leader Mary Richard discussed:

In the late 1960s and early 1970s, we did not get much response from lobbying by Aboriginal parents and Aboriginal organizations to the board of the Winnipeg School Division concerning Aboriginal education. We went to many meetings and wrote many briefs but without much result. Even if the complaints were accepted, there never seemed to be effective action. It took years and years to gain any recognition that there was a problem.

Large numbers of Aboriginal students were in special education or alternative programs that were not going to lead them to high school graduation. Several Winnipeg principals described the way that T.B. Russell vocational high school was used to stream Aboriginal students. Former Winnipeg principal Brian O'Leary remembered that: '[In the late 1970s] there were very few Aboriginal students in regular stream schools or classes in the secondary system in Winnipeg. You can look at the grad photos in the school when I became principal ... and see very few Aboriginal faces among the graduates. It was a "dirty little secret" that nobody really wanted to know.'

A Conservative Turn: 1975 to 1988

The political climate changed during the late 1970s. In 1977, Manitoba voters replaced the NDP with a Conservative government led by Sterling Lyon, who came into office on a platform of 'acute, protracted restraint.' One of Lyon's first acts was to fire deputy minister of education Lionel Orlikow. That same fall, some of the leaders of the more progressive faction on the WSD board were defeated in the municipal elections. Over the next few years, much of the work that had been done in inner-city Winnipeg in the late 1960s and early 1970s dissipated. The special programs that had been supported by provincial funds and staff dried up, and the division itself was under more financial pressure.

The Community Education Development Association (CEDA) survived the late 1970s by altering its funding and governance to respond to changing social and political conditions. It had been funded by the Department of Education, and as the government looked to cut expenditures, its future was uncertain. There was ongoing friction between the administrations of CEDA and the WSD. CEDA leaders saw the division as resisting local input from parents, and the board was divided on the merits of the organization, often with the same five-four split vote that existed in other areas. In this climate, Greg Selinger, then-head of CEDA, undertook a complex series of negotiations, using research on the effects of the programs. He convinced the United Way to provide funding, and the Department of Education to keep its funding flowing through the WSD. It was a major accomplishment by a skilled politician and negotiator. Selinger explained it thus:

> I wound up negotiating with [the board chair] for permanent funding, which did not entirely materialize ... she was always ambivalent; she always received messages encouraging her to quash the program, but she did not want to eliminate the program. She did, however, want a good deal, which is why I had to get United Way funding so that she could say to the board that for every dollar it funded, the United Way would match it.
>
> Mary Kardash [a north-end communist trustee] was always supportive and understood the model very well. She formed part of a radical tradition which saw the north end having its own institutions of resistance,

including her own . . . She saw results from our program. A lot of the schools in which we were involved were in her ward. The problem with her support was that there automatically arose at least four votes against such support merely because it was she who supported the program.

Despite the tenuous relations with the board, I was able to combine partial funding from the division with United Way funding to convert the community-schools program into a non-profit organization that was governed by inner-city people: two-thirds inner-city people and one-third inner-city activists and professionals on a board of twenty-five people. The United Way, therefore, became a resource that allowed inner-city programs to survive during the first wave of neo-Conservative downsizing of government.

To give the United Way credit, we were fairly controversial, but they were willing to fund us because they saw results. We had research to support our achievements; we had several people hired in the schools; we had a nutrition program; we were fighting glue-sniffing; and we were fighting housing issues.

Although the board of the WSD funded CEDA, the organization had its own board of directors that acted independently. It was a kind of contract between the Division and a third party non-profit organization to deliver services to the schools. The WSD was always fundamentally opposed to having organizations that were not fully under its control delivering services in the schools.

This difficult relationship between the board and CEDA continued, since CEDA often pressured the board on behalf of inner-city groups. Anita Neville, a long-time trustee in the 1980s and 1990s and a strong advocate for inner-city issues, saw both the virtues and problems of CEDA:

> Part of the political pressure around inner-city issues was driven by CEDA and by some community activists. CEDA co-opted most of the outspoken community activists. It is unfortunate that there was not another countervailing force in the community to CEDA. CEDA was a major player, both positively and negatively. They pushed the board hard and had many agendas. There were many votes at the board as to whether the Division should continue to fund them or not. Ultimately, it was cut back. CEDA was behind a number of challenges to the board, such as candidates running against incumbents, as well as organizing groups in opposition to the board. That got the board members' backs up, some more than others.

There is a question of how hard an external political body can push and how actively you can lobby and run against incumbents in an overt way when dependent on funding from that same board.

In the 1990s, the board eliminated its funding of CEDA. However CEDA survives today as a community development organization in central Winnipeg.

Even at the height of restraint, inner-city issues never disappeared entirely from the policy agenda. The board always had some members who were advocates for greater equity. When the NDP were re-elected as the provincial government in 1981, Maureen Hemphill, the minister of education from 1981 to 1986, represented an inner-city constituency in Winnipeg and prioritized inner-city and immigrant issues. As a result, the Department of Education paid renewed attention to inner-city issues including providing additional provincial funds to the WSD and developing policy and program supports related to Aboriginal education, English as a second language, and parent engagement.

In the late 1970s and early 1980s, the board went through several changes in leadership in a short time. As a result of the five-four split among trustees, two chief superintendents were hired and then fired within a couple of years, creating considerable instability. In 1981, the board appointed Jack Smyth as chief superintendent, a position he would hold for twenty years. During his time in office, Smyth became increasingly convinced that the inner city had needs that could not be addressed through the policies and approaches that characterized the WSD as a whole. He began to build capacity within the teaching and board staff. He described his approach:

> At both levels I realized that there was little being done in terms of addressing the needs of inner-city children since the research suggested that they were different and that, consequently, their problems should be addressed differently. Little was done for them for about two or three years. I then began to ask the superintendents what was being done for inner-city schools. The answer was: not very much. A year later the status quo still persisted. There was no focus at all on inner-city schools.

In an effort to improve the situation, Smyth gave Pauline Clarke, then his executive assistant, the responsibility to work with about a dozen of the most needy inner-city schools. The idea was to get a group of inner-city schools together, led by somebody familiar with inner-city educational problems. Later, he created the position of superintendent of inner-city schools, to which Clarke was appointed.

Although Smyth made continuing efforts to support inner-city schools in various ways, he was always cognizant of the initiatives his trustees would support:

> Some trustees did see that inner-city education had unique needs, but some resented the idea. I made sure the resources were there to allow those schools to contribute to their success. Sometimes they got a little extra money. Some of the trustees were not very supportive of that. We had a staffing model based on what we called inner-city criteria. All the schools were ranked, but the inner city received a bonus and had the best staff ratio in comparison to others. The south-end had the lowest teacher-student ratio. That caused some problems with some of the south-end trustees. It also caused problems with some of the superintendents. I could justify our decisions based on data that we or the province had produced. I tried not to appear arbitrary or to play favourites. I felt that there was a real need in the inner city.

Another key inner-city initiative of the 1980s was a tri-level agreement between the federal, provincial, and municipal governments in 1981 that led to the creation of the Core Area Initiative. The CAI put in place a number of programs and supports for the inner city, including parent involvement, nutrition programs, and parent-child pre-school programs. Many of these initiatives were similar to those of a decade earlier, and though the amount of money involved was modest, it did support many initiatives such as early literacy, parent-child centres, increased community outreach, and improvements in Aboriginal education.

Pat Rowantree, who was a manager with CAI, said, 'I borrowed all the ideas from the 1970s.' However, the CAI was a time-limited agreement (five years, later extended by two more) that had difficulty changing activity in the schools. When the first agreement expired, its replacement, negotiated by the Filmon Conservative provincial government and a more conservative city administration, focused on physical infrastructure with very little funding for social or educational programs.

In 1987, Smyth appointed Pauline Clarke as superintendent of inner-city schools, further affirming a deliberate effort to address inner-city education issues in a distinctive way. The appointment was controversial, he said: 'There was a split on the board and lots of politics behind the scene, but the board eventually confirmed the position.' Initially sixteen schools were involved, selected on the basis of demographic data produced by Paul Madak, the board's research officer.

Both the Aboriginal and immigrant communities in Winnipeg became increasingly organized and powerful politically during the 1970s and 1980s. A growing number of Aboriginal people with higher levels of education provided much stronger indigenous leadership to the community, which became increasingly adept and articulate in its political participation. The Aboriginal community increasingly organized its own institutions and programs, both through the governance structures on reserves and through organizations of urban Aboriginal people, such as the Centre for Aboriginal Human Resource Development (CAHRD). But the degree of change was still small. Poor, immigrant, and Aboriginal groups and communities still had much less political influence than more affluent ones. They were less likely to be active in the political process and sometimes lacked the skills of political participation in a large system, such as preparing briefs or organizing delegations.

The Development of Inner-City Education after 1988

The division was increasingly recognizing the challenges that the diversity of its student body created for educational programs. While attempts had been made in the previous decades to improve services for immigrants and minorities, language policies, such as the development of bilingual schools, addressed well-established groups rather than recent immigrants. Bilingual schools taught half the day in English and the other half in German, Ukrainian, or Hebrew, but no bilingual programs represented a new group of immigrants or Aboriginal students.

In 1988, the board established the Task Force on Race Relations, led by trustee and board chair Anita Neville. The task force consisted of about twenty people including board members, WSD administrators, and people from the community. Two of its members were of Aboriginal origin. Although the mandate was around race relations across the whole division, much of the work eventually focused on Aboriginal and inner-city issues. The task force coincided with the very high profile Aboriginal Justice Inquiry launched in Manitoba as a result of the deaths of several Aboriginal people, including the shooting of J.J. Harper by a Winnipeg police officer.

In her interview, Neville described how the task force developed and some of its main results:

The focus of the task force shifted to be primarily on Aboriginal education. It very clearly and very quickly brought to the fore many of the issues related to the education of Aboriginal children in the division in a way that had never been highlighted before. Issues about transportation, migrancy, children not completing secondary school – a whole host of issues dealing with the inner city. On Monday nights all the television cameras would be at the Aboriginal Justice Inquiry, and the next night the task force would have a meeting with all the television cameras present. This had not been anticipated.

There was a lot of pain, anger, and hostility that came out of the task force. Parents came forward to talk about racism in the schools, either their own experiences or those of their children. Even if their child did not have a problem, they brought their own negative experiences into it. Such criticism had a demoralizing effect on some in the schools, which were doing their best, as they knew it. However, it showed that the efforts had not been enough.

We heard from staff who felt that they had been bypassed because they were Aboriginal or persons of colour. We heard about a lack of curricula to which children could relate.

The Task Force on Race Relations reported in 1989 and was a significant catalyst for change: 'it turned the system inside out.' The process of the task force was as important as its report, because of the public education it produced. The recommendations contained in the report were acted upon. Among the substantive results of the task force were reviews of the curriculum and a review of all school division policies to see if there was any inherent racism. However, the review of the curriculum was not as thorough as it might have been, and problems with books and issues recurred for years afterwards. As a result of the task force, the board also revised WSD policies to make them anti-racist, adopted a multicultural policy, and developed employment equity strategies.

The response to the Task Force on Race Relations revealed the extent of the alienation between the school system and some of its main constituencies. In the early 1990s, the division elected its first two Aboriginal board members, but neither served a second term and there have been no others. Although new Aboriginal organizations emerged, they remained relatively small and fragile. Aboriginal community leader Mary Richard explained the situation:

> One of the problems is that there is no political pressure because our com-
> munity has neither political will nor political voice. We tried to pressure
> the division through the Urban Aboriginal Education Coalition ... There
> was insufficient political will and organization. For one thing, there are not
> enough Aboriginal people with awareness of potential change. Secondly,
> most of the Aboriginal people who are in education have jobs in the inner
> city; consequently, they are stifled in what they can say.

There was ongoing political tension in the WSD between the needs of the inner city and those of the rest of the division. That tension was acute when the system as a whole was facing declines in budget, as happened again in the early 1990s. But both the superintendent and the board maintained some focus on inner-city schools. Neville's account is consistent with Jack Smyth's recollection of his time as superintendent:

> After 1990, the board was consistent in maintaining a lower pupil-teacher
> ratio as well as in maintaining additional funding in the inner city. The
> ward 1 trustees were instrumental in advancing that agenda. I do not even
> know whether people [voters] were aware of the differential treatment
> of inner-city schools. For the most part, it [the south end of the city] is a
> socially conscious community that understands the importance of bring-
> ing children along and giving children opportunities, and was willing to
> support additional resources for the inner city.

The task force and the creation of the inner city superintendent position also marked a renewed effort by the WSD to address some of its
challenges. There has been a gradual shift over time to paying more
systematic attention to instructional practice.

When Pauline Clarke was appointed as the superintendent of inner-
city schools in 1988, she began to work with principals and teachers to
develop a distinctive shared approach to teaching and learning based
on a common set of principles. Winnipeg made some significant progress during these years, despite rather unfavourable social and political
conditions, including a Conservative provincial government from 1988
to 1999 that was not very interested in the inner city and was making
overall budget reductions for education and other social services. It is
worth quoting at length the approach that inner-city superintendent
Clarke (now chief superintendent of the WSD) took:

We have developed a series of basic beliefs – 'principles' – which we use to underpin our work including program strategies. The first set of principles we developed were the principles of learning. In 1989–1990, a group of administrators, the inner city curriculum committee, examined the four core curricula that were in place at the time ... From the four core curricula, eleven principles of learning were developed. My responsibility was to ensure that all the administrators understood these eleven principles of learning and their connection to the four core curricula so that the administrators could determine whether the principles were being applied in the classroom and in their schools. The principals integrated, to varying degrees, the inner-city principles into their schools.

The inner city district principles of learning were finalized in 1992; in 1993–1994 we began developing the principles of assessment ... This work evolved into the Feedback for Learning Project, which has been in ten of the schools since 1999, improving their knowledge about good assessment practices and good programming and the relationship between the two. This work has been shared with all the schools in the inner city district and has reinforced our knowledge of students as learners.

Many other programs have evolved out of this work. One of our learning principles is to have children learn through doing. Beginning in the early 1990s, the Inner City Arts Training Program integrated arts with curricula areas ... It has been very successful. It is an effective model for professional development [in which] teachers attend four professional development sessions a year and in between they apply the strategies in the classroom. They also write personal reflections in their journal and share with others teachers at the next session.

In 2001, we became part of the Learning Through the Arts (LTTA) program, which has reinforced the value of the arts in the learning life of the children. Other programs we have initiated include fetal alcohol syndrome programs, off-campus, addressing student migrancy, technology, and school-to-work.

Above all, our programs depend on good teaching and assessment practices. [We have] emphasized the development of the skills of teachers in Assessment for Learning. Another initiative, the Comprehensive Assessment Program (CAP), has also been an important tool in making sure we know our children as learners and can strategize appropriately. We're using the CAP to benchmark ourselves against other schools in the division in terms of student progress.

[More recently, some] schools wanted to try and integrate the general principles and effective practices through a clustering into groups of three schools with a learning support teacher to support them. The role of the learning support teacher is to work with the classroom teachers in the three schools on many of the principles and practices that we have learned which are relevant and work in maximizing student learning.

We have developed shared ownership throughout the schools – a key factor in school improvement. The emphasis on children's learning is the key task of inner-city schools.

The focus on Aboriginal education in the work of the Task Force on Race Relations led to a growing understanding of the challenges facing the division in that area. Since then, the WSD has continuously made Aboriginal education one of its top priorities. Changes were made in a number of areas, including staffing, curriculum, and community outreach. Two consultant positions were created in the early 1990s to support development of more materials and resources around Aboriginal education. In 1990, Clarke established a pilot project for Aboriginal languages in three elementary schools. Initially, there were insufficient Aboriginal teachers, curriculum, and materials to teach Aboriginal languages. (Both Cree and Ojibway continue to be vital languages in Manitoba, spoken by substantial numbers of people.) However, gradually curriculum materials were developed, and more Aboriginal teachers and principals were hired. Inner-city teachers and principals received more professional development on Aboriginal education, and more efforts were made to reach out to Aboriginal parents. As Clarke described:

> The inner city district Aboriginal education committee took a lead role in working with inner-city administrators as a group. As our inner-city administrators group changed, we could not assume that the new administrators understand the issues around Aboriginal education. For example, we requested the establishment of Aboriginal school support worker in the mid-1990s. We approached Jack [Smyth] and said that we need this connection to the community. We also recommended that the board develop an Aboriginal education policy. We developed a publication to the community that described many of the initiatives we were undertaking in Aboriginal education.

Brian O'Leary, who left the WSD in 1991, also noted the positive efforts:

> A big feature of the history of the inner city in the Winnipeg School division was slowness in responding to a rapidly growing Aboriginal population.

By 1990, Winnipeg had a very conscious approach to Aboriginal issues, partly, I must say, due to pressure from that community. In the last decade the division has really turned this around and done a huge amount in Aboriginal education, including affirmative action in hiring, substantial staff training, and promoting Aboriginal awareness among all staff and students.

Some Aboriginal leaders in Winnipeg believed that the WSD was not responsive to their needs and that they should operate their own schools, or even their own school system in the city. Rhonda McCorriston, an Aboriginal educator who was formerly a teacher in the WSD, described how she felt driven out of the division by its lack of flexibility:

I decided that the best thing for me to do was to work with our Aboriginal children outside the school system. So I developed Songide'ewin, which is an at-risk youth program. Songide'ewin means 'courage' or 'strong heart.' Only one or two of the students were non-Aboriginal. The students were supposed to be sixteen to nineteen years old, but they turned out to be fourteen to nineteen years old. The first time I was there we had 125 students. We were supposed to have forty, but I could not say no to them. They were coming from probation, or they were just getting released from custody. The other schools would turn them away. Others were single mothers or dropouts returning to school. If we did not take them in, no one would . . .

I received funding from Pathways and from Winnipeg Development Agreement. The staff consisted of a teacher assistant, another teacher, and me. I had set it up so that the entire curriculum was in folders. Within each curriculum we developed Aboriginal content. To get their credit, students had individual tutoring from the staff, so they could work through the material in the evening and on Saturdays. We fed them soup every day at lunch. This was around 1993 or 1994.

In the early 1990s, Winnipeg Aboriginal leaders began to investigate setting up their own school system in the city. Mary Richard described this work:

We received at one point a mandate from the Aboriginal council to research the establishment of our own schools, so we went to Alberta to look at charter schools as one possibility. The council and CAHRD researched all the legislation. We told the provincial government that we had a legal right to establish a charter school. Our communication to the government just followed on the heels of the creation of the French School Division. The momentum consequently existed. The government was more right wing at the time – not better or worse but different. Consequently, we thought that it was the perfect time to establish our own charter school. The minister told us to think over the situation before taking full control of the establishment of a charter school; there was a potential partner in the Morris-Macdonald School Division since the latter had already established [several adult learning centres]. We said we would look into the matter, and that is how we became affiliated with Morris-Macdonald School Division in 1997.

The Morris-Macdonald connection allowed the CAHRD to offer high school programs and diplomas to Aboriginal students through their centre in central Winnipeg. CAHRD became one of the largest providers of high school completion in the province. Later, serious problems arose in that connection; the Department of Education took over the school division when it was revealed that it had falsified enrolments in its many adult education programs to receive more funding. Eventually a new adult learning policy framework was created, and the Adult Learning Centres Act was passed by the legislature (Levin, 2005). CAHRD, however, continues to be an important provider of high school completion programs to Aboriginal youth and adults in Winnipeg.

While this work was going on, other Aboriginal educators and leaders wanted to work with existing schools. Out of these currents emerged the proposal in the early 1990s to create an Aboriginal-focus school or schools. The Task Force on Race Relations had drawn attention to the relatively poor performance of Aboriginal students in Winnipeg and had suggested that the division consider creating what was called an 'Aboriginal survival school,' similar to those in several other western Canadian cities, as a response to the high dropout rates among Aboriginal youth. Instead, a new Aboriginal organization, the Thunder Eagle Society, led a drive to create schools that would be governed and run, including selection of principal and staff, by the Aboriginal community rather than by the board. The schools, while open to all, would place considerable emphasis on Aboriginal languages and culture.

The politics around setting up separate Aboriginal schools were very difficult. The debate was highly public, with a great deal of media coverage. Concerns were expressed about segregation of students and potential 'apartheid.' Feelings ran very high and communities were split; although the proposals for the school were advanced by a coalition of Aboriginal activists, other Aboriginal people resisted them as exclusionary.

One of the most difficult aspects of the discussion was the demand of the Thunder Eagle Society, the organization created to represent the Aboriginal community in these discussions, that the schools should be managed by Aboriginal people. Both the political and administrative leadership of the board saw this as problematic. As Jack Smyth, the superintendent, said:

> The Aboriginal community was often looking for more than we could give them. It was not an easy process . . . What they started out with was a desire to have their own Aboriginal school outside the public school system but financed by the Winnipeg School Division. One of them, Bill Sanderson, ended up being elected as a trustee. They would not accept that we could only go so far as the Public Schools Act would allow. The division could not just give them the money. The discussions were difficult. The way it turned out was the division would finance the basic school, and the Thunder Eagle Society would find money to support cultural activities. That was the only way that the Aboriginal community could address its needs within the public school system. There could not be absolute control of the school by the Aboriginal community.

Board member Anita Neville also recalled the discussions:

> The Thunder Eagle Society wanted to be the governing or controlling body of the school. There were prolonged negotiations in developing a governing model for it, with lawyers on both sides . . . We ultimately came up with a model of governance. It included representation from the community; that was the overarching principle, as was parental involvement. The board was not willing to give up control of the school. There were many hours of discussion in the community to determine representation from the community: the tribal councils, the parents, the Aboriginal Center.
>
> I did receive a few phone calls – not a lot – from constituents, saying such things as, 'Why are you setting up an apartheid school?' I understood the concerns about segregating kids by background, but continue to believe that the Aboriginal schools provide an important focus and choice for some parents and students.

The trustees were publicly split on the issue, especially when the proposal was made to lodge the program in a new building that housed Argyle Alternative High School, which would then have to move to another location. The location debate created lasting bad feelings among people within the division who had previously been united in their concerns for Aboriginal education. Gerry Moore, then the principal of Argyle, publicly supported using that site for the new Aboriginal-focused high school, which caused considerable consternation:

> When the Thunder Eagle Society finally approached the superintendents with their response [to the board's first proposal on a site] it was with a rejection of the original offer of the elementary school in the warehouse district and a demand for the new Argyle building. They were told it was not possible. Then began the process of lobbying the board. When the staff [at Argyle] became aware of [my support for this] they invited the area superintendent to a staff meeting. At that meeting they voted unanimously to request my removal as principal of Argyle High School. The superintendents made an effort to remove me from my position as principal. They did not have the support of the board to do so. There was an incredible amount of agitation around the issue – petitions, marches, protests, delegations to the board, letter-writing campaigns, etc. Eventually the board voted in favour of the idea of converting the new Argyle school into an Aboriginal survival school. The Thunder Eagle Society moved on, designed the operational model for the new school and had everything in place for the fall of 1991 when it opened as Children of the Earth School.

Once Children of the Earth was established, the creation the following year of an elementary school, Niji Mahkwa, was much less contentious, in part because the building in which it was housed was a school that was already more than 90 per cent Aboriginal. Still, the debates over apartheid in education continued.

The creation of these two schools was important symbolically, but the political struggle exhausted all parties and the issue died down. While both schools still exist, their enrolment is fairly small and no Aboriginal schools have been established since. Some of the Aboriginal leaders with whom we spoke felt that the WSD never really wanted these schools to work; the co-management model gradually dissipated so that after a few years the schools were managed like all other Winnipeg schools, though they did retain their Aboriginal staffing and curriculum focus. Yet the vast majority of Aboriginal children in the

WSD are not in these two schools, and outcomes for Aboriginal children continue to lag behind provincial and national averages. Nor, despite some ongoing discussion in the community, have there been any substantive steps to create an 'urban reserve' or Aboriginal school authority in Winnipeg.

Conclusions

Winnipeg's struggle to address the challenges of its inner city was continuous betwen the late 1960s and the early 1990s. It is marked by ebbs and flows in political attention, public will, and support from senior governments, but there was no time during which a considerable number of educators and community leaders were not deeply concerned with how the schools could be more effective. The early burst of effort in the late 1960s and early 1970s largely did not survive the changing political landscape of the later 1970s, and reforms were never adopted in Winnipeg as systematically as they were in Toronto. Developments in curriculum, community engagement, and Aboriginal education were counterbalanced by political fighting among trustees and by difficult relationships between the division and the province. The board was often as concerned with control and consistency as with improved results for students, a point on which there was never substantial evidence.

Winnipeg's inner city today is as deprived as ever, and local students continue to have educational outcomes that are significantly worse than city or provincial averages. There is no public comparative longitudinal data that provide a reliable basis for assessing student outcomes over time in Winnipeg, and it would be impossible to separate the impact of particular programs or policies from the impact of broad social changes.

Many of our respondents, looking back on these years, seemed disappointed that more progress had not been made. However, there were some important and lasting achievements, including new modes of teacher preparation, increased outreach to the community, a much stronger focus on Aboriginal education, growing sensitivity to the diversity of the population, and a stronger set of principles and teaching practices to guide inner-city schools.

3 Reform at the Toronto Board of Education

Toronto is Ontario's capital city, and the largest city in Canada. The Greater Toronto Area has a population of over five million people, and Toronto itself has a population of more than 2.5 million. This makes it somewhere between the fifth and eighth largest metropolitan region in North America (depending on the data); the financial, educational, and industrial centre of Canada; and the engine of a great deal of Canada's prosperity.

Toronto began as 'muddy little York,' a small, Protestant, English settlement established in the mid-eighteenth century on Huron land, where the Don River reached the northern banks of Lake Ontario. York changed its name to Toronto in 1834. It attracted first British settlers, and then 'refugees from the revolted States of America' (Cochrane, 1950). In 1850, an elected school board replaced various appointed boards and introduced a compulsory school tax. Since that time, the board has governed an expanding school system and, through its schools, battled 'vice, poverty, and ignorance' with great energy.

The recent story of Toronto is the story of increasing, and increasingly diverse immigration. At the turn of the twentieth century, the census showed that 92 per cent of Toronto's people were ethnically British. By 1950, the non-British population had grown to almost a quarter, and represented many European cultures and languages. The city was a 'vertical mosaic,' with British Canadians holding considerably more power and wealth than Italian, Greek, Polish, and Portuguese immigrants. In the 1960s, Canada began to dismantle restrictions on the immigration of those who were from developing countries and those who were not white. Immigration from around the world increased, and many of these new immigrants settled in Toronto. The percentage of Metro Toronto's population that was of European heritage fell from

96 per cent in 1971, to 60 per cent in 2001 (Ornstein, 2006). Muddy little York had grown into 'the world in a city,' a metropolis that describes itself as the most diverse city in the world (Troper, 2003).

Today, half of Toronto's citizens are foreign-born, contrasted, for example, to only 20 per cent in New York City. Toronto journalist John Barber (1988) described the change a generation of Toronto-born residents experienced: 'I grew up in a tidy, prosperous, narrow-minded town where Catholicism was considered exotic; my children are growing up in the most cosmopolitan city on Earth. The same place' (Barber, 1998). This also describes Gaskell's experience of the city where she grew up in the 1950s and 1960s, and to which she returned at the beginning of the new century.

Toronto sees itself as a city of neighbourhoods, which are signaled in street banners and real estate guides and reflected in electoral wards and voting patterns. Neighbourhoods relate to the availability of social services, transportation, school attendance, health outcomes, and levels of well-being. As the population grew and diversified, neighbourhoods in Toronto became increasingly distinct and polarized in terms of income and wealth (Hulchanski, 2007).

Poverty in the city is linked to neighbourhoods and immigration patterns. As wealth has increased, so has inequality among families and neighbourhoods. The correlation of recent immigration with living in census tracts containing a high proportion of low-income families is significant: it grew from about 0.5 in 1971 to 0.6 in 1991 (Ley & Smith, 1997). In 1971, poverty in Toronto was strongly localized in eight contiguous census tracts in the central city. Over the following decades, gentrification and reinvestment displaced some of the poverty in this area, while immigrants and the poor settled across the metropolitan region. A number of immigrant groups are now more concentrated in outlying areas of Toronto than in the city itself. The gap in income and wealth among Toronto's neighbourhoods increased so that both poorer and wealthier neighbourhoods were more numerous in 2000 than in 1970, while mixed- and middle-income neighbourhoods were less common (Hulchanski, 2007). Today, the inner suburbs include greater diversity and more extreme poverty than the downtown area.

The Toronto Board of Education

The geographic boundaries of the City of Toronto and the Toronto Board of Education (TBE) changed as the city grew and diversified. In 1969, the province reduced thirteen Toronto area school boards to six; the TBE incorporated the formerly independent areas of Forest Hill and Swansea. At the same time, the power of the boards increased as provincial school inspections ended and local boards were granted more power to lead program development responsive to local conditions. School boards also decided on the rate of school taxation, despite some attempts by the province to make things more equal and rein in increases.

The Metropolitan School Board was established in 1953 with a mandate to increase communication among Toronto area boards and share the tax resources available from the businesses in Toronto with the families of downtown workers who lived in the suburbs. The TBE was a member of 'Metro,' as it was called, along with five other boards from the Greater Toronto Area (North York, Scarborough, York, Etobicoke, and East York).

From 1969 to 1995, the TBE was made up of eleven electoral wards. The more northerly wards (10 and 11) contained relatively wealthy and white neighbourhoods: Rosedale, Forest Hill, and Lawrence Park. The downtown wards (3, 4, 6, 7, and 8) contained pockets of extreme poverty, marked by public housing projects such as Regent Park and Moss Park. Other wards to the west towards High Park (1 and 2), to the east toward the Beaches (ward 9), and by the University of Toronto in the Annex (ward 5) had a more mixed demographic, including both working-class immigrants as well as secure middle-class families. These wards have become gentrified since 1970.

From the late 1960s to the late 1990s, the TBE had twenty-four trustees. Two were elected from each of the eleven wards and two represented the separate (Catholic) school system. Although there was a publicly funded Catholic system in Toronto, it was only funded through grade 10 until 1985. Trustees were paid $7,500 in 1970, a significant sum that allowed some trustees to treat their jobs as full-time employment, and their salaries continued to increase, reaching $50,000 before amalgamation. The TBE functioned like a municipal government. Trustees often worked twelve-hour days, and the chair of the Board made more money than new principals and had an executive assistant.

Public school enrolment in the TBE reached its peak in 1976. In 1971, 25 per cent of the Toronto population consisted of young people under age fourteen who were attending public schools; by 1981, this had dropped to 18 per cent, and it continued to fall as families with children moved to the suburbs and Catholic and private schools enrolled more students (Lemon, 1985, p. 195).

The school district of Toronto was relatively wealthy and had a sub-stantial and growing business tax base. It could increase revenue and expand programs despite falling enrolment, as long as it had the sup-port of voters, which it did. Although the province experimented with placing ceilings on the TBE's educational expenditures in the early 1970s, it abandoned the attempt in 1975. Toronto trustees increased tax rates and staff became skilled at negotiating financial formulae with other levels of government. They argued that immigration and poverty were concentrated in Toronto, so funding for Toronto's inner city school initiatives was critical. As a result of the arguments, the skill of accoun-tants, and the tax base in the city, Toronto's programs were funded at a rate substantially higher than those of other boards in the province. This eventually resulted in provincial threats of 'negative grants,' in which Metro would pay money to the province instead of the other way around.

In the 1950s and 1960s, the Toronto Board of Education was considered a strikingly progressive board. After the Second World War, trustees emphasized the role of education in promoting democracy, intercul-tural understanding, and citizenship. Toronto trustees funded music, health, and art programs to broaden the curriculum, and expressed concern about the experiences of disadvantaged and immigrant chil-dren. In 1950, Cecil Charles Goldring, the director of education, was paying attention to the fact that 'unusual names, such as Wolfgang, make the pupils self-conscious' (Lind, 1974, p. 29). In 1965, a research department report titled *Immigrants and Their Education* pointed out that: 'It has reached the point where there are Greeks learning Italian so that they can get along in Toronto' (Lind, 1974, p. 30). Toward the end of the 1960s, under the leadership of Z.S. Phimister, the director of edu-cation, an inner city funding program gave more money to schools in disadvantaged communities. The program also supported some exper-imental schools, notably the Main Street School, which was established in 1965 to teach English to immigrant children in innovative, culturally grounded ways. By 1970, the TBE had twenty teachers who worked exclusively with immigrant children and a hot school lunch program in poorer areas of the city.

The TBE supported child-centred pedagogy, although the practice of teaching in most schools remained traditionally teacher-centred. The recommendations of the 1968 provincial Hall-Dennis report, which championed a child-centred approach and progressive ideas, resulted from a study of curriculum innovations pioneered in the TBE. The report, *Living and Learning,* quoted Phimister's addresses to the board with approval: 'Inventiveness, adaptability and creativity are characteristics which are extremely valuable at present. Yet much of our schooling has to do with memorizing, repeating and following directions' (Committee on the Aims and Objectives of the Schools of Ontario, 1968, p. 71).

The TBE was not a staid and conservative board for the time, although it could still be described as 'ordered, disciplined and hierarchical' (Axelrod, 2005, p. 240) with an attitude of strict paternalism (Llewellyn, 2006). Only property owners could vote in municipal elections until 1958, so the poor were not represented. The overall goals articulated by the board were to assimilate immigrants, improve the educational standing of the poor, and socialize all children according to the norms of the Anglo-Saxon elite. This was done using progressive pedagogical methods in a few schools, and drills, spelling tests, and worksheets in most schools. Students were sorted into classes and programs based on their potential as determined by tests and grades. Trustees supported the strap, joined a campaign against comic books, and barred Communists from working for the TBE – a controversial move, given that at least one trustee, Edna Ryerson, was elected with the support of the Communist Party (Clarke, 2002). Cultural assimilation and intellectual ranking were the order of the day.

The 1970s ushered in a new era of policy initiatives focused on equity. Newly elected reform trustees challenged the system, its administrators, its principals, and its teachers. They wanted more attention on the experience of students growing up in poverty, more involvement of local communities in decision making, the teaching of languages other than English, and a system-wide critique of racism, sexism, homophobia, and class bias. The TBE identified the most disadvantaged neighbourhoods, allocated additional staff and resources to schools in those neighbourhoods, and provided staff committed to curriculum innovation with opportunities to do things differently. It actively mobilized parents and involved them in choosing principals and making policy. It restructured its staff and created equity advisers, inner-city coordinators, and community liaison officers who reported to the TBE, rather than to local principals. These advisers were activists who developed close working relationships with ward trustees, felt protected by those relationships, and worked informally with trustees to develop new policies. Work groups composed of trustees and staff, often with differing politics, produced some of the most effective and progressive policies, as they made provisions for implementation as well as overall policy direction. This equity-focused direction prevailed from 1969 to 1998, despite political turmoil and gradually declining resources. The rest of this chapter provides an overview of the Toronto experience, discussing the key changes in people, policies, and politics between 1970 and 1998.

Gradually, the political and financial independence of the TBE was constrained. In the mid-1980s, the province, through Bill 127, forced the TBE into unified collective bargaining across Metro. As collective bargaining, especially with elementary teachers, had been a major strategy for securing more teachers in inner-city areas, the TBE's capacity to act independently of other 'suburban' and more conservative boards was substantially reduced. In 1995, the newly-elected Conservative provincial government, under premier Mike Harris, announced its intention to amalgamate all Metro boards into the Toronto District School Board (TDSB). The amalgamation was accomplished by 1998, despite overwhelming opposition from within the old TBE and city. The result was the largest school board in the country, funded according to a financial formula determined by the province (Gidney, 1999). This is the point at which our study ends and educational reform in the city changed direction as a new, larger group of trustees had to renegotiate their commitments and find new ways forward.

The 1970s: Setting an Agenda for Reform

In 1968, a group of parents from a public housing development, known as the Trefann Court mothers, presented a brief to the Toronto school board arguing that the system was failing their children. It was written with the help of the community activists who were steeped in the radical politics of the 1960s and later became reform school trustees, and it articulated a significant shift in assumptions about education. It stated:

> What we are increasingly led to think is that the school system – with Opportunity Class as its dead-end division – just isn't set up to be meaningful for our kids. It doesn't relate to the things they know about and care about. It doesn't touch the world as it's experienced by people who don't have much money, who are constantly threatened by unemployment, who are harassed by welfare officers or the police. It doesn't understand what it means to be a person with integrity under these circumstances, or where you find life and friendship. So the kids slide away, and turn their minds

and their hearts off. And many of those who turn off the most end up in Opportunity Class. (Martell, 1974, p. 41)

These parents argued that the curriculum did not engage and educate their children and the teachers unfairly streamed them into special needs and vocational classes that became an academic dead end. They took issue with the idea that their children were not intelligent (titling their brief *Downtown Kids Aren't Dumb*). They argued that teachers' notions of academic and social success were far too limited, narrow, and biased, and served to undermine the confidence and enthusiasm their children brought to school. They wanted schools to recognize their children's existing skills and knowledge, not just provide compensatory programs to lift them up or fit them in. This brief became one of the foundational texts for the movement for school reform in Toronto. It placed the onus of change on school personnel, not disadvantaged families, and made the voices of parents in marginalized communities pivotal in how these changes were defined and brought about.

In 1969, a slate of reform trustees who shared, and in some cases had helped to advance, the views of the Trefann Court mothers was elected to the TBE. The new trustees were variously described in the press as 'young,' 'radical,' 'cerebral,' 'firebrands,' 'blue denim radicals,' and 'distrustful of the system.' They had absorbed the intellectual and political currents of the 1960s. They read Saul Alinsky, the American organizer of low-income communities; Ivan Illich, who proposed 'deschooling'; and the political and economic ideas of Karl Marx. They worked and lived in alternative communities like Everdale and Point Blank, and they were skilled at using media. They were young, energetic, and committed to social revolution.

The election marked what one trustee described as a 'sea change,' both in the substance of the TBE's policies and in the processes it used to arrive at policy. The reformers, loosely defined, had organized carefully, looking at the demographics of who voted in trustee elections and realizing that voter turnout was so low that a little political organizing could turn into a lot of seats. They won a majority position that allowed them to elect the chair of the TBE. Some of the best known reform trustees elected to the 1970 board were Fiona Nelson (ward 5), Gordon Cressey (ward 7), and Doc Yip (ward 6). In 1973, they were joined by Sheila Meagher (ward 9), Dan Leckie and Bob Spencer (ward 6), and Doug Barr (ward 7). In 1978, Penny Moss (ward 5), George Martell (ward 7), Pat Case and Peter Davis (ward 4), and

Tony Silipo (ward 3) were elected. Later, Olivia Chow (ward 6), David Clandfield (ward 7), Fran Endicott (ward 7), Pam McConnell (ward 7), and Tam Goosen (ward 8), among others, carried on the progressive policy mandate. They did not always agree, but they could often find common positions. Most of the reformers were associated with the New Democratic Party, although some, notably Doc Yip, Fiona Nelson, and Penny Moss, identified as independents or liberals and at least one, Pat Case, was a member of the Communist Party. They were primarily elected in the downtown wards and from the Annex.

Several Toronto Reform Trustees in Brief

Fiona Nelson was an elementary school teacher in the 1960s, and resigned when her principal told her she could not take her students on field trips: 'I was furious that he would interfere with my program, which was successful and based on the needs of the children.' She ran as a trustee in 1966 to change the rules. She was not elected, took another teaching job, was fired, fought it, won reinstatement, ('it never occurred to me that I should back off; they should back off'), and then quit and was elected as a trustee in 1969. She was a feisty trustee, dedicated to promoting good education and healthy living. She remained a trustee over several different periods until amalgamation, chaired the school board several times, and had a major impact on Toronto politics.

Gord Cressey grew up in north Toronto, went to the West Indies with the Canadian University Service Overseas (CUSO), and attended university in Chicago. Returning to Toronto as a social worker with a social conscience, he was running a group home for troubled kids and 'woke up one morning and decided to run' for the TBE. He was elected in 1969, and became an effective and well-known chair. He joined the NDP in 1977, well into his political career, and left the Board to run for provincial politics and city council.

George Martell came to Toronto after getting a doctorate from the London School of Economics in 1965, 'a very unhappy camper with academic life.' He worked as a CBC radio producer, joined the Company of Young Canadians to work with young people, founded an alternative school called Point Blank, and rejoined academia as a sociology professor at York University. His political views were to the left of most of the other trustees, and he had a very important impact through editing *This Magazine Is about Schools* and through his powerful writing on community schools. He was an elected trustee for only two years, in 1979 and 1980, and chaired the NDP caucus even after he decided to leave his role as a trustee.

Penny Moss was a parent who had been involved in stopping the closure of her children's school. When the trustees in her ward, who were members of the NDP, decided to step down in 1978, they were looking for a candidate with a progressive edge. Moss explained her campaign: 'When I ran for the school board, I didn't know about inner-city issues, I was a young mother, I think my eldest was probably in grade 3, and I was a fairly active parent in a local school.' She worked closely with Fiona Nelson, who was elected in the same ward, acting as an independent but left-leaning trustee who brokered compromises until she left the TBE in the mid-1980s, disillusioned with the lack of progress on ending streaming in schools.

David Clandfield started his involvement in Toronto politics through supporting his children's right to go to francophone schools. He was a French professor at the University of Toronto from a working-class British background that predisposed him to sympathize with the left. He became friendly with George Martell, which led to his election: 'The francophone community wanted a stand-alone school, not sharing as they had been for two years, and a large enough school. And that got me well enough known that when George stepped down, he said, why don't I run.' David became an important resource for the TBE in linguistics, but left when he found his role as trustee was too demanding in light of his professorial duties.

Pat Case was recruited to run for the TBE by the Communist Party in 1979. In his account of the events, he said: 'I got involved with the school board because the Communist Party said, "We want you to run for the school board." I was involved with some of the schools in the neighbourhood. And I thought OK, fine, cool. So I got elected to the school board and after I got elected I decided what I was going to do.' He remained as an active trustee (though not a member of the Communist Party) until 1985, when he decided that attending law school along with being a trustee was too much. After graduating from law school, he returned to the TBE as a staff member and worked on improving equity programs.

The Reformers' Program

Under the new regime, the assumption that the existing practices of teachers' and principals' were worthy of support was gone. Gone also were the days of easily approving recommendations from TBE staff and of any consensus as the trustees divided along ideological lines. As one member of the Toronto Teachers' Federation was quoted as saying in the *Globe and Mail,* 'ever since the new board was elected in December, it has been divided into two opposing camps. One supports the school system and the administration, and one does not.' The reformers did not, and they had a bare majority, so coalitions were unstable and a swing trustee could make a big difference.

In 1970, David Bonham, described as 'a soft-spoken grandfather with a sunny smile' by journalist Loren Lind, defeated Fiona Nelson, a reformer, for chair of the TBE on the first ballot. Lind (1974), writing about that first year, concluded: 'A year of bitter battles has left the would-be-reformers splintered and weak with moderates firmly in charge.' Bonham noted these tensions in his address to the school board: '1970 has in some respects been a difficult year. Some new trustees were unfamiliar with the administrative structure and present programs of the board ... The new members brought in many creative ideas. These ideas have been studied; some have come into fruition, others are still under consideration' (board minutes, 1971).

During the first year, debates ranged over reform of inner-city schools, expansion of early childhood education, and the power of the principal to determine student dress codes and hair length. The passage of a resolution, 'that the use of the strap be abolished in the secondary and elementary schools of the City of Toronto,' signaled the changes that were coming. As Bill Quinn, a superintendent at the time, put it: 'I'll never forget the removal of the strap from the classroom. I think, if I had to do it again, I'd go about it a little more gently. That was removing their authority in the eyes of many teachers' (Toronto Board of Education, 1950, p. 59). But the new trustees aspired exactly to tip the balance of power in the schools in favour of parents and students and elected trustees ('the people'), away from teachers and administrators and board staff ('the system'). As Penny Moss, a former trustee, gently put it: 'I still have a bit of a cynical streak about senior administration of school boards.' George Martell was more blunt: 'I just assumed these guys were my enemies. So you went after them in public, you didn't just do it behind the scenes, you assumed that these guys were conning you or not telling you the truth or doing bad stuff, and you'd say so.' Gord Cressey commented: 'To begin with in the early days, we weren't worried about the administration being on-side. What we finally realized, is the goal was implementation.' To achieve that goal, they had to get the support of the staff.

The new politics shook up the administrative staff at the TBE, upsetting some and energizing others. Many staff saw the reformers as a major impetus for trouble. As Duncan Green and Ned McEwan said in their interviews: 'The new board had less respect than they should have for some of the people that were working there; they just tarred them all with the same brush.' 'They were very simplistic in their approach to things and often cruel in their dealings with people.' 'They were impatient to do things. I used to say they'd pass it on Thursday night and expect it to be done by Friday morning, and you can't do that.'

There were different views among the existing staff. As John Bates, the inner-city coordinator, said:

> Everybody had a different agenda. I'm not going to name names, because the tape's on. But some wanted the left looked after; they wanted someone to keep them away from 155 College Street (the board office). Keep them busy! And another person just wanted to know what they were doing. And another one felt that if they had their way and with a bit of guidance, we would be able to do great things! And they did! They did marvelous things! There is no doubt about that!

Don Rutledge was a staff member who found the new trustees very helpful. Even though he and his staff had been working on new curriculum and particularly language policies since the mid-1960s, he said, 'I don't think we would have gotten off the mark if the trustees hadn't shaken things up.' Duncan Greene also discussed the new trustees: 'They were the most exciting, diverse, and progressive group of people that I ever worked with. And the Board as a collective made, from my point of view, the right decisions 90 per cent of the time. It really did restore your faith in democracy, if it needed to be restored.'

Given these views, it is not surprising that the new board members wanted new staff. They voted to hire John Bremer, a well-known progressive educator from Philadelphia, as director of the board. The introduction to his book reads, 'The fundamental contention of this book and of the Parkway Program is that no changes in a educational system will be of any significance unless the social organization of education is totally changed, that is, unless the system itself is changed. Nothing less will do' (Bremer & von Moschzisker, 1971, p. 11). He was not approved by the province, as was then required; officially, he did not have appropriate Ontario qualifications, and politically, there was substantial provincial opposition to his appointment. Instead, Ron Jones, an internal candidate, became director. He was succeeded in 1974 by Duncan Green, a skilful politician and articulate educator, who had risen in the TBE from secondary teacher to principal to president of the teachers' federation. He wanted a more flexible and responsive system that served students better: 'The thing that really bugged me all the time was the promotion system and the compulsory subjects.'

New staff positions and departments were added to focus on research, community relations, equity, and the inner city. The relations between the staff, the trustees, and the community were restructured. At a speech to the Canadian Education Association in 1975, Duncan Green discussed how dramatically the decision-making style of the TBE had changed: 'Community involvement arrived in Toronto some years ago; indeed it was always present. Those of you who are responsible for jurisdictions which have a nucleus of wealthy or politically influential people will know what I mean. The school system has been sensitive to needs expressed by such groups. New to Toronto was the insistence of groups who previously had lacked political influence on the scene.' He also discussed how widely the TBE had come to involve parents in issues as mundane as school construction, curriculum, and language instruction: 'Our parents were not slow to let us know their concerns ... All these processes of community involvement are time-consuming and slow. They make it very hard to run a system.' But he concludes that educators must 'recognize as legitimate partners in the educational process the students and parents that the school is established to serve.'

As a result of the restructuring, the boundaries between the senior staff and trustees were porous and relationships trumped hierarchy. There was a great deal of debate that engaged a wide community. Working groups consisting of school trustees, administrators, and community members were established to study and make recommendations on difficult issues. The new working relations demanded a great deal from everyone involved. For the trustees, it was a full-time job to be effective. For the staff, as Duncan Green described, 'it was exhausting. Most weeks were seventy-hour weeks; we were really going full tilt. Because the teacher stuff was all on weekends, the board stuff was on weekends, the job was during the week.'

After an initial change to include trustee input in hiring principals, trustee and parent involvement in what had been staff decisions, according to Green,

increased and expanded; they grafted on parents and staff and everybody, the caretaker, everybody. The first principal appointment we made under that agreement, trustees were there, I was there. We interviewed the applicants, chose an applicant. Everybody was happy, the applicant goes forward, recommended to the board, no problem. About four months later, I get a call from one of the trustees, 'We've got a problem.' 'What's the problem?' 'Well some people aren't happy with the new principal.' I said, 'So?' 'Well,' he said, 'What are you going to do about it?' I said, 'I am not going to do a thing about it. What you are going to do about it, however, is go out there and defend that guy. You chose him. And if you could have appointed God himself to be principal of the school, you'd be getting complaints about something in a month. Remember now, you're part of the process. And you don't just get the privileges, you get the responsibilities too.'

Some of the most outspoken new trustees became well known advocates of social reform in the city, becoming public intellectuals and in several cases, successfully running for city council, which had also changed its political stripes with the election of 'tiny, perfect,' and progressive mayor David Crombie in 1972, and John Sewell, a central figure in the Trefann Court fight, in 1978. In 1973, Fiona Nelson became vice chair of the TBE, and in 1974 she became chair. Gord Cressey was vice chair, then became chair in 1975. Dan Leckie took over the position in 1977. As one interviewee put it: 'The combination of Cressy, Barr, and Leckie was pretty formidable. They had the agenda that you are writing about [poverty] very much at the centre of their heart. And they had close links with City Hall, with Sewell.'

Speeches at the first board meeting of 1974 provide insight into the new board's operations. Nelson's presentation looked back on the 'halcyon' days of the 1960s when municipal boards' budgetary prerogatives were not questioned and equality of opportunity and freedom of choice were accepted. She displayed her erudition by quoting the Club of Rome, *Deuteronomy*, and Edmund Burke, among others, lambasting the moral vacuum of technocrats and supporting the values of the local community. Duncan Green spoke more pragmatically about new work groups the board had set up on student rights, vocational schools, day care, and early childhood education. He noted his concern about relations with Metro, cooperation with other city groups, and curriculum reform.

The new board focused on the effects of poverty in education. In 1970, the director of research, E.O. Wright, conducted the first Every Student Survey to provide a description of the demographic, social, and academic characteristics of students in the TBE, including their language, parental occupation, place of birth, special education status, and level of secondary school courses. The survey had a 97 per cent return rate, reflecting the remarkable power of the board to command teachers and principals. It found that 40 per cent of students spoke a language other than English in their homes, and that one quarter had been born outside Canada. The analysis showed that being born outside Canada, speaking a language other than English, and having low socio-economic status reduced the likelihood that a student would be in a high-status academic program. This provided concrete local data to support what a great deal of sociology of education was reporting at the time: academic success was linked to socio-economic status (Coleman, 1966; Jencks, 1972). The Every Student Survey was repeated in 1975 (Deosaran & Wright, n.d.) and periodically after that. Its affirmation of the relationship between demographic variables and academic status laid the foundation for an agenda to try to provide more opportunities for vulnerable children.

In 1971, the TBE created an inner-city department, which began small but had a budget and number of staff that gradually increased over time. The staff initiated area-specific programs and monitored every new city-wide initiative for its effect on the inner city. They started a new reader series geared to the experiences of inner-city children, and they funded the Inner City Angels to bring art and cultural performances into the schools. They developed the After Four program and other community school programs, expanded early childhood education, and began tutoring and parenting programs in inner-city areas.

A formula was calculated to rank schools according to their degree of need. The rankings used census data on income, rental housing, visible minority status, single parent families, education, employment, mobility, non-English language spoken at home, and immigration status. These indicators were debated and changed over time, as more and better data and analyses became available, but the policy remained to allocate additional teaching staff, paraprofessional staff, and funding to schools that scored lowest on the school needs index.

Reform also meant support for alternative programs, like SEED, ALPHA, CONTACT, City School, and Laneway, which provided more flexible pathways for students who did not flourish in normal schooling. Alternative, 'free' schools were a major commitment of radical educators in the 1960s, and of the reformers associated with *This Magazine*, whose editors spent a lot of their time setting up new kinds of schools, incuding Everdale, Superschool, and Point Blank, and publishing analyses of how these alternatives worked (Repo, 1970). Support for alternative schooling was a key part of the new trustees' reform agenda, and it was reinforced by a commitment to parent voice, local community building, and non-hierarchical power relations. Alternative schools never displaced the focus on reform across the system, but they continued to attract and nurture innovative teachers.

Reform also meant challenging the streaming of students from elementary schools into rigid secondary school programs, or 'tracks,' that produced very different outcomes for students. Vocational education was seen as a dead end, a second-class education, and a dumping ground for the poor. Streaming was a difficult practice to change. Despite concern, several reports, and school board debates about its effects, it continued to have strong support from teachers, principals, and many students and parents.

More action took place at the elementary level. The major innovation was to create a few schools, eventually called 'inner-city project schools,' which would model a different way of interacting with students in poor neighbourhoods. The Dundas project was the first one, begun in 1975 to 'evolve new methods of instruction in an effort to raise academic achievement in a pilot downtown elementary school.' The program included new approaches to language teaching, weekend school-based professional development programs for staff, parental participation, and collective decision-making. This became the model on which the TBE built its approach to elementary education over time.

Inner city project schools were schools in areas of need, and had staff who applied to receive extra funding and become both experiments and exemplars. They were committed to developing a distinctive curricular approach and to ensuring a close connection between the school staff, the parents, and the community. These schools attracted some of the best teachers to the inner city. They had more autonomy than other schools. They were able to fund school-based professional development and select teachers who shared a basic philosophy of education. They also had extra staff and community liaison officers. The principal of one project school described them as places where teachers 'believed that inner-city kids could do well at school . . . believed that the connection with the community and the parents would make a big difference. And there was a big focus on literacy.'

The focus on literacy had historical roots at the board. Don Rutledge, an Ontario English teacher who undertook doctoral studies under Jimmy Britton, a well-known British professor, had been hired in the mid-1960s. Britton promoted a child-centred approach to language learning, which included having students learn to read by writing their own stories. He wanted teachers to insist on students writing drafts, editing in groups, and treating language as the medium for learning in every school subject. Rutledge brought Britton to speak to the directors of education in 1965, and had him return to Toronto for many years to coach teachers at the inner-city project schools, to instruct teachers from across the province at OISE, and to meet with trustees about educational theory and practice.

The TBE's focus on equal opportunity for all students was conceptualized as a concern for equity. Equity expanded beyond a focus on poverty to include equal opportunity for students with different cultures, languages, skin colours, genders and, later on, sexual orientations. The social movements of the time provided energy, ideas, and networks that were harnessed to change at the Board. Curriculum materials and personnel policies were examined for bias. Staff positions were created to encourage curriculum change, to promote gender equality, and to attack racism in personnel policies. Some argued that the Board's increasing focus on 'identity politics' diminished its attention to poverty, but a broad commitment to equity engaged a wide and active community on the left, as well as responding to the community pressures and demographic shifts that were changing the city.

In 1976, a report on multiculturalism encapsulated the debate about how the schools should approach cultural difference. A working group of staff, trustees, and community activists had developed a draft that had a:

> very comprehensive rationale for the inclusion of languages and culture maintenance programs as a segment of the school's regular program. The rationale is based on the recognition that such programs are necessary to the educational well-being of students from a cultural and linguistic heritage other than British or French. The necessity arises because schools very naturally reflect a dominant culture, which is alien to these children. The draft report's position is that culture and language maintenance programs would function to help to dispel the negative impact of the dominant culture on the personal development of these children. (Report of the Multiculturalism Task Force, 1976, p. 21)

There was still concern about this elision of the dominant culture and oppression. The board as a whole was not willing to agree with the task force that English instruction constituted a bias and assimilation was not a goal. However, they did support the development of culturally sensitive curriculum materials, and experimented with Italian, Greek, and Chinese bilingual programs. Reception classes and transition programs for new immigrants increased. The School Community Relations Department (SCR) was established as a result of this report, to build bridges to new ethnic communities in the city by hiring and supporting community liaison officers.

An SRC director (first John Piper, then Charles Novogrodsky) was appointed to report to the TBE. He hired community activists who reported to him, and who frequently caused 'trouble' for local principals. As George Martell put it, 'We hired all these Portuguese and Italians and Chinese and Greeks and all sorts of folks and they went out and organized their communities. And they'd come back yelling and hollering at us, and we thought that was just fine.' Duncan Green commented, 'By and large, I think they did a lot to improve the understandings between those communities and the schools. And, well, some of them were spies for trustees, sure.'

The SCR gave concrete form to the belief held by the reformers that power should be removed from principals and teachers, and placed in the hands of disadvantaged communities and the community leaders who worked with them. Green estimated that by 1978, there were at least 625 parent organizations involved in the schools of Toronto. Parents were not only given a voice in the selection of principals, they were put on working groups at the board and involved in policy discussions, if they were articulate and willing to devote the time. The political process at the TBE increasingly used advisory committees that consisted of community members. This additional, and very active, community involvement meant that meetings lasted late into the evening or early morning. Trustees and staff studied issues at length and argued publicly as they attempted to reach agreements on policy matters.

By the end of the 1970s, the processes, staffing, and policies of the TBE had changed substantially. Its hallmarks included attention to the inner city, to diversity, to community involvement, and to equity in its many guises. Keeping this focus alive in the more conservative 1980s was going to be a challenge.

The 1980s: Institutionalizing Change

The political and economic climate in Canada and in Ontario changed in the 1980s. The early 1980s were a time of economic recession.

Taxation and government intervention became more unpopular as the zeitgeist became more conservative. The election of the conservative governments of prime minister Margaret Thatcher in the United Kingdom, president Ronald Reagan in the United States, and prime minister Brian Mulroney in Canada signaled an era in which politicians encouraged belief in market forces and suspicion of government programs, especially if they were targeted at equity. Provincial and federal governments were interested in education as an economic lever for global competitiveness and national prosperity, while its role in local community-building and providing equal opportunity became less salient. This was the advent of what came to be labeled 'neo-liberalism.'

During this period, local educational expenditures rose substantially faster than federal transfer payments and provincial funding. The financial and policy autonomy that the TBE had enjoyed was challenged more often by provincial governments, both because the expenses kept rising, and because provincial premiers wanted to make their mark on education, raising standards and ensuring quality. In 1987, there was a teachers' strike across Metro as unions and management struggled over scarcer and scarcer educational resources.

At the TBE, political conflict among trustees and staff increased. Left-leaning trustees now had substantial experience and strong roots in the system, but were challenged by more conservative candidates with support from some news media, especially the *Toronto Sun*. Some of the initial reform trustees, like Cressey, Martell, and Leckie moved on, but others, like Nelson, Moss, and Case, stayed and new reforming trustees were elected. In 1980, Doug Little, Tony Silipo, Pat Case, Peter Davis, David Clandfield, Penny Moss, Fran Endicott, and Fiona Nelson were elected to the Board. Penny Moss and Fiona Nelson had no opposition in ward 5, and meant that Toronto maintained its left leaning policies.

The staff now included well-known activists, as well as career educators. Activists like Myra Novogrodsky, Tony Souza, Charles Novogrodsky, Tim McCaskell, and later Pat Case and Terezia Zoric, had important jobs, and they hired others to advance the agenda of equity in the TBE. As McCaskell (2005) argued, 'There was a good group of activists that you could count on behind the scenes to be allies.' His book, *Race to Equity*, illustrates the sense some staff had that they were fighting for social justice and equitable education in the face of a recalcitrant administration and conservative trustees who would not move quickly enough. Case, originally elected as a trustee, returned as a staff member later in the 1980s after completing law school. He understood the difficult relations between trustees and staff: 'If staff working within the school board got a little bit too far ahead of what the elected officials or the senior admin felt, you certainly were reminded of it. There were few, but a couple of firings.'

The inner-city emphasis and the community involvement ideology remained dominant, but there were clear and increasingly obvious divisions. The left-leaning members on the TBE and the staff aligned with them wanted more radical changes and engendered increased opposition. The right wanted more accountability and less spending. The atmosphere was politically volatile, and implementing new programs required compromise.

The staff and the trustees' collaborative processes were tested when an NDP caucus formed in the early 1980s. As George Martell, who chaired the caucus, said, 'We wanted to be the government of the board; we wanted parliamentary democracy to function at the board.' The caucus was very contentious, as independent trustees who tended to vote with NDP trustees were excluded from it, and board staff saw it as a means of keeping them out of discussions and decision-making. As one interviewee put it: 'The Caucus used to meet in Room 249, which is on the second floor of 155 College, and they'd meet and plan or plot, depending on your point of view, what would be done with the board agenda.' Ann Vanstone, a more conservative trustee who was not part of the caucus, remarked, 'We had about four years of really tough sledding. The NDP caucus, which held formal meetings and took formal stances on stuff had a slim majority. And they focused, to the exclusion of all else, I think, on inner-city issues and immigration issues.' Pat Case described the caucus as 'endless, endless meetings' around internal politics.

Independent trustees such as Penny Moss or Fiona Nelson played an important mediating role. As Moss remarked, 'Early on I learned that there is no change if it's passed by a majority of the left. It just doesn't happen. The administration waits you out. I always worked to include and find consensus, which sometimes broke down after a subsequent election.' Others adopted the language of struggle and advocacy, tapping into social movements to define a 'we' that took on the 'they' of everyday education.

The decade began with a report to the inner-city committee from senior staff on the continuing strong relationship between socio-economic status and achievement in school. The Toronto data from the Every Student Survey was presented with the comment that 'this pattern has been observed for many years now, not only in Toronto but elsewhere.' The report summarized international research, including the Coleman report, Basil Bernstein and William Labov on language, Michael Rutter et al. on effective schools, and reviews of Head Start. It also pointed to research on Toronto's programs and the importance of 'the individual school as the locus of energy, because of both the learnings from the Toronto projects and the research indications quoted in this report.' The report concluded that effective inner-city schools need strong administrative leadership with on-site curriculum assistance, an emphasis on academic achievement, high expectations of pupils, a calm atmosphere, and a belief in and responsibility for local improvement.

This was not a radical analysis, but a well-informed one that emphasized whole school reform, local responsibility, and school-level innovation, particularly in inner-city areas. John Bates had taken over as inner-city coordinator in 1979, and increased the resources available to his department. John Piper commented that 'Bates would go around like Santa Claus and put these funds wherever there were activist teachers wanting to do things.' He was a person who achieved goals and worked with community agencies and the new literacy initiatives. He could influence curriculum development across the TBE and made sure it served students in the inner city. He hired staff who understood literacy, were committed to increasing the achievement of inner-city students, and avoided a negative analysis of children from poor homes. His hiring decisions considered not only competence, but also political and ethical commitments.

The equity agenda also continued to expand. In 1980, the TBE appointed two equity advisers, one for race relations and one for gender equity. Employment equity for staff was the original focus, but it expanded into curriculum change for students. Much of the focus of the race relations adviser, Tony Souza, was on curriculum change, workshops for students and staff, and teacher professional development. The affirmative action adviser (Myra Mather, who was followed by Myra Novogrodsky in 1984) was hired to work on hiring and promoting women. But Myra was soon joined by Gail Posen, who developed curriculum initiatives to promote gender equity. They also became the periodic focus for some politically charged identity politics as racism and gender equity competed for space and resources.

Equity was promoted through workshops for students and teachers and focused on changing ideas. According to Tim McCaskell, these workshops were 'fundamentally different from other student leadership experiences. Not content with simply building skills or hoping that a shared experience would encourage diverse students to learn to like each other more, [the] goal was to forge a social analysis out of the collective sharing of experience' (2005, p. 29). Students learned to treat each others' experience with respect, and to understand why activism was important for citizenship. Workshops, conferences, and talks on literacy for teachers were aimed at getting students to write more, ending the ritual of spelling tests and dictation on Fridays, and making connections among like-minded teachers and community members so they would work for social, political, and educational change.

In the early 1980s, there was a heated debate about heritage languages among several groups. Immigrant parents, organized by the SCR and supported by several researchers, trustees, and staff, requested that Toronto schools teach heritage languages during the regular school day. They argued that immigrant children would benefit academically from having their language recognized as part of the core curriculum, and from continuing to learn in that language. Moreover, TBE staff realized that such a policy would retain immigrant students who might have otherwise gone to the Toronto Catholic District School Board, which had a similar language program already in place. Opposition came from the teachers' unions, which did not want extended work hours, and a segment of the community who believed that the program would undermine the priority and teaching of English and French. The fight was described as 'bloody' and 'divisive.' It led to a court challenge, a teachers' boycott of extracurricular activities, and several meetings that went on all night. A compromise was reached in 1984, whereby the programs would be offered in schools where a majority of parents requested them, and teachers were exempt from direct involvement.

In 1984, there were significant staff changes at the TBE. John Bates, head of the inner-city schools division, moved to be the director at the school board in Kingston. Duncan Green moved to the provincial government to work on curriculum reform, and Ned McKeown, a deputy director who had worked closely with Green, took over as director. Interviewees described McKeown as 'a bit of a wizard with the money,' 'really good with budgets, with strategic planning and particularly with tactics with the board,' and very effective at 'getting things done,' but he was less interested than Green had been in the philosophical debates that animated the TBE.

McKeown had been around for a long time, and he had his own political constituency. He was straightforward in his opposition to many of
the ideas put forward by the left-leaning members of the board, even
while he recognized the importance of reform. As he put it: 'While I
didn't change their mind very often, many times I was able to say to
them, "We will, as staff, try to structure processes to minimize the dam-
age that I think your harebrained ideas are going to cause." We had that
kind of open communication and it worked out.'

The left wing trustees were both impressed and sceptical. George
Martell commented: 'McKeown was a total politician. I'd go to tree
plantings outside my school and there was McKeown. He was an
astonishing politician; he knew more people in my ward than I did and
I lived there for years.' Relations between McKeown and the reform
trustees at the TBE were sometimes strained because the philosophical
differences were large (whether acknowledged or not), but they were
always interesting. In part of his interview, McKeown discussed how
trustees needed good relations with the staff to be effective:

> Philosophically, neither of the two of us [McKeown and Green] was par-
> ticularly at odds with them [the trustees]. Sometimes they wanted to be
> too extreme, we felt. I remember one night at the board, they were grum-
> bling about the recommendations of the vocational schools work group
> not being implemented. And we'd obfuscated for a while and finally they
> asked me again. And I stood up and said, 'You know, madam chair, the
> recommendations were not implemented because the staff thought they
> were wrong and chose not to implement' and sat down. Interestingly
> enough, they knew that; they were just surprised that I would admit it.
> But then we went along and said, 'All right now, let's review these things
> and see what can be salvaged out of this.' And then we had a go at selling
> the idea to the secondary schools, saying we've gone as far as we can go in
> dragging our feet. We've got to implement certain aspects of the report. So
> we went ahead and did that.

Another of McKeown's anecdotes illustrates his street smarts and
effectiveness:

> We were far into daycare, more than any other board in the province, cer-
> tainly more than any other board in Metro. We had a daycare in almost
> every elementary school. They were almost all parent-run daycares. I got
> a panic call at home on a Sunday saying that the parent who was treasurer

had disappeared with the contents of the bank account, around $6,000. And they couldn't pay the staff and they weren't going to be able to open. I got a call the same night from John Sewell, who was then mayor, and whose son was in the daycare. What were we going to do about it? I tried to explain to him it wasn't our thing to do. But what we ended up doing was buying the furniture that was there (it was the same size as junior kindergarten furniture) for $6,000 and leasing it back to them at a dollar a year. The board meeting was the following Thursday and somebody asked what had happened and I gave them the answer. And one of the trustees said, 'Mr. Director, is this legal?' And I said, 'I'm not really sure, madam chair, but it certainly was the right thing to do.' And I suspect one of them called the ministry and the ministry told them no, it wasn't legal, but the ministry knew better than to pursue it.

In 1985, a more conservative group of school board trustees, who organized as the 'positive alternative' and were interested in more standardized testing, won a majority of seats in the school board election. The positive alternative trustees abolished the SCR and downplayed the de-streaming of secondary education. Some of our interviewees pointed to 1985 as the end of the reform era at the TBE, but others saw a good deal of continuity in direction, even after the election.

When the SRC was eliminated by majority vote at a board meeting in April 1985, its controversial but energetic leader, Charles Novogrodsky, lost his job. School community advisors would now report to the local superintendents, not to staff at the TBE. Tim McCaskell (2005) describes this as 'the shift in the balance of power away from community activism and the reassertion of the traditional paradigms of entrenched educational bureaucracy.' Certainly, the power of community activism was diminished, but the educational bureaucracy had never been inoperative.

Activist staff, along with left-leaning trustees who regained a majority position by the late 1980s, maintained a commitment to equity. Over the next five years, sexual orientation was included in the TBE's anti-discrimination statement, and the education of black students was a major focus of discussion. Inner-city project schools remained in place, an affirmative action plan was adopted, and innovative curriculum projects continued to find support.

The persistence of streaming in secondary schools, despite a provincial report by Radwanski (1987) critiquing it and a board-level task force questioning it, was the biggest failure of the original reform agenda.

The streaming of working-class students into vocational schools had been the focus of the original Trefan Court brief from years earlier, but had not yet been satisfactorily addressed. The provincial government was torn between the teacher unions, which supported streaming students in secondary schools, and reformers, armed with research that supported ending it. There was evidence that streaming negatively impacted students in lower streams and made no difference to the achievement of those in higher streams. But a more conservative group of trustees combined with opposition from teachers succeeded in protecting the status quo.

The Liberal provincial government elected in 1985 under premier David Peterson was pursuing accountability and testing in education, and hoped to 'raise standards' in Ontario schools. The TBE, under Rutledge's leadership, developed a system of 'benchmarking' student achievement through classroom activities that remained consistent with their philosophy. The TBE was arguably responsible for the strong resistance to high-stakes standardized testing in Ontario, and for the gentler, curriculum-based form it ultimately took in the 1990s.

Twenty years after the election of several radical trustees, their legacy remained, though it was increasingly contested. The reforms were most notable in schools where there was support for it: elementary schools and schools in poorer areas of the city where new resources, community involvement, and committed educators enabled significant innovation. But the district remained distinctive in its commitment to inner-city education.

1990s: Struggle and Amalgamation

In 1990, a provincial NDP government was sworn in. It was the most left-wing government Ontario had seen, but it faced a severe recession, a taxpayers' revolt, and teacher strikes. The premier, Bob Rae, was under pressure to improve education across the province, which meant school boards lost some of their power. In 1992, the *Toronto Star* reported that 'the province's over-managed and over-priced school board system badly needs a shake up' (Gidney, 1999, p. 195). Tony Silipo, who had been an NDP trustee and chair of the TBE in the late 1980s, was now minister of education. Silipo called for 'comprehensive reform' and Rae set up a Royal Commission on Learning to examine the state of education in Ontario.

The Rae government was defeated in 1995, and Mike Harris's Conservative government, arguably the most right-wing government the province had seen, was elected to bring about a 'Common Sense Revolution.' Their platform focused on reducing and equalizing educational expenditures, introducing province-wide testing and challenging the working conditions embedded in teachers' contracts. The Royal Commission on Learning, which was tabled just before the government changed, included some of these goals, and called for provincial testing and more equal province-wide school board funding. In 1996, the government introduced legislation to amalgamate the city of Toronto with six suburban cities to create a new megacity, and amalgamate the Toronto Board of Education with other school boards in Metro, making it the largest one in Canada. The new legislation also ended the ability of school boards to raise local taxes and restricted trustees' salaries. The province's schools were thrown into turmoil, with widespread teacher strikes and an increase in the early retirements of teachers.

During the 1990s, the TBE trustees remained divided, but basic policy commitments to inner-city schools, equity, active community involvement, and language as the centre of curriculum remained. The NDP provincial government's emphasis on employment equity policies and citizen involvement encouraged the TBE to move forward in these areas. Trustee salaries had reached $49,000, not including expense allowances, allowing trustees to approach their positions as full-time jobs. Joan Green, who had been a student of Jimmy Britton, became the director of the board from 1990 to 1995. She continued the TBE's commitment to innovative literacy approaches and heritage language policies, and noted that this focus on literacy and equity 'were just kind of givens; that was in the water we drank.' Despite this commitment, programs were still reduced: 'The heydays of the 1980s were over and the fiscal reality was that things were being chipped away.' Green left to become the first head of the Educational Quality Assurance of Ontario (EQAO), the provincial testing agency in 1995, and John Davies took over as director. He had worked effectively with the black community in Toronto, with early childhood education, and on de-streaming secondary schools. He was impressed by the continuity of the commitments of the board:

I used to be really surprised talking to people outside of Toronto. They would say, 'how on earth do you manage in that political zoo?' The reality was that it was not a political zoo. The trustees were very experienced and had been there a long time. They knew the issues. They knew them very well. They were full-time. And in that context, it was very predictable. They knew what they could get through the board and what they couldn't. I knew what I could get and what I couldn't.

Under Davies, the equity policy remained strong, inner-city and model schools continued, and the TBE developed alternative schools for black, Aboriginal, and gay and lesbian youth. Secondary school streaming remained controversial and in place, supported by the teachers' unions, despite attempts by both the TBE and the NDP government to ameliorate its effects and push it into later grades. A vote on de-streaming the early years of secondary schools – following the lead of the Radwanski commission – passed by one vote, but implementation remained a problem.

When the provincial Conservative government was elected, attention turned to its plan to amalgamate school boards across the Greater Toronto Area (GTA). Opposition to amalgamation was strongest in the old City of Toronto, where people were worried about higher property taxes, an erosion of services, and the end of their access to local governments. A large citizen's movement, organized by a group called Citizens for Local Democracy, rallied to oppose the megacity. The movement was composed of 'largely white, British stock,' reflecting both the fact that the central city had become steadily wealthier and whiter than the suburban municipalities, and the fact that the elite were more easily mobilized in civic protest (Siemiatycki & Isin, 1997). By 1997, 48 per cent of residents in the GTA were foreign born, while only 39 per cent of residents in the old city of Toronto were foreign born. The percentage varied across the amalgamating municipalities, but in North York, for example, it reached 52 per cent. Despite strong resistance in old Toronto, the province proceeded with its plan to amalgamate municipal governments, and the Toronto District School Board was created in place of the TBE.

Amalgamation created a board with twenty-two school trustees, one elected from each of twenty-two wards, which had the same boundaries as provincial and federal constituencies. A trustee now represented the same electorate as a member of parliament or of the Ontario legislature. The trustees had to align policies from six legacy boards and to reorganize staffing to serve more than 600 schools and a quarter of a million students. While some of the trustees from the TBE were elected to the new board, the overall composition changed. Many activists left their staff positions after finding there was little support for their activities. The focus turned, at least for the next few years, from poverty, democracy, and cultural difference to balancing the budget and working out the logistics of a new internal organization.

Conclusions

The Toronto Board of Education had a well-deserved reputation for innovative policy in relation to poverty and cultural and linguistic diversity from 1970 to the end of the century. Innovation was driven by the election of local school trustees with strong community ties, the ability to agree on progressive policy directions, and the power to obtain the necessary resources. Despite differences and conflict, the basic direction of the board remained in place over almost thirty years. As the city became wealthier and more diverse, its neighbouring districts became relatively poorer and even more diverse, making it a target of resentment and leading to the provincial action that destroyed it.

The policies of the TBE developed over time as trustees learned, staff implemented new programs, and the city changed. There was a consistent and strong focus on providing equal education for all: for children from disadvantaged families, for women, for gays and lesbians, and for children who did not share in the dominant culture and language. Racism was consciously named and combated. The debate was about making the schools more humane places, where students and parents were engaged and literate; it was not specifically about testing and achievement scores, although modes of instruction were challenged and changed to be more student focused.

Board level policies provided direction and resources, while schools tried out new forms of instruction and communication. The focus was on whole school reform, where staff and parents worked together. Research was designed to examine how successful reform was, but it never provided clear evidence that a particular strategy was more or less effective. Instead, it provided a reading of the landscape, while policy decisions were based on deeply held beliefs about the purpose of education and the meaning of social justice.

4 Ideas Matter: The Impact of Evidence and Belief

In this chapter, we explore the way ideas shaped educational politics and policy at the Toronto and Winnipeg school boards. We consider not only the ideas expressed by leaders in the two districts, but the sources of these ideas and the ways in which they were taken up in the political processes in each district. We give more prominence to Toronto, as the Toronto Board of Education had a more explicit and sustained focus on articulating ideas about equality in education and using empirical analysis to shape and argue for policy proposals. It built a more substantial system to bring important ideas and local research into its work, and so is richer ground for analysis.

Reformers in both boards were motivated by their ideas about education, which grew out of their experiences, research, and discussions. We outline some of the thinking of reformers about the purposes of education and the relation between education and equity, and show how those ideas were shaped and expressed. We then explore how ideas became resources for policy, programs, and institutional change in each board. It is not surprising to find that these ideas were neither completely developed in terms of their implications for action, nor were they entirely consistent. However, they were debated, and their articulation was crucial to defining educational problems and legitimating policy responses. Although the ability of reformers to bring their ideas into policy and practice depended not only on what they believed, but also on the conditions around them, ideas mattered to both their aspirations and their approach to change.

How Do Ideas Matter? Social Movements and Evidence-Informed Policy

Ideas play an important role in politics, but which ideas matter and why are complicated questions. There is substantial literature on the impact of ideas in politics (e.g., Stone, 2002; Edelman, 1988; Lindblom, 1990). Work discussed in chapter 1 (e.g., Silver & Silver, 1991) illustrates some of the ways ideas about urban education and equity have been described and influenced political choices.

There is a rich tradition in sociology and in political science that explores the interaction between power, ideas, and social change. Analysts have sometimes treated ideas as a smokescreen for power or self-interest, or reduced them to a consensual political culture or national zeitgeist. From Mannheim to Weber to Marx, sociologists have wondered about the connections between social and political structures and the beliefs that can sustain or undermine them. Ideas are a vital resource for political life.

Beliefs and ideas about education come from many places. They are deeply rooted in upbringing and experience; religious, political, and ethical commitments influence what people believe children should learn and how they should be treated. Religious beliefs are, for many people, shaped in childhood and can remain unquestioned. Political ideas may be deeply influenced by experiences in youth, when people have their first encounters with and thoughts about the organization of society. But ideas also change with external political events or social movements that reframe experience and provide new explanations, friends, colleagues, and debates. Ideas are shaped by political and social processes. Changing the law is an effective way to change what people believe is right, as the desegregation of the American South and the requirement to wear seatbelts illustrate. March's classic work (Cohen, March, & Olsen, 1972) on the 'garbage can model' illustrates how ideas can be adopted because they serve particular interests in particular contexts. The result is that trends in ideas, like clothing styles, go in and out of favour depending on their resonance in various contexts (Levin, 1998).

Although many ideas are in circulation at any given moment, only a few of them garner enough momentum and support to be influential. Some ideas are deeply held by a few people but are never widely disseminated, while others are embraced by a variety of groups and come to have an important public life. Some ideas are actively promoted by individuals and groups, in more or less effective ways. They are made available through public media, academic publications, policy entre-preneurs, informal conversations, or administrative practices. Ideas, and the evidence to support them, are also adopted by interest groups ranging from political parties to lobby groups to civil society organiza-tions. Research and ideas are important to political engagement in any policy field, including education.

Some ideas are more likely to make sense to certain audiences, at certain times; their resonance depends on their fit with prior ideas, their coherence with a group's interests, and their ability to help people make sense of new circumstances. Max Weber described this as 'elec-tive affinity.' The literature on social movements explores how new belief systems radically alter the worldview of groups of people who then work to advance a social agenda, often ignoring the pragmatic politics of institutional change in the face of fervent beliefs about how the world should change (Melucci, 1989). For instance, the civil rights movement and the women's movement germinated, explored, and cir-culated new meaning for the term equality of educational opportunity, and are part of the story in the Toronto and Winnipeg boards. Social science research and academic analysis are important to generating and clarifying ideas. Academics are often disappointed to find that evi-dence, even when it seems compelling, and argument, even when it seems definitive, are not enough to change someone's mind, let alone affect their behaviour. There are many reasons for this. Research pro-vides only partial or tentative answers to fairly narrow questions and must work with assumptions rooted in everyday discourse (Lindblom & Cohen, 1979). Beliefs can be resistant to evidence, especially when those beliefs are key parts of a person's identity (Gawande, 2007). In the short term, evidence can have relatively little effect and be safely ignored by more powerful members of society.

In the longer term, ideas generated by social science research mat-ter, and effective social systems are open to critique and analysis. Some people change their ideas and beliefs, sometimes quite dramatically. Many more people change their views on particular issues as a result of evidence and its public discussion. Evidence plays an important role, if a slow one, in changing public attitudes (Gaskell, 1988). Witness chang-ing views in Canada on issues such as corporal punishment, drinking and driving, or the dangers of smoking. Evidence linking inequality in educational outcomes to the longer-term welfare of countries and soci-eties has increased the salience of educational policy for governments (e.g., OECD, 2007b).

The intersection of evidence and belief in the formation of educational policy is complex, but nonetheless influenced both boards. The next section will closely examine both cases in order to draw conclusions about the conditions that are likely to sustain reform directed at equal educational outcomes.

Frameworks for Thinking about Education and Equity

Stone et al. (2001) suggest that education is 'an ill-structured problem space.' While it is often thought that education needs improvement,' it is difficult to agree on what improvement entails. The problem could be low test scores, disengaged parents, the competence of the local superintendent, or teachers' inadequate pedagogy. The solution could be a new curriculum, more charter schools, or better teacher education. Different people at different times define the challenges in their own ways, and offer many policy answers. Sometimes policy makers start with a solution – such as decentralization – and seek to apply it to multiple problems. Successful educational reform depends on establishing shared ideas and having organizations, documents, and discussions that develop them to create change. In some instances, as seen in Toronto and Winnipeg, agreement on new ideas can be mobilized to bring about successful change. Similarly, disagreement on both the nature of the problems and their solutions can derail reform.

There is no universal agreement on the fundamental idea that unequal outcomes in education, especially if they are linked to poverty and cultural or racial difference, are a problem. For many years, the orthodox view was that these outcomes reflected differences in children's intelligence and capacity, while they also stabilized and reproduced the social order. In post-war Canada, the common belief was that schools should teach young children the norms and beliefs of their elders. This view underpinned a school curriculum and a system of governance based in the dominant and self-confident (even self-congratulatory) culture of the anglo-Canadian elite. It was reflected in the annual reports of school boards and departments of education, as well as in the academy, which taught the classic functionalist sociology of education of Emile Durkheim, along with a more current analysis by people such as Talcott Parsons and Robert Dreeben.

Providing equal educational opportunity in this context meant striving for a meritocracy. All children should attend school. Immigrants were to be socialized into the mainstream values of Canada. Aboriginal people would be fully assimilated. Children from disadvantaged families should not be set different tasks than children from wealthier families, unless, of course, they displayed different talents. The teacher was responsible for judging children's ability to quickly assimilate and reproduce the knowledge, comprehension, and skills required by the curriculum, and the school graded and streamed students on that basis. Supporters of this meritocratic system argued that it would separate more-able from less-able students and place them in programs that would provide the appropriate kind of learning for their abilities and destinations as adults.

The 1960s and 1970s were a time of great intellectual and cultural ferment in Western democracies as these orthodoxies were challenged by new social movements. People felt – some with excitement and others with dismay – that historic social transformation was taking place. Growing numbers of young people, post-war prosperity, and the rapid growth of education provided the conditions for intellectual and political unrest. The civil rights movement, the war on poverty, and the women's movement articulated powerful critiques of the status quo in government, family, and schools.

In Canada, popular movements to protest the war in Vietnam, resist Toronto's proposed Spadina expressway, and fight for women's rights engaged many Canadians in local community activism. The Front de Liberation de Quebec struggled for Quebec independence and the nationalist Waffle faction of the New Democratic Party attacked American cultural and economic imperialism. Draft dodgers fled to Canada. The Student Christian Movement was left wing. Social reformers – including university students, both authors of this book, and many of our interviewees – were rethinking the social order. The Company of Young Canadians and Opportunities for Youth, which were both government programs, funded young people who worked to reshape the country's identity as bilingual, multicultural, and more egalitarian. The energy and excitement of the era meant that debates were sharp, loud, and pervasive.

These debates critiqued the assumption that traditional education policy met the requirements of all students and the country. This critique was not new; opposition to inequality had been strong in Canadian cities in the beginning of the century, and rose again during the Great Depression. But in the 1960s, such critical views had new momentum and were supported by evidence from the burgeoning university social science departments. The dominant anglo-Canadian culture was revealed as partial, oppressive, patriarchal, and racist – notably in Porter's *Vertical Mosaic* (1965). Treating all children alike was increasingly viewed as favouring children from middle-class and culturally privileged homes. 'Blaming the victims' for their own failure was replaced with a critique of schooling as responsible for the failure of working class and minority children.

The widespread interest in new ideas about education challenged urban school boards across the country. Many activists and reformers ran for office or were hired into the system. Levin was elected as a school trustee in a suburban Winnipeg district in 1971 at age nineteen, the same year in which reformers won control of the WSD.

Pedagogically speaking, the education reform movement rejected the idea that children are vessels that teachers should fill with knowledge and understanding. The 1960s embraced a student-centred view of education that started with understanding the active role that children play in their own development. The Hall-Dennis report of 1968 in Ontario (Provincial Committee on the Aims and Objectives of Education in the Schools of Ontario, 1968) is often seen as the official statement of this new ideology. Although the report never received official provincial approval, it legitimized and widely disseminated the ideas pivotal to a child-centred approach to pedagogy. Supporters argued that children are naturally curious; that all children can learn; that teachers should guide learning, but not control it; and that nurturing the joy of learning would produce citizens who were confident, knowledgeable, and able to realize their dreams.

Reformers argued that the school curriculum needed to embrace more points of view, that teachers should value all children and respond to their specific needs, and that school outcomes should become more equal for children from different socioeconomic, cultural, and linguistic backgrounds. There was enormous optimism about the possibility of change. In addition to better schools, reformers wanted a better, more equal world. Education seemed as if it might lead to that world, as children who could become intellectually able and socially aware could also work for social change. The energy and commitment that educational reform generated came from its links to social transformation. Critics agreed that social change could be approached through educational change, with social transformation and equality as the ideal; school, and curriculum reform as the means; and child-centred, community-based pedagogy as the foundation. Parents, educators, and activists believed that changing education was the way to change class inequality, gender inequality, racism, homophobia, and the dominance of anglo-Canadian culture.

Every social movement contains contradictory and conflicting views, and a unified public stance is fragile when it is achieved. School reformers had a full spectrum of opinions and contributed to the larger political debates of the day, offering different views on the scope, nature, and speed of change required. Some reformers saw school change as the way to create an entirely new kind of society reflected in some of the communitarian political and social movements of the time. This stance was often based on a class analysis rooted in Marxism and influenced by writers such as Herbert Marcuse or Paulo Freire, and was rooted in the idea that the entire social system needed radical reconstruction. Others were more drawn to classical liberal reformism and saw school improvement as important in its own right as well as part of a gradual improvement in social conditions. There was also a strong interest in anarchism and individual liberation, in the vein of *Deschooling Society* (Illich, 1970) and 'free' schools based on Summerhill (Neill, 1968).

The critique of education was taken up, with different emphases, by teacher unions, academics, and community activists. Popular Canadian magazines and journals dealing with education, including *This Magazine Is about Schools, Community Schools, Canadian Dimension,* and *Working Teacher,* were started to promote discussion. The number of teaching jobs was expanding rapidly, and the field attracted idealistic young people. Teacher unions grappled with their role beyond salaries and working conditions. They created task forces, advisors, and position papers to explore and articulate radical new views on educational issues. The Centrale de l'Enseignement du Québec developed a curriculum that encouraged class analysis; the British Columbia Teachers Federation elected 'red diaper babies' (children of members of the Communist Party) to the executive and ran workshops and conferences on the status of women and racism. The Federation of Women Teachers' Associations of Ontario encouraged the development and dissemination of feminist ideas.

University-based education faculties also grew, and educational scholarship became more sophisticated in examining how factors such as social class and race affected educational attainment. Academics in new and expanding faculties of education provided the capacity for increased research, offered graduate courses for teachers, and published critical articles on educational policy and practice. Canadian universities grew rapidly, with many of their faculty drawn from the

United States and other countries, bringing those ideas to Canada. In Manitoba, Ken Osborne, Terry Morrison, Lionel Orlikow, and others critiqued class and racial biases in schools and supported various movements to bring change. In Toronto, the mid-1960s creation of the Ontario Institute for Studies in Education as a stand-alone graduate education and research institution provided a critical mass of academics and researchers focused on education. Jan Loubser, John Porter, W.G. Fleming, and Ray Breton, among others, analysed sociological data on the relationship between educational opportunities and class. Orlikow worked at OISE for a time. Jim Cummins, Mary Ashworth, and Keith Davey began a conversation about what was happening to immigrant children. Dorothy Smith, Margrit Eichler, and Jane Gaskell wrote and taught about the patriarchal assumptions of schooling. Ed Sullivan, David Livingstone, and George Smith introduced Marxist and critical theory to teachers. The journal *Interchange* started at OISE as a forum for critical thinking about education.

Perhaps the most important site for bringing these ideas together, at least in print, was a monthly magazine called *This Magazine Is about Schools*, which began publishing in Toronto in 1966. The editors were a group of radical educators based at an alternative school called Everdale, and they wanted to change the world. In one issue, they wrote: 'It is important for our readers to know that the editors of *This Magazine* are not professional journalists who think that writing about schools is more important than actually changing them' (1966, p. 1). The front page requested submissions of all kinds from readers, ranging from articles to children's poems to pictures on subjects such as children, education, and popular culture.

The magazine was eclectic, fun, well-written, and controversial; it soon had a circulation of 10,000 and an international audience. Articles provided analysis and made concrete suggestions about guerilla tactics, curriculum changes, and political organizing strategies that would replace the power of the privileged with the power of the working class and the dispossessed. The first issue included an article by then-weatherman and now university professor Bill Ayers, as well as an account by Daniel Cohn Bendit of 'notre commune du 10 Mai.' The spring 1972 issue, for example, included an article by Herb Gintis that critiqued Ivan Illich's *Deschooling Society* from a Marxist position, which was reprinted from the *Harvard Educational Review* (the editors wrote, 'It is, we think, a very valuable contribution to current educational theory, and we wanted to let our readers have it as soon as possible'). It included a discussion of jazz in Cuba, drawings, poetry by Milton Acorn, 'short notes on three books for downtown teachers,' advertisements for new books ranging from David Cameron on the schools in Ontario to the current issue of *Socialist Revolution*, and the possibility of an education book club that would provide them monthly: *Free Schools*, by Jonothan Kozol, *'You Won't Remember Me': The Schoolboys of Barbiana Speak Today*, by Marvin Hoffman, *Crisis in the Classroom*, by Charles Silberman, and *Jules Henry on Education*, by Jules Henry. It also included a good deal of Canadian political economy literature, such as Mel Watkins' account of his experience and belief in the Waffle, and selections from the Quebec teachers' white paper on unionization, language policy, and the Quiet Revolution.

This Magazine, with George Martell as one of its editors, combined the academic with the popular, the theoretical with the aesthetic, and the personal anecdote with the analytic treatise. It had a socialist angle, but aspired to be more than 'an in-group newsletter for converted radicals.' On the back cover of its second issue are plaudits from George Grant (a Canadian conservative nationalist), Herbert Marcuse (a U.S. psychoanalytic theorist), Robert Fulford (a Canadian journalist), and Edgar Friedenberg (a U.S. academic who later worked at Dalhousie University). The magazine was a key source of ideas for reformers in education and an important site of debate about educational change and its role in social reform.

Such new ideas affected mainstream institutions. Over time, ideas that seemed novel in the 1960s and 1970s became more powerful as they were taken up by educators, spread by social movements, and incorporated into school board debates. The ideas for reform at the Toronto and Winnipeg school boards were drawn not just from individual advocates for change, but from an international social movement that circulated critique across a variety of spheres of political and cultural action. Changing the school boards was tied to widespread rethinking of the role of education and of the meaning of equality.

Educational Analysis in the Toronto and Winnipeg Boards

The social movement that shaped the beliefs of many education reformers took different forms and had different results in Toronto and Winnipeg, but it had a substantial influence in both cities. Stone et al. (2001) point out that educational professionals tend to see fewer problems in education than do community leaders and activists. This was particularly true in Toronto, where elected trustees with community and activist backgrounds took control of policy formation and focused on articulating their values and reforming the system. Over time, the people changed, but the social movement, in one form or another, continued to animate debate and reform efforts and gave the TBE its sense of being special, progressive, and reformist. In Winnipeg, there were reforming trustees who could enumerate many problems with the system they were governing, and who identified themselves as revolutionary or were simply tired of the way the system shortchanged parents and youth from disadvantaged backgrounds. But such trustees were less organized, and at times there were only one or two on a nine-person board. Instead, activist staff were often leaders on reform issues and organized in local school communities, but found it difficult to get central support.

In both provinces, school boards and ministries of education carried out research, and produced and circulated documents on new ideas that served as the basis for decisions on how to move forward. In Toronto, interest in new ideas and research led to a substantial investment in an infrastructure for producing local studies, and a process for discussing theories, position papers, and policies. The TBE could act on its own conclusions, using external documents when they were relevant, but primarily funding its own initiatives and inquiry. Contrasted with Toronto, Winnipeg was a smaller, less-wealthy board with fewer radical trustees and a less-developed infrastructure for discussing research and ideas. Winnipeg did have a research department that carried out studies, but on a much smaller scale and without the political salience of those in Toronto. However, compared with most other boards in Manitoba and elsewhere in Canada, Winnipeg was a highly politicized setting where ideas and evidence mattered.

Ideas as a Resource for Change in Toronto

In Toronto, many trustees were committed to the study of educational theory and the practice of educational research. In our interviews, they made it clear that debate over ideas and understanding was an important part of their reform effort. Some were more focused on changing hearts and minds than on changing specific policies and actions at the TBE. The battle over ideas was waged energetically, as trustees, staff, teachers, and students received reports, created task forces, and attended workshops. The process of debate was institutionalized.

In 1975, Gordon Cressey, the chairman of the Toronto board, expressed his excitement about ideas for change in his annual address to the trustees:

> I am not a historian, but I am a student and youth worker of the 1960s, and a politician and teacher of the 1970s, so I believe I know the time frame well – I have lived it intimately. The sixties were an exciting time for us all – especially the young. The Economic Council of Canada stated that education was our most important investment. Money was abundant. The protest movement was in full swing both north and south of the border. There was a type of euphoria around. The existing institutions were accused of being irrelevant and their value system bankrupt. Free schools were leap-frogging into existence. The just society was just around the corner – and the Hall-Dennis report arrived on the scene telling us that each child had the right 'to learn, to play, to laugh, to dream, to dissent, to reach upward, to be himself and to be regarded by the schools as the unique individual he is.' We knew that the war on poverty would win and the educational arena would be the major battleground. The seeds of the sixties did not go away and in many ways have become firmly rooted in the seventies … Although we as trustees are often critics of our own system, we are here because we believe in the public system and want to make it better for our young people.

Some remarkable staff worked at the TBE; many of them wrote about their experiences and views on education. Don Rutledge, described by a number of our respondents as the leading intellectual among the staff, was deeply steeped in new British research on literacy. He worked at the TBE from 1960 until his retirement in 1988, starting as director of publications, then becoming director of the language studies centre, superintendent of curriculum, and associate director of education. Myra Novogrodsky was a teacher who wrote for *Community Schools*, a local school publication funded by a federal government grant early in her career, and later co-authored, with Gaskell, a book on gender issues published by *This Magazine*. She became a senior staff member at the TBE with responsibility for gender equity and attempted to combine the various equity groups into a coherent structure. Tim McCaskell, a self-described Marxist who worked in the equity unit and organized retreats for high school students, was hired into a position in the School Community Relations department in the late 1970s. His book, *Race to Equity* (McCaskell, 2005), describes his experience and his struggles to move the board forward on an equity agenda that reflected his world-view. Many other staff had deep roots in left politics and knew each other well from those experiences.

The Toronto trustees and staff were also committed to using local research to inform their practice and communicate their concerns. The board's research department at one time had fifty staff under the leadership of Ed Wright. Duncan Green, the director of the board in the early 1980s, believed in the importance of research: 'I used to read Jonathan Kozol, I loved Jonathon Kozol. But local data is much more persuasive.' He outlined the uses of research in a speech to the Ontario Educational Research Council in 1977: 'During the past twenty years, there have been thousands of studies in journals, scholarly papers, books, etc., all of them designed to help us learn better, or teach better, or both.' But, he argued, 'we don't use what we've got,' because unless the research is based in local concerns and schools, and has questions and answers that are politically appropriate, it is not listened to. In Toronto, local research reports were responsive to the politics of the board and were used in the process of developing shared ideas.

Such research included the results of the Every Student Survey, discussed above, which provided local data on the relationship between poverty, language, and school achievement every five years from 1970 to 1997. The analysis of the data showed, as one trustee put it, that the situation in urban schools 'was worse than the Trefann Court mothers thought.' The research reports included cross-tabulated data on student background with data on school success. The many follow-up reports all showed a negative relationship between poverty, immigrant status, and school success. On two occasions, the surveys included the entire secondary school population and were linked to course marks as well as the credits earned by every student. This data represented a significant investment in documenting the effects of poverty and diversity on school achievement. While it did not show the effectiveness of the board's policy, track students over time, link achievement to particular school initiatives, or show changes in the effects of demographic variables on school outcomes, it did justify the continuing need for a focus on equity at the board.

Another example that illustrates how central the clarification and debate of ideas were to the Toronto board was a seminar on literacy convened in the early 1980s. It transported trustees and staff to Trent University for several days to hear and discuss the work of two world-renowned scholars with very different ideas about why children from disadvantaged backgrounds failed in school. William Labov, a Philadelphia sociolinguist who had studied the language use of black youth, argued that teachers should recognize a variety of forms of English in the classroom, and that each form had its own integrity and rules. Basil Bernstein, a sociologist from the University of London, argued that children from disadvantaged backgrounds failed in school because they failed to produce the appropriate linguistic forms, and that these should therefore be explicitly taught. The conference was exciting and memorable. In his interview, David Clandfield, a trustee present at the gathering, described the context: There was a dancercise conference going on next door, and 'lots of people were wearing leotards and dancing around in the room next to us, separated only by glass partitions.' The two academics 'had said horrible things about each other and one of them was suing the other.' One of them 'wouldn't have dinner with us, so he joined the other conference.' The story ends with Bernstein and Labov going for a long walk, finding common ground, and moving the trustees forward with their literacy policy. The account makes vivid both the drama and the highly personal nature of the politics of ideas at the time.

Conceptions of multiculturalism and racism also led to the lively exchange of ideas, and eventually the development of an official board position, complete with many citations of the literature. The first multicultural report, *The Bias of Culture*, was developed by a working group that included trustees, staff, and community volunteers. It was circulated as a draft in seven languages: Chinese, English, Greek, Italian, Polish, Portuguese, and Spanish. This first draft developed a comprehensive rationale for including languages other than English and French in the schools' curriculum and culture maintenance programs. It argued that such programs are necessary to the educational well-being of students from a cultural and linguistic heritage other than British or French, because schools otherwise reflect a dominant culture which is alien to such children:

> The draft report's position is that culture and language maintenance programs would function to help to dispel the negative impact of the dominant culture on the personal development of these children.
>
> In accepting the reality of multiculturalism in Canada, the work group on multicultural programs for the TBE believes in the right of each person to cultural integrity, to a positive self image, and to an understanding of and respect for differences. If we are to appreciate differences and

commonalities, multicultural education must be a basis of our school system and must be directed to all students and teachers. (1976, p. 21)

The report led to a wide-ranging debate on whether schools should develop multiculturalism or devote resources to knowledge from the dominant culture. Those opposed to the draft report argued that students must assimilate, that the programs were too expensive, and that while families and communities should maintain other languages and cultures, they were not the responsibility of the education system.

The final report in 1976 was a compromise. It recommended increasing the resources for teaching English, while recognizing the value of instruction in other languages, especially during the transition to English. It provided five pages of references that included many research reports from the board, many scholarly journal articles, articles from *This Magazine Is about Schools*, Michael Novak's *The Rise of the Unmeltable Ethics*, and U.S. reports such as *Beyond Compensatory Education* from Far West Labs. It also included dissenting views.

The work of OISE professor Jim Cummins was often quoted in the Toronto debate. In commenting on the debate, he remembered:

> Some community groups drew on work that I had done in terms of positive effects of bilingualism, linkages between the development of students' first language and English literacy. And so some of that research got drawn into the debate and was quoted on a fairly regular basis by some of the trustees who were in favour of more adequate provision.

The debate continued for years as the policy gradually changed. Ten years later, the board was considering the introduction of heritage language programs into the school day. There was no consensus among staff, trustees, parents, or teachers, and the debate continued into the early hours of the morning. Many argued that English should remain the sole language of instruction. Parents who supported French argued that English was already first, and that French was second. Others argued that to maximize the intellectual development of the child and the involvement of parents, a variety of languages should be integral to the curriculum.

The politics of ideas at the TBE was unusual. It could be described as a version of deliberative democracy or as an engaged learning organization. Political debate was the norm, and while it was often constructive and educational, it could also be bitter and divisive. The concern with theory, data, and discussion was resisted by those impatient to 'get it done.' The culture of open debate meant long, heated meetings. Debates were exhausting and trying. They also energized people, created a sense of urgency, and ensured that innovation, concern for the poor, and critical awareness of dominant cultural assumptions remained a focus of policy discussions.

McCaskell describes his experience in this atmosphere as 'a period of significant social struggle, cultural transformation, and deep learning' (2005, p. vii). He saw his work as 'forging a social analysis' through political struggle with fights, allies, and enemies. His account is about the struggle of ideas. Myra Novogrodsky, in reviewing his book, questions his pedagogy, while respecting his commitments: 'The modus operandi which McCaskell and many of his allies used, which involved shaming teachers and administrators, was fraught with difficulties. Good educators know that real learning takes time. Embarrassment, force and humiliation will not win friends. Sound experiential based pedagogy, a safe environment in which to air differences, and a sense of humor are better ingredients for adult and adolescent education which sticks' (2006, p. 156).

The difficulties and acrimony should not diminish the extent to which the TBE was, for many years, an organization in which ideas and the debate over ideas mattered a great deal, and an organization committed to the learning of adults as well as of students.

Ideas as a Resource for Change in Winnipeg

Winnipeg reformers were also influenced by many of the ideals of the 1960s. Staff members with a commitment to community activism played key roles, while trustees with reformist tendencies were elected for the NDP. In the early 1970s, Winnipeg had several assistant superintendents, including Marcel Pelletier, Reevan Cramer, and Keith Cooper, with well-developed analyses of inner-city school issues. Future leaders such as Pat Rowantree, Greg Selinger, and Brian O'Leary were deeply influenced early in their careers by their commitments to equality for inner-city youth, as were many of the Winnipeg School Division's later leaders, including Jack Smyth, Jan Schubert, and Pauline Clarke.

The provincial infrastructure was more developed than the school-board infrastructure. Lionel Orlikow's provincial planning and research branch, established under the NDP, sponsored community organizing and alternative teacher education as well as new curricula and materials for teachers. In the early 1970s, the provincial Department of Education involved Levin in organizing conferences of high school student leaders that involved substantial critiques of the existing order in schools. But the WSD was involved in bringing Toronto trustees and staff from the Toronto inner-city school projects for conferences to share ideas and experience. Radical teachers with a background in community organizing and an interest in Saul Alinsky's radical community organizing ideas (Alinsky, 1969) were recruited to lead inner-city initiatives, and an Alinsky organizer spent an entire year in Winnipeg working with inner-city staff. The development of CEDA and the community development initiatives of the 1970s were as radical as anything the TBE attempted, but did not have the same longevity. Not all the NDP trustees supported the party's official positions on issues, which meant that even when there was an NDP majority on the board, compromises had to be made on particular issues. On the other hand, some of the non-NDP trustees were as left-leaning as most NDP members, so the actions of the board were not predictable from the party affiliations of its members.

Manitoba politics remained polarized between a social democratic NDP sympathetic to the language of equality and participation, and a Conservative Party, which was and is not – although when in government both parties are usually closer to the centre than their platforms and rhetoric might suggest. Neither the NDP nor the Conservatives in Manitoba were internally united in their beliefs about educational ideas and policy. A group of activist educators animated by community development and social reform wrote the official NDP education policy in the 1970s, which called for community controlled schools; democratic decision making in each school involving parents, teachers, administrators, students, and community; extended school programs; safeguards to protect minority rights and interests; and the coordination of school and family services with the community school. However, when the NDP took power provincially from 1969 to 1977 and again in the early 1980s, it acted cautiously. Similarly, the Lyon government, beyond disbanding much of the planning and research effort of the early 1970s, made few significant changes in education policy, and the Filmon government's 'blueprint' of the mid-1990s was neither very radical (compared, for example, to the Ontario Harris Conservative government), nor was it fully implemented.

The early 1970s in Manitoba were a period of positive change that then lapsed. Orlikow argues that they were a time of 'intense public debate over the closure of small rural schools, inadequate vocational facilities, aid to private schools, anti-government demonstrations by teachers and the organization of high school education' (1988, p. 135). He argues that 'peace broke out' in the 1980s, as grass-roots politics became less relevant and concern for expertise and political stability replaced an appetite for debate and change:

> The government lacked a socialist vision of any sort, and saw education not as one means of social transformation, but rather as a political mine field to be negotiated with extreme care. Left wing manifestos, like the old NDP education policy, were no longer politically acceptable. Neither the faculties of education nor the school divisions had the staff to research or evaluate whether programs were working, who was being affected by them, and how. Around the world, democratic socialist parties treat education very seriously, recognizing its social and political potential. This unfortunately, has not been the case in Manitoba. (1988, p. 139–41)

In Winnipeg, the early ideas of the reformers were overtaken by the more conservative views of education that dominated both political parties trying to get elected in the 1980s. As a result, many reformers were dissatisfied with what they saw as the relatively slow pace of government policy.

Winnipeg did have intellectual battles over key issues, though not with the same frequency or level of analysis as in Toronto. The WSD board did not have a group of trustees who consistently advanced a class analysis of education. Board meetings could also be long, but were not as frequent, and debates were often animated by personal animosities as much as by theoretical differences. However, in the 1970s, ideas animated the WSD to implement a range of programs intended to reduce inequities, with support from the Department of Education. These included compensatory funding, summer enrichment for children in disadvantaged communities, training inner-city residents as teachers, integrated social services, and efforts to increase parent participation and influence, among others.

Winnipeg also debated issues of multiculturalism and diversity, as described in chapter 2. These issues were frequently on the WSD agenda in various forms. However, as was typical of the difference between the two districts, the debate was not as organized, open, or sharp as it was in Toronto. In the early 1970s, there were public debates about the creation of bilingual Hebrew, German, and Ukrainian programs in Winnipeg schools. Discussion of diversity was most alive in the late 1980s, when the Task Force on Race Relations was in operation, and in the early 1990s, when the two Aboriginal focus schools were created. The work of the task force was a flash point for different but strongly-held views on the WSD's efforts to address the diverse student population. The same issues were salient in the lively and public debate in the early 1990s over the creation of two Aboriginal-focused schools, described earlier. Although the political struggles in Winnipeg were less likely to be framed in academic or research terms than those in Toronto, and were not led in the same way by a consistent group of political activists, similar issues came to the table to be discussed and decided.

Conclusions

This chapter has explored the ways in which changing ideas about education, equality, and social transformation provided a platform for change in policy and practice in both school districts. The boards were strongly influenced by the social movements that swept across North America, and much of the world, in the 1960s. Active individuals in these movements turned their attention to educational change; the organizations they started and worked in provided resources and networks to disseminate these new views. Shared and personally-compelling beliefs about equality, and about the role of schools in creating it, were the foundation for reforms.

These beliefs were not universally shared, but they, and the practices they supported, were seriously debated and, at least in Toronto, studied and written about. Research and other evidence played an important role in shaping what reformers believed, how they tried to convince others, and how they shaped their ideas into specific proposals and actions.

Policy was, to some extent, evidence-based, and research was brought into dialogue with policy and practice in the TBE. However, research still had a limited role. It did not examine the effectiveness of particular reforms or determine the appropriate policies. It posed questions within a framework that accepted the new definitions of equality and the new premises of literacy teaching. Research that had been based on different assumptions would neither have been carried out nor would it have been heeded. Research helped to frame questions, provided descriptions of local conditions, and forced decision makers to consider alternative approaches to problems. It helped to develop new curriculum materials and new articulations of policy. But ultimately, to use the current language, policy was evidence-informed but not evidence-based. Even with the more advanced data-gathering tools and statistical modeling currently available, research can only work within a framework of belief about what a good education should look like.

Reformers in both cities were unable to act on everything they wanted. Although the basic assumptions of the TBE persisted for twenty-five years in a large, diverse, and left-leaning city, they were upended by a provincial government elected with a very different view of education. Efficiency, testing, and competitiveness replaced equity, community, and literacy as watchwords for reform. In Winnipeg, change was more pragmatic and incremental, and consistently depended more on wide public acceptance than on research and scholarship framed by a concern for equity. There were fewer sudden reversals, but also less steady progress and innovation. In the consensus politics typical of Canadian school boards, the TBE's consistent concern for equity is rarely found, to the detriment of educational politics and of education itself. The conditions that produced it are also difficult to replicate, although this chapter has pointed to several lessons for moving forward.

5 Politics, Conflict, and Civic Capacity

While ideas are important in shaping public opinion, defining educational problems, and suggesting what might be done about them, political and institutional capacity is needed to create and sustain programs that will make a difference for children. This chapter focuses on the creation of civic capacity for greater educational equity in Toronto and Winnipeg, and on the political challenges that often threatened it.

Politics is at the centre of educational change. The trustees and community activists in our study viewed politics as the basis for their work, and the basis for the way they pursued change and other goals. For educators, politics shaped what they were able to do and how they were able to do it, including the resources available to them and the conditions under which they operated.

These cases embody several key political tensions. The first is between partisan politics and non-partisan collaboration at the school-board level. While political parties are expected in provincial or federal politics, their involvement in school boards is controversial. There is also tension between local school board governance and provincial authority, as both levels often want, and have a case for, a legitimate role. In both cities, the relative power and political commitments of the school boards and provincial governments fluctuated, creating conflicting agendas and cooperation at different moments.

A third tension is between the desire for local community involvement and the boards' need for central direction and authority. Both boards struggled with community engagement while balancing central and local structures, and political strength and professional expertise. Finally, there is tension between elected school trustees and the staff they work with (Levin, 2005). Trustees are elected to make a difference, but to do so they must have positive relationships with senior staff, teachers, support staff, and their unions.

The Role of Partisan Politics

While politics certainly has a role in education, there is significant disagreement about the nature of that role. Many educators and members of the public regard politics as an evil in education that should be kept away so that educators can work. A common refrain is that education should be about what is good for students, as if it were a self-evident matter. Plank and Boyd (1994) describe this desire for a governance process without politics as 'the flight from democracy.'

During the progressive era of school reform in the early 1900s, reformers in US cities tried to eliminate the corrupt politics that dominated big city districts by making school board elections non-partisan. Supporters argued that civic leaders should run schools on the principles of business efficiency and educational science (Tyack, 1974). That implicit call to minimize the role of party politics and maximize the role of expertise remains powerful today.

School board elections in Canada are typically not defined by partisan politics, reflecting the belief that independence, competence, and caring about children should be the key qualifications for trustees. Mario Santos, a trustee in Winnipeg in the 1990s, said that he ran to improve education and his goal was to do what was good for children: 'People can accuse me of many things, but I hope people believe that I was there for the children. Whatever was good for the children was good for me. I kept reminding the trustees of that. That was why we were trustees. I did not care at all whether the feelings of some administrators or some teachers were hurt if the best interests of children were served.'

Non-partisanship was also appealing in Toronto. Penny Moss reported: 'The city in general, or lots of parts of the city, had no qualms about progressive education and progressive municipal politics, but they weren't prepared for the overlay of the provincial party system. Their biggest fear was that their local trustee would not be independent in formulating their own positions on the issues.'

While eliminating partisan politics and having responsive local trustees can seem attractive, such a scenario ignores the role that legitimate differences about ideas and interests play in educational issues. Citizens disagree about the meaning of a good life for their children and can prefer different approaches to obtaining it. Some people think children are served by more discipline, while others prefer more freedom. Some people want more diverse schools, while others want more homogeneous ones. Some value the broad intellectual role of schooling, while others are more concerned about vocational preparation. Educational policies and research must make assumptions about these kinds of values and priorities, but individual beliefs play an important and legitimate part in the work of schools and districts.

Most trustees can be placed on a political spectrum from the left to the right. Those on the left are often more committed to the reform ideas of the 1960s, including increasing resources for schools, especially those in poor neighbourhoods; improving the diversity and flexibility of curriculum offerings; community involvement in school governance; and student-centred learning. Those on the right tend to favour more traditional forms of schooling and fewer extensions of the role of the school beyond the classroom. These ideological differences may not be clear to voters who do not pay close attention, however, unless trustee positions are signaled in some clear way. Party affiliation is a shorthand that voters understand, while low voter turnout in trustee elections and complex political differences make it a challenge to understand what the public 'really' wants.

In both cities, the NDP took an active role in school board politics. The party recruited candidates, supported them, and publicized their positions on the issues. In Toronto, the influence of the NDP was variable over time. To begin with, reform trustees were not associated with the party; later, more candidates were party members, and the NDP caucus played an active role in coming up with policy positions. Although no other parties were active, in 1985 a more conservative group of candidates was organized under the label of a 'positive alternative.' This slate garnered enough votes to form a majority, if only for a short period of time. In Winnipeg, the NDP was more consistently active, but it did not manage to control the votes of its candidates once they were elected. While partisan politics was present in both cities, it was not terribly strong in either.

It is both impossible and undesirable to treat education governance as if it were not affected by values and by the politics in which those values are embedded. There is no neutral stance on education, no universally accepted idea of what will benefit students, and no research program that can make those decisions. At the same time, excessive partisanship is also problematic. In order to develop policy, launch programs for the inner city, and effectively run schools, boards must reach agreements that have support externally, in the polity of the city and beyond, as well as internally, among staff, teachers, and principals. As Stone et al. (2001) argue, 'successful educational reform ultimately requires a broad and sustainable coalition of support, and the route to this goes directly through, and not around politics' (p. 1). Consensus has often been difficult to achieve as differing interests, divisive politics, and personal animosities get in the way of decisions on important issues.

The challenge for urban school boards, given the diverse and sometimes fractured nature of their communities, is to be aware of the range of views in the community, and to allow those differences expression, even heated expression, yet also to build coalitions and inclusive approaches to policy that encourage people with different positions to work together. This is a challenging balancing act for any political leader.

Central and Local: Relationships between
Districts and Provincial Governments

The politics of education takes place at the federal, provincial, municipal, and school levels. In most countries, schools are funded, managed, and held accountable in several of these jurisdictions, sometimes in conflicting ways. Politics takes different forms at different levels, and local school politics usually do not involve the same loyalties, issues, or people as those of municipal, provincial, or national politics. Different countries have different ways of organizing school governance, not all of which involve a role for the local level. Local school boards have a long history in North America, but they do not exist in some democratic countries with public educational systems (e.g., Australia, India, and France), and they have been substantially marginalized in others (e.g., England).

In North America, however, local school boards have been central to the philosophy, financing, and direction of public education since its inception in the nineteenth century. As North America was settled by Europeans, elected school boards were established everywhere to create and manage local schools. They embody the 'democratic wish' (Morone, 1998) of direct citizen participation in the politics of their local communities. Although the number of local boards has been reduced in both the United States and Canada over the last century, there are still more than 14,000 school boards, or 'ten thousand democracies' (Berkman & Plutzer, 2005), in the United States, and almost 500 in Canada. Canadian school districts range from very small – some have only one school – to very large, with several having more than 100,000 students. Local boards recognize that communities and parents have an important stake in their children's well-being. People like having schools run by people from their own communities.

Education must respond to more than local concerns. The rhetoric around education has focused increasingly on the significance of education for human capital development, which is thought to affect both countries' economic strength and social cohesion (although as we suggest in chapter 1, social cohesion itself can lead to economic strength). Differences in the capacity of local districts to finance and manage schools have repercussions in contexts beyond the local, which justify an active role for more senior governments. As a result, small school districts have been consolidated across Canada and governments have tried to create more consistency across districts by establishing curriculum guidelines, testing regimes, and funding policies.

The United States has an even stronger commitment to local school governance, and has a much larger number of school districts relative to population. However, as was the case a century ago, the belief that elected school boards meet the requirements of large cities is under attack (Boyd, Kerchner, & Blyth, 2008). Mayoral control and direct state takeovers have replaced elected school boards in a number of large cities, while in others, charter schools with their own governing structures have proliferated, or boards have contracted many of their functions to private companies. The impact of the federal government on local educational policy has also increased dramatically, as the No Child Left Behind legislation mandates testing, qualified teachers, and consequences for schools that do not meet expected standards.

In Canada, the picture is very different. The constitution makes education a provincial responsibility, although the federal government has, at various times, funded vocational programs, French language programs, and education research. Entrepreneurialism has not yet replaced the public's belief in a well-governed public system. Elected school boards remain in all large urban centres, although their size and power varies and a few large boards have been temporarily taken over by provincially appointed trustees. School boards have been gradually but steadily losing power to provincial governments for decades (Levin & Ungerleider, 2007). School districts have substantially less financial and curricular autonomy than they did fifty years ago. Many provinces have changed their legislation to give themselves more control over local boards. Almost all of the provinces now provide nearly all of the funding for public schools, and the boards' resulting lack of economic power has seriously diminished their influence. Collective bargaining is still carried out at the local level, but within a provincial financial framework that allows little flexibility. Some would argue that boards have become, for the most part, a means of executing provincial government policy. But in every province, local school boards continue to ensure that schools reflect local priorities and beliefs about education. Provincial governments remain reluctant to intervene in local board decisions, and can benefit from having local authorities to blame when things go wrong.

There is inevitable tension between school boards and provinces based on the desire of local politicians and administrators to manage their own affairs with minimal interference from the Department or Ministry of Education, and the conflicting desire of provincial politicians to motivate and take credit for educational improvement at the local level. At the same time, provincial governments are reluctant to cede too much autonomy in high-profile policy areas to local governments, since this can compromise their own ability to manage programs and demonstrate leadership. A provincial government cannot be elected in Ontario or Manitoba without support in the capital, which means that provincial politicians must be involved in local issues in those cities. Events in these cities may set province-wide trends that cannot be ignored by provincial governments. Capital cities are also provincial media centres, and so events in their school systems recieve closer scrutiny than they might otherwise.

Toronto and Winnipeg are provincial capitals and the largest cities in their provinces, and factors at play within them include political actors, media coverage, and dramatic demographic shifts with increasing poverty and immigration. These districts saw themselves as having a special status in their provincial systems, with particular needs for local autonomy and extra resources. In the late 1960s, local school board autonomy was on the rise, though it was not as powerful as it had been early in the century. Many of the controls of earlier periods, such as inspectors and provincial examinations, were removed in the 1960s as Canada's increasingly large and sophisticated school boards were given more autonomy. Ontario abolished province-wide grade 13 exams in 1968, and provincial inspectors had disappeared before that. In 1969, the Davis Conservative government reduced the number of school boards, but also granted more control over curriculum to those that remained. The government also introduced a new, more flexible credit system for secondary schools (HS1) in 1972 and a new, progressive elementary framework (The Formative Years) in 1975. In Manitoba, from the late 1960s to the late 1990s, the provincial government gave school boards more authority but later sought greater control. Manitoba abolished provincial exams in 1969 although, unlike Ontario, it reinstated some high school exit exams in the 1990s.

The peak of local control lasted longer in Ontario than in Manitoba, but both provinces faced economic pressures to centralize. In the 1960s and 1970s, educational expenditures grew as enrolment increased and costs spiraled. As a result of these pressures, along with more limited revenues, provincial governments tried to step in more insistently to control costs and provide direction. In the 1990s, provincial governments exerted more control over educational policy. Ontario amalgamated the Toronto boards in 1998, and Manitoba amalgamated some districts in 2001. Manitoba is now the only province that allows significant local taxation by school boards.

Although there are some broad similarities between the two provinces, the political party in power at each level also made a difference. In Ontario, the Conservatives were in office from the 1940s to 1985; the Liberals and NDP governed from 1985 to 1999. For most of the late 1960s and onward, the provincial government had a relatively hands-off approach to school districts, including Toronto. Eventually, in the late 1990s, the Harris Conservative government brought in the most far-reaching changes in decades to Ontario education and the role of school boards, including the amalgamation of the Toronto Board of Education with five others to form the gigantic Toronto District School Board. This amalgamation disrupted the existing programs and policies of the TBE by creating a much larger entity with less coherent politics.

In Manitoba, on the other hand, power moved back and forth between the Conservatives, who were in office for more than a decade prior to 1969, then from 1977 to 1981 and again from 1988 to 1999; and the NPD, who were in office from 1969 to 1977, 1981 to 1988, and 1999 to the time of publication. The two parties had very different attitudes to central Winnipeg, which largely elected NDP members to the legislature. Each change in government meant changes in the approach and resources available to the Winnipeg School Division.

Both the Winnipeg and Toronto school boards wanted autonomy from their provincial governments, but also needed provincial support for their initiatives. Both boards argued that the provincial funding system was not meeting their needs, especially around inner-city poverty and ethnicity issues. Lack of provincial funding, the boards claimed, was why local property taxes for education were high. The media typically reported this conflict every year at budget time as boards criticized provincial funding.

In Toronto, the financial discussion was complicated by the Metropolitan Toronto School Board, which was designed to share tax revenue among the seven Toronto school boards (six public and one Catholic). Despite efforts to use Metro to control expenditures, Toronto trustees lobbied to keep the Metro formula tilted towards their own needs. Collective bargaining shifted to Metro in 1985, reducing the power of the TBE. By 1995, Toronto received no revenue from the province, and municipal tax revenues supported its schools and helped fund those in other Metro districts according to an equalization formula. Only in 1997 did the provincial government eliminate local property taxing by school boards, which meant that all funding for schools was to come from provincial revenues, including several billion dollars from provincial property taxes.

As long as both Winnipeg and Toronto boards had the ability to raise money locally, they did so. Worried about rising costs and taxpayer resistance, both provinces tried at various times to impose ceilings on local spending, but failed to hold onto them over the protests of the two boards. The boards, despite vigorous debates in which some trustees predicted dire consequences and taxpayer revolts, had the ability and support of the electorate to raise their own property taxes, and regularly did so with little voter resistance. Much of the taxation was levied on businesses, which protected home owners from excessive mill rates.

Both boards increased local taxation in order to fund programs that the province did not support. Nursery schools and enriched staffing levels, as well as supports for Aboriginal education, were funded this way in Winnipeg, while the equity advisors, increased staffing in inner-city schools, and community workers, along with school swimming pools, were funded locally in Toronto. The trustees we interviewed never felt significant public resistance to these taxes.

For much of the period of this study, the TBE paid relatively little attention to the Ontario Ministry of Education on educational policy issues other than funding. The board was an important site of program innovation. Duncan Green, director of the TBE, pointed out: 'The boards were more responsible for progressive ideas in education than was the Ministry of Education. If you look at junior kindergartens, if you look at vocational schools, or technical schools, if you look at curriculum, if you look at the credit system, always it came from the bottom to the top.'

When the Ontario education ministry initiated reforms the TBE supported, like encouraging non-sexist or anti-racist curriculum and introducing employment equity policies, the board took advantage of the resources and legitimacy the province provided. Only in the 1990s did the province try to impose significant curriculum reform, in the form of de-streaming secondary schooling and introducing province wide testing for public accountability. Neither of these initiatives were particularly popular at TBE, and they led to much discussion as the board tried to adapt the initiatives.

In Manitoba, the relationship between the WSD and the Department of Education was affected by the political party in office. In the 1970s, the NDP provincial government tried to force the WSD board into a more proactive stance on inner-city issues. The government's strong interest in inner-city issues was resented by the board. In the early 1970s, the province directly organized and funded a whole range of initiatives in the WSD, sometimes without going through the board. Some of the left-wing trustees were closely connected to the NDP and made common cause with the province on these issues, which regularly went against the wishes of their own district administrators.

When the Pawley NDP government came into office in 1981, it tried to work more closely with the WSD, supporting generic measures such as compensatory funding to high poverty areas across the province rather than a whole series of program initiatives specifically in Winnipeg, but also, with the city and federal government, supporting the Core Area Initiative that had been developed under the Lyon government. The mood in the early 1980s was very different than it had been a decade earlier, and the political connections between Winnipeg trustees and provincial cabinet ministers did not exist to nearly the same extent. Beginning in 1984, the NDP government gave Winnipeg a $2 million grant to recognize inner-city needs, although provincial civil servants (of whom Levin was one) were always suspicious about whether Winnipeg used that money for the inner city, since the board's politics at that time, as under the earlier NDP government, were less oriented towards poverty than the province's. On the other hand, the WSD leaders did not always see the department as helpful:

> I never felt that the Department of Education provided the kind of leadership and support for which I would have hoped. Admittedly, we were asking for money, but we also wanted autonomy to formulate our own policies. Most of the time we were practically on our own. We had our own Aboriginal consultants who produced the Aboriginal education curriculum materials, but we received no help. On the other hand, in other cases we sincerely wanted to work with other people.

The Conservatives held office in Manitoba for most of the 1990s. They were generally unsympathetic to new investments in the inner city, where they did not win many seats, but the Filmon government was quite interventionist on education. Some of its policies were primarily fiscal, such as the funding cuts and enforced days without pay for teachers (along with other public sector workers) that were major issues in Manitoba in the 1990s. However, in the mid-1990s, the Conservatives also changed curricula, introduced provincial testing and examinations, mandated parent councils, changed special education policies, and made a variety of other significant policy shifts. As a result, the Winnipeg board found itself in opposition to the province on many issues. One WSD educator commented on the newfound tension between the government and the trustees:

> The Dark Ages of education, when the Conservative government, during its eleven-year reign, set out to destroy public education, involved provincial neglect for inner-city education, Aboriginal education, and public education in general. The trustees, though, really fought to maintain the resources. They presented budgets that maintained the integrity of the educational system. They were not prepared to just lie down and accept the direction of the Conservative government. They did not implement days without pay for teachers ...
> I was really disappointed with the Conservative government. They caused some hard times with their fiscal policies on education as well as the whole business with increased testing.

These cases demonstrate the fluctuating relationship between large districts and provincial governments over the course of our study. Each resisted giving the other influence, especially when their political allegiances and directions differed, yet each needed the other to accomplish its goals. From a public policy standpoint, strong partnerships between the two levels were desirable. However, they required understanding and good will on both sides, as well as the ability to make compromises. That ability was in short supply, as politicians at all levels used partisan issues to get support. Similarly, officials at the two levels did not always work together easily, and neither side invested the necessary time and energy into building partnerships. In both situations, it was clear that the provincial government could, if sufficiently determined, force the district to follow its policy direction, but that this would not always have good long-term consequences.

Trustees and Boards

School board elections in Canada are generally modest affairs, with low voter turnout and relatively little media coverage. In Winnipeg, being a trustee on the school board is a part-time position with relatively low pay. In Toronto, trustees steadily increased their compensation from $7,000 in the late 1960s to the equivalent of a full-time salary by the early 1990s, and a number of them treated their trustee role as their main employment. This encouraged community activists to run for office, but it also meant that trustees with other jobs found being on the board a great deal of work, and burned out quickly.

As described in chapters 2 and 3, both Winnipeg and Toronto had, and still have, ward systems for electing trustees, though the wards are quite large. The Winnipeg School Division had a board of nine trustees, with two from each of three wards, while the former Toronto Board of Education had twenty-two members, with two from each of eleven wards. Toronto was a larger community, with about 750,000 residents in 1975, contrasted to about 220,000 in Winnipeg, which meant that a ward in each city had approximately 70,000 residents who elected two (in Toronto) or three (in Winnipeg) trustees.

The fact that the wards were large and that voter and media interest was low created different electoral politics than at the provincial or federal level. In Toronto, at times, popular trustees were elected by acclamation. At other times, ten or more candidates would run in a ward, with the least popular candidates receiving only a few hundred votes. The leading trustees in Toronto over the period of our study received about 9,000 or 10,000 votes from a population of approximately 70,000. Some candidates were elected with as few as 2,000 votes. In the 1994 election, the last for the TBE, the number of votes for those elected as trustees ranged from fewer than 2,000 to a maximum of more than 8,000. The average for elected trustees was around 4,000 votes, or about 6 per cent of the electorate.

Low turnout meant that trustees could be elected with support from a relatively small group of people, if the voters in a particular community, parent group, or employee group were motivated to turn out for the election. According to one Toronto participant, the low turnout was exploited by those involved, as it 'was so low that you could do a little bit of political organizing and get a lot of seats for it. And so it wasn't random. It was very, very deliberate.'

Some trustees were chosen by acclamation, especially if they were well-known or, in some wards, supported by the NDP; so that the chances of other candidates being elected were slim. In 1974, Gord Cressey and Doug Barr – both popular, progressive trustees – were acclaimed in ward 7. The next election, Dan Leckie and Bob Spencer were acclaimed in ward 6, while Doug Barr had to run again, but easily won in ward 7, because Gord Cressey had left a seat open in his run for city council. Fiona Nelson and Penny Moss were acclaimed in ward 5 in 1980.

Winnipeg voter turnout was similar; a 25 or 30 per cent turnout was considered very good, which meant that trustees were also elected with relatively few votes. There were rarely acclamations for trustees in Winnipeg, but incumbent trustees had a large advantage, though there were a few occasions where incumbents were defeated in elections.

Reflecting the interests of local constituents was important for getting elected. Many trustees had been involved in local educational struggles and had worked to stop school closings, organized for an alternative school, represented ethnic communities, led parent organizations, or supported heritage language programs. Through this work they became known – and were sometimes recruited to run – by various parties, or decided to run as a way to exercise, they hoped, greater influence. Once elected, connections to community groups gave individual trustees more influence on the board as a whole.

In Winnipeg, trustees regularly came from ethnic – especially Portuguese, Filipino, and Ukrainian – communities, in part because high turnout from even a relatively small but geographically concentrated community could ensure electoral success. The Aboriginal community, however, has never been well represented on the WSD's board. Although some 10 per cent of Winnipeg's population is Aboriginal, and the proportion is much higher in the central and north wards of the division, only two Aboriginal trustees were elected – both in the early 1990s, and both for only one term.

Many Toronto trustees were well-educated, and a substantial minority had graduate degrees. According to one trustee, 'the calibre of trustees on both sides of the spectrum, the capacity to think, to understand' was very high. Many were also young, at least at the start of their careers. In 1975, 80 per cent of the TBE was under the age of forty, and half a dozen members were in their twenties (Nagle, 1975). Demonstrated community involvement, wide social connections, and the support of ethnic communities and organizations were also important for many trustees.

Trustees who found political life rewarding sometimes went on to municipal, provincial, or federal politics: in Toronto, these included Gord Cressey, Olivia Chow, Tony Silipo, and Kathleen Wynne. Others, such as George Martell, Pat Case, and Penny Moss, remained local activists in other organizations and were more interested in pushing forward their ideas than in getting into elected office. The same pattern happened in Winnipeg. Maryanne Mihychuk, an NDP trustee, became a provincial MLA and cabinet minister. Anita Neville became a federal member of parliament. Mira Spivak was appointed to the Senate of Canada. This is not surprising, given the community leadership skills and interests of former trustees.

On the other hand, the role of the school trustee could be very frustrating. Contrasted with politicians elected at the provincial or federal level, school trustees have few supports, less ability to change the system, work in a setting in which overt politics are either derided or ignored, and depend on being able to garner votes on any given issue. One year into his trusteeship, Levin wrote:

> The lesson that has been most deeply implanted is that school boards really have no function ... They do not do anything which could not be done just as well if they ceased to exist ...
>
> After all, trustees are part-time nonprofessionals trying to control a system of full-time specialists ...
>
> My feeling so far is that although I have enjoyed myself and learned a great deal, I have had no impact. (Levin, 1973, pp. 306–7)

The ability of a board to define and implement a coherent strategy is critical. Both the Winnipeg and Toronto districts had a historical division between the political left and right, and an ongoing struggle as to which side would have a majority and control the agenda. In both cities, there were moments of acrimony at a personal and political level, though these seemed more glaring in Winnipeg, perhaps because they are more apparent on a nine-person board.

The NDP nominated or endorsed candidates and lent the support of its electoral machinery to school board campaigns at various times in both cities. Other parties were much less interested in local politics, and concentrated their resources on successful provincial and federal campaigns; the non-NDP camp in both Winnipeg and Toronto ran candidates either as independents or under non-party labels, such as the Independent Citizens Election Committee (ICEC) in Winnipeg in the 1970s and 1980s. In Winnipeg, the NDP ran candidates and elected trustees throughout the period between the late 1960s and the late 1990s. In Toronto, many of the trustees between 1970 and 1978 were members of the NDP, but they did not necessarily run as NDP candidates. Later, the party became more formally involved in electing trustees. In instances where the party only had one NDP candidate, up to four or five non-NDP candidates might split the rest of the vote, so the NDP candidate was likely to win.

No matter who was elected, maintaining party discipline on the board was difficult in both cities. The formal NDP caucus established in Toronto in the early 1980s in an attempt to force more consistent policy positions was seen as divisive by many trustees, including some who were sympathetic on many policy issues. Ann Vanstone, who was more conservative, and who chaired the Board in the mid-1980s, felt the caucus created too much 'strict ideological control, and caused a lot of fighting for a lot of years.' Staff felt excluded and independent trustees felt it prevented the development of consensus and understanding. After the NDP lost an election in 1985, 'party politics sort of died,' and the board's agenda emerged from looser groupings of trustees. According to one interviewee: 'Most of them were individualists anyhow, they didn't like fitting in the mold. So these were loose alliances that went along.'

The WSD had either four or five NDP-nominated trustees throughout most of the period of this study, splitting the nine member board almost evenly with non-NDP trustees – who by no means held a consistent ideological position. Most of the NDP trustees in Winnipeg came from the poorer and more diverse neighbourhoods in the centre and north of the city. However, the NDP also regularly elected candidates in the wealthier, southern ward of the WSD – for example, Lionel Orlikow was elected for a decade in ward 1 – and sometimes the north end would elect conservative but populist candidates.

Party discipline did not operate once trustees were elected in Winnipeg. In 1971, five of the nine trustees were NDP-nominated, but only four of them, plus one independent who usually supported them, were part of the board's dominant coalition. At a later time, the coalition was made up mainly of non-aligned but progressive south-end trustees with a couple of NDP supporters. Yet there were times in Winnipeg when an NDP caucus exercised control over the board, sometimes, as in Toronto, provoking the ire of other trustees.

Changes in control of the WSD did matter to policy. In 1977, a more conservative majority took control and had a palpable impact on ideas and initiatives. One inner-city administrator described it this way:

> A huge change happened in the division in the summer of 1979, when the Division effectively killed community schools. A new, more conservative board had been elected in 1977, as had a Conservative provincial government. The new superintendent was not in favour of these initiatives. Keith Cooper left the Division instead of being fired and went to head Children's Home. At one point the new superintendent had a package ready for the board of appointments of principals as advocated by Cooper then pulled them at the last minute.

In Toronto, the agenda was more consistently left-leaning, with a focus on the inner city, even though trustees changed and the NDP caucus came and went. In part, this was because on a board of twenty-two trustees, a change in one person mattered less, and coalitions had to be put together on most issues. Although agreement could rarely be taken for granted, trustees worked to create coalitions and consensus in order to drive things forward. They also gradually learned that they needed the administration's support to get things done. In 1975, one Toronto trustee wrote that:

> a group of trustees with radical tendencies not only serves to reinforce the positions and behavior of its individual members, but also can move an entire system ... The ability and philosophical intent of trustees to work with their communities augur well for a democratic education system. (Nagle, 1975, p. 37)

Even after the 1985 election, when the left-wing group of trustees lost its majority and the School Community Relations department was disbanded, the basic direction of the board continued unchanged. The staff, including those working on equity and inner-city schools, had job descriptions that kept things going. Irene Atkinson, the first chair under the 'positive alternative' group that had a majority after 1985, said: 'By and large, and I think that the NDP trustees would say the same thing, it didn't work too badly for a number of years.' Left-leaning trustees agreed that the right wing had adopted many of their practices for running the board.

In school boards, as in all politics, public support is essential. A school board must operate within the parameters that voters accept. Still, the views and skills of trustees also matter. These cases show that a school board can build and sustain a policy direction over time, even when political or economic conditions are not entirely favourable, if the elected trustees have the appropriate combination of will and skill to do so. Toronto and Winnipeg elected more progressive trustees than did smaller or rural districts, and they had more progressive policies as a result. Although ideological and political affiliations were important, they were balanced with considerations of what is required to move things along under a given set of circumstances. In both boards, sustaining policy required trustees to cooperate across party or ideological lines in a way that did not occur at the provincial or federal level. The boards were most successful when trustees and their senior staff could work together. Given large wards, part-time and low-salaried work, complex issues, and fractious policies, being a good school trustee politician requires dedication and cooperation across partisan lines.

Community Involvement

In 1970, education reformers were focused on community schools, parental involvement, decentralization, and community organizing. These approaches, it was thought, would provide a voice for the poor in the face of intransigent educators who listened closely to powerful, middle-class parents and who were accountable to an equally intransigent bureaucracy. The most vivid example of these approaches in action was in 1967, when New York City mayor John Lindsay decentralized the NYC school district in response to demands from the city's African-American and Latino communities, a move that led to a great deal of conflict with teachers' unions. Creating more community involvement was important to both the Toronto and Winnipeg boards.

The movement towards 'community control' went far beyond schooling and was deeply rooted in larger political movements of the 1960s and 1970s, which called for power redistribution and local control of public institutions. These intentions were everywhere in public policy. In 1970, Canada had a Royal Commission on Youth that set out a framework – which was never implemented – for youth engagement and participation in public decisions. The first efforts were made to move control of education on First Nations reserves from the federal government to local First Nations. In 1971, the University of Manitoba Act created a university and community council that was intended to be a strong community voice for the university, although it was abolished a few years later. In 1970, in addition to creating a single city from ten municipalities, the City of Winnipeg Act included a bold vision for large-scale community participation – though this vision, too, was later greatly scaled back. Lloyd Axworthy, then a professor at the University of Winnipeg, founded the Institute of Urban Studies, which helped to organize local communities. Jane Jacobs' writing on cities and activism to preserve neighbourhoods in Toronto reflected the same impulses.

The problems and contradictions of community involvement became evident over time. Community involvement was challenging. Parents were not always ready or eager to participate in school governance, even when they had high aspirations for their own children. Middle-class and professional parents were often both most able and most willing to take political action on education issues. Additionally, local school councils did not always make choices that adhered to the reformist impulse behind board policy. A Toronto leader worried about how wealthier communities might respond if it were clear how much of the budget was allocated to poorer areas:

I always resisted those comparisons that said if you lived in Regent Park the school board spent x thousand dollars per student [versus] if you lived in north Toronto it was y. Because I knew what that data was and how dramatic the differences were, and I knew that politically it would be very difficult to maintain should that information become public. It wasn't that we were trying to suppress it, but I certainly didn't do anything to encourage the collection and publication of that data on a school by school basis.

Finally, and most importantly, there was inevitable tension between community control and professional autonomy within and control over the organizations in which they both worked. The result could be heated debate and extensive conflict, which some trustees and staff welcomed, and which others managed and mediated as best they could.

Winnipeg's initial efforts to engage parents more fully were community school initiatives, which were largely promoted by Orlikow's Planning and Research Division in the Manitoba Department of Education, and were supported by the reform trustees who took office in Winnipeg in 1971. A few schools were selected for intensive effort that was rooted in a very explicit analysis of value of community organizing. These efforts did not last more than a few years, as they were too demanding of staff and school leaders. However, attempts to involve parents did continue through most of the 1970s and lead to the creation of CEDA, discussed in chapter 2, which still operates as an inner-city community agency in Winnipeg.

In the 1980s, another community engagement effort was made through the Core Area Initiative, although in general the CAI had more of a program focus. It supported parent-child centres in a number of central Winnipeg schools as a way of getting parents involved, even before their children started attending. At around the same time, the WSD created a system of advisory committees, based on either geography or on issues (such as special education) as a way of getting regular community input. Over time, these committees became an established part of the decision-making process and the board often consulted them on developing issues. As one trustee remarked:

> Stability at the board level was gradually achieved because of the creation of advisory committees. There [were], at the beginning of my time on the board ... many delegations who focused primarily on the budget because earlier the [WSD] did not have the apparatus to listen to people ... The creation of advisory committees was meant to address a specific problem in areas of the division that were growing, and yet there were very few facilities in those schools. We wanted to work with parents there so that we could find solutions. We then used [this] idea of advisory committees across the division ... As a consequence of the advisory committees, people began to see decision makers come to their schools and their areas to listen to their concerns.

In the mid-1990s, Manitoba's Conservative government mandated parent advisory councils in all schools, but these had little impact, in part because they had no real authority and so were similar to existing parent organizations. The explicit politics of transferring power had disappeared from the effort.

Some Winnipeg educators with community development experience tried to extend the role of their school into areas such as adult education, integrated social services, and training and employment for local residents meant to generate local economic activity. Hunter (2000) describes her efforts as an inner-city principal in the early 1990s to move in this direction, including developing a food cooperative and an employment cooperative to generate economic activity in her poor, mainly Aboriginal community. However, these efforts were the product of exceptional individuals and were not generalized across the district.

In Toronto, community engagement strategies were very significant throughout the period of this study. The protests against excessive streaming and poor results for their children by low income mothers living in Trefann Court are credited with starting reform at the TBE. The Park Street community school council, which had a Donner foundation grant to hire parent aides in the classroom, led to another influential brief called *Downtown Kids Aren't Dumb*. The new board in Toronto in the early 1970s quickly set about involving more parents and community activists in committees, advisory groups, and community schools as part of their strategy to transform the system. In an essay in *This Magazine Is about Schools* that captured the spirit of reformers, George Martell, who had worked with such groups, wrote:

> It seems to me that we're not serious about our belief in democratic government unless we come out strongly for a school system where parents, teachers and students collectively make the all over policy for the school in which they or their children live and work . . . this belief says that if people have power over their lives, then they will make the best decisions about life in that community; they will make mistakes, but the mistakes hurt them . . . [and] it can be a very effective means of starting to turn back the class bias in our educational system. (1971, p. 80)

The TBE brought in a number of specific policies to encourage and legitimate parent involvement. Parents and students were brought into decisions on matters such as staffing, budgeting, and hiring principals. A number of alternative schools were established, often at the initiative of parent groups (Nelson, 1973). Parent council leaders were extensively involved in policy discussions. Duncan Green, the board director from 1975 to 1985, noted that the heads of local parent organizations in Toronto often had more power than trustees, as they could make public statements with less concern about the next election. These measures had a significant impact, and often bridged the differences between various parts of the community and the professional staff. As Dehli (1996) argued:

> During the late 1970s and early 1980s, a culturally and racially diverse movement of working and middle class parents in Toronto was quite successful in enlisting the support of mainly Anglo-European teachers around a series of organizing efforts to improve the schooling of working class, immigrant and minority children. This coalition was able to prevent lay-offs of teachers and it was instrumental in bringing a greater degree of parent participation into school decision making. (p. 78)

The establishment of the School Community Relations department was the clearest expression of the Board's commitment to enhancing community input. Community liaison officers helped parents articulate concerns about their schools (Lenskyj, 2005). The department also provided for direct communication between trustees and central staff on the one hand, and parent communities in poorer downtown areas on the other. The SCR was sometimes resented by principals because it helped parents organize to put pressure on schools, which illustrates the tension between citizen involvement and professional autonomy.

The debate about heritage language programs, discussed in chapter 3, illustrated how contentious wide-ranging community input could become, and set teachers against community organizers and staff against each other in very public ways. There was intense activism on all sides of the debate, and the open disagreement was not restricted to trustees or an inner circle of staff. Meetings ran late into the night so every group could be heard. Resolving the issue eventually required board votes, court appeals, and school-by-school decision making. The discussions created animosity and accusations of racism, but were also a learning experience that gradually led to the acceptance of the value of languages other than English in Toronto schools.

Community engagement efforts were always partial. Neither the Toronto nor Winnipeg boards gave local communities full control of their schools, although in both districts vocal and determined parents had considerable influence on many matters. While those inside the system experienced such input as a positive change, many communities felt they had achieved little. The Aboriginal community in Winnipeg, in particular, continued to feel marginalized after years of effort by the Division. Increasing community involvement did not meet the goals of the activists. Achievement gaps and streaming students by class, ethnicity, and race continued; professional educators continued to have much more power than parents, and could often sideline parent concerns; and parent activists sometimes took up issues of choice and excellence rather than equity and poverty. Nevertheless, the idea that politics was part of schooling and that different kinds of communities should have a direct say in educational policy became much more widely accepted. Between the late 1960s and late 1990s, inner-city communities had increasing power as they developed their capacities and found reasons to speak out.

Relations with Board Administrators

In all governments, the relations between elected officials and their professional staff are vital to the organization's success but are problematic to some degree. Politicians and staff have different time frames, different incentives, different sources of information, and different frames for understanding the work of schooling (Levin, 2005). Trustees are elected for a few years, and relatively few serve more than a couple of terms, while staff invest their careers in the system. Trustees are also primarily focused on the concerns of their electors and communities, while staff are primarily focused on the concerns of professional colleagues. These differences produce friction.

Many of the trustees elected in the political ferment of the late 1960s and early 1970s were activists who regarded the school system as an oppressive institution that needed to change. These trustees saw the board administration as anywhere from being unhelpful to being opponents who needed to be put firmly in their place. After all, the administrators were the people responsible for all the failures of the system that the new trustees were there to correct.

Such views did not make for easy working relationships, and there were intense power struggles. Both Winnipeg and Toronto were organized as hierarchies under a chief superintendent (Winnipeg) or director of education (Toronto) appointed by the board. Both districts had people in other leadership roles, such as assistant superintendents in Winnipeg or directors of particular program areas in Toronto. The staff structure of each board shifted over time, and the number of staff positions grew. Both boards had a set of managers for financial and administrative matters, some, but not all, of whom were educators by background. Both boards also had innumerable committees, made up of staff from across the district and often of parents as well. However, as in most organizations, the nature and character of the CEO was critical.

In 1968, the WSD board hired Carmen Moir, a progressive new chief superintendent from Nova Scotia. When Moir returned to Nova Scotia in 1975, the board went through three chief superintendents in five years, two of whom were fired after a relatively short tenure (both on five-to-four votes), until Jack Smyth was hired in 1982 and remained in the position for the next twenty years.

The TBE changed directors more regularly. When the reform board was first elected in 1970, they tried to hire a reform director to drive change. Their choice, John Bremer, was a prominent and innovative educator who had run a 'school without walls' in Philadelphia. His appointment was vetoed by the provincial government, ostensibly because he did not have Ontario certification. Ron Jones, an internal candidate with a background in special education, got the job instead. In 1973, Duncan Green took over and stayed until he moved to the provincial level to lead secondary school curriculum reform in 1985. His deputy, Ned McKeown, took over at that point. McKeown described their working relationship in a way that others agree with: 'As we often said, [Green] led the system and I ran it, because the associate director's job was to deal with money and buildings and politics.' This meant substantial continuity over a period of almost fifteen years. In 1990, Joan Green had the job for five years before moving to EQAO; John Davies then held the job until amalgamation.

Each of these people had somewhat different approaches to the job, but they all came from within the GTA, knew the context well, and shared a belief in the directions the board was moving. Duncan Green, who was the longest serving director, was a creative and reform-oriented educator particularly concerned about the low success rate of students and the rigidity of the secondary system. He worked closely with McKeown, who took responsibility for operations. Joan Green, the first female director, came from North York Board and, as a follower of Don Rutledge's theories of language, provided continuity in direction. John Davies also came from a suburban Toronto board, where he had been deeply immersed in parent participation and success for low-income students. Moving to Toronto meant working on a board where he would have more support for his priorities.

The directors tried to keep the trustees from 'meddling,' but trustees had an impact on staffing below the director level. The director reported to the TBE, and the rest of the staff reported to the director, but the trustees recognized the importance of other managers to the implementation of their agendas. In Toronto, when things weren't moving fast enough, the impulse was to hire new staff or create a new division to move things forward. In many cases, trustees developed close relationships with staff who shared their commitments throughout the organization – not just with the central administration, but with school principals as well. According to one interviewee, trustees and staff 'in many cases belonged to the same political party, attended the same political events, had breakfast together, and so on. So a lot of things happened.' Staff and trustees sat on committees together, worked on reports together, and often learned about issues collaboratively. The hierarchy was not well-entrenched, and personal relationships and politics often trumped formal workplace relationships. In Toronto, local trustees were frequently involved, even if informally, in hiring principals in their wards.

The same pattern occurred in Winnipeg. Trustees were directly involved in hiring two key outsiders as assistant superintendents in the 1970s. Throughout the 1980s, trustees were lobbied and got involved in decisions not only about district level appointments, but also about principal appointments. Levin, who was politically connected to some WSD leaders, can remember being involved in discussions with trustees and influential advisors about who would be hired into which principal positions in Winnipeg.

Change for the inner city depended not only on policy decisions, but also on implementation, and the commitment of staff was crucial. Both boards found ways to reorganize departments and hire staff to move the inner-city agenda forward. Both boards also created inner-city divisions that had resources and a mandate in relation to the success of students who came from poor families, who were racialized, Aboriginal, or did not speak English. Toronto created divisions responsible for equity and community development, and worked in a collaborative way that often upended the official hierarchy. Winnipeg, as a smaller board with less consistent politics, was less able to create distinct divisions, although it did create dedicated positions to work on Aboriginal education issues and it did support CEDA as a community development arm for many years.

The Toronto school board created a staffing structure that focused on the inner city, encouraged a culture of political awareness, and created new units and roles to be filled by activists. The inner-city department, the equity advisors, the research department, and the school community relations department had discretionary funds and were able to hire new staff. John Bates, head of the inner-city department, said that: 'When I became inner-city coordinator, the inner-city schools had $15,000 to spend over a three-year period . . . The first thing we did was vote ourselves a million dollars.' The money allowed strategic hiring into a staff culture where issues of poverty, power, and privilege were constantly examined. For the people who were hired, Bates said, 'it was an invigorating place to work, because despite the stress, you were working in an environment where people were trying to make things better rather than simply reproducing all of the inequities that existed. And there was always a good learning environment.' There were also tensions and disagreements, but productive working relationships: 'We always reported to people; either an equity advisor or someone in the equal opportunity office. And I remember it being quite collaborative. Even though we got direction from people, they allowed you to go off and design strategies.'

Our respondents often used the word 'collaborative' to describe their experiences, even in the face of disagreement and conflict. However, disagreements were inevitable, especially among those who were politically most engaged and committed. According to one interviewee:

In 1991, we suggested that it was ridiculous to have people scattered all over in the same organization, and what we needed was not a coordinator of Women in Labour Studies, whose office was next to the coordinator of Multicultural Feminism Anti-Racism, but we needed a department. We had nobody dealing with homophobia. [So we tried] to create an Equity Studies Centre. [That meeting] was one of the worst nights of my life because the trade unionists didn't think that it was important to deal with homophobia, and the Aboriginal group refused to come because they certainly didn't think that anti-racism was the way to think about their situation. People from the Status of Women Committee were utterly contemptuous of the trade unionists who came with their dirty hands or whatever. [People were] pounding tables and saying, 'It's all going to get watered down. Our issue will disappear if these other issues are dealt with.' It was horrible.

In Winnipeg, debates about organizing the district were ongoing throughout the period of this study. The board created a regional superintendent structure in the early 1970s, in part as a way to place people the trustees thought would support their agenda for the WSD in strategic positions. Winnipeg reverted to elementary/secondary organization in 1980, but returned to regional divisions in 1990. In part, the changes were based on the high tolerance for different policies and practices in different parts of the WSD. Much of this debate was over whether the inner city would have its own superintendent, but part of it was over which administrators would have which roles. School districts, like other organizations, use organizational restructuring as a way to move individuals into or out of important positions. In one Toronto case, a senior official of the board sued a number of trustees over a change in his position that he felt marginalized him within the board.

Senior administrators in these very politicized districts had to be adept at understanding political pressures, regardless of the stability of the environment. Issues could emerge suddenly, and the vote could be difficult to predict. Senior administrators could influence policy, and were able to advise trustees, argue their position, and point out difficulties and opportunities with each possible result. They also had to recognize when the board had made a decision, and the administration would have to accommodate it.

Despite the tough rhetoric that sometimes characterized relations between trustees and senior officials, for the most part the Toronto and Winnipeg boards had strong and consistent leaders.

Conclusions

Politics permeated virtually every aspect these districts as they struggled to confront challenges and organize for change. As occurs often in politics, the pressures were contradictory. Reformers wanted to define clear alternatives to the existing system and ideas, but also wanted consensus and support for their policies. They wanted local control of resources and policy, but had to work with provincial governments that were increasingly interested in education. They wanted to decentralize the system, but also ensure their goals and priorities were given attention. They wanted greater respect and autonomy for professional staff, yet also greater trustee and community participation. Reformers had to come to terms with opposing forces and conflicting agendas, and find ways to work with diverse groups and interests. These tensions are endemic to every political setting. The ability to work together creates the civic capacity necessary to sustain effective programs for inner-city schools.

Change in schools does not happen quickly. The ability to build coalitions and get things done requires some continuity of policy direction and staffing, as well as the resources and climate to motivate people to follow through. It involves those outside and inside schools working together with trust, willingness to learn, and shared beliefs, even in situations that often degrade to partisan politics and fighting over policy and programs. Despite a great deal of conflict, there was cooperation in Toronto over most of the period we studied. In Winnipeg, a similar level of cooperation was only seen in the 1990s, when long-serving staff committed to inner-city reform found common direction with trustees and the provincial government. Talented political and staff leadership, voter support, and willingness to resolve conflict were key factors.

Both boards developed the civic capacity to manage issues in inner-city education. The voices of the relatively powerless were heard early on in both cities. In Toronto, trustees and staff collaborated to move the board in the directions parents consistently advocated for. Yet even after decades of work, reform was fragile and was later undermined by provincial politics. Change was less consistent in Winnipeg, but the infrastructure that the WSD eventually built remains robust and relatively effective. Neither board has resolved its political or educational challenges, but each was effective in moments when it found common cause.

The goal of reform is to change students' experience of learning so that they learn more and become better citizens. The reformers in Winnipeg and Toronto had strong views about the specific goals of reform, but they were less clear on the instructional strategies that could lead to them, which resulted in a trial-and-error approach in many cases. As a result, the two districts had limited success in transforming the classroom experience, although changes did take place in some areas.

The reformers in Toronto and Winnipeg defined the new student learning outcomes they wanted in broad terms. The problems of urban education had come to their attention because of school practices they considered wrong. They saw the lack of academic success, coupled with many stories of poor treatment of students from impoverished, immigrant, and Aboriginal backgrounds, as deeply problematic. They wanted more humane, inclusive, and respectful learning environments. They wanted more literacy, fewer dropouts, better high school graduation rates, and more intellectually and socially engaged students. They wanted less tracking and streaming of students. They wanted parents to be more involved with teachers and principals.

In Toronto, trustees came into office with a social class analysis that addressed the fact that working class and visible minority students were being streamed into vocational and special education programs. They also recognized the Toronto Board of Education had to respond more effectively to the large proportion of students and parents who did not speak English as a first language. This response would require, among other things, different approaches to teaching literacy, to English language learning, and to daily interactions with students and parents.

In Winnipeg, trustees concerned about the inner city argued for experimental and alternative programs, community involvement, and structural changes focused on the success of Aboriginal and students from low-income backgrounds. Their response focused on changing relationships in schools and improving the achievement of students from poor families and from Aboriginal communities.

Reaching these goals was, and remains, very challenging for many reasons. Research shows that it is difficult for educational leaders at the board level to alter student-teacher interactions. Despite changing ideas about education, political agreements, and new policies, teaching and learning can proceed remarkably untouched (e.g., Cuban & Usdan, 2003; Tyack, 1974). In light of the stability of teaching practice, one of the first challenges for reformers is agreeing that current practices are not effective and need to change. Especially in the earlier years of this study, there were few widely accepted markers of good student achievement, and even less data on levels of performance. It was hard to know which groups were or were not succeeding, or at what level. This lack of knowledge was the impetus behind the Every Student Survey in Toronto, which used institutional markers, notably measures of streaming and completion rates, to measure student progress and highlight existing problems.

A growing body of work (e.g., Fullan, 2007; Elmore, 2004; Levin, 2008) has explored the difficulties of changing teaching and learning practices in a large system in a meaningful and sustainable way. Teaching and learning takes place mostly within individual teachers' classrooms. Education has not been an activity in which consistency of practice is always valued or reinforced; individual professional autonomy is the norm. As professionals, teachers want and need the ability to make instructional decisions based on their students' needs and local context, but this can lead to inconsistent practices within a school, or to failing to adopt new practices with strong evidence of effectiveness. In many cases, the research is not sufficient to provide clear guidance for practice, and professional development is often ineffective in changing teaching practices. Education is also a field that everyone has experienced through their own schooling, so teachers, students, and parents often have strong ideas about what it should look like, and these ideas are powerfully informed by specific contextual norms.

Overall, the Toronto and Winnipeg districts had some, but limited, success in changing educational practices in the classroom. Part of this was because classroom practice was not always a priority. Attention had to be paid to changes in organization, funding, policy, and program offerings, even if their connection to student experience was indirect. The most controversial, pressing, and politically important issues were not necessarily related to everyday teaching and learning. Necessarily, then, efforts to change teaching and learning played a variable role over time in both districts. Sometimes they were at the centre of each board's attention, while at other times they were overshadowed by other issues.

When teaching and learning was a central focus, trustees and staff faced dilemmas about how best to organize and support the changes they wanted. Given limited time and energy, they first had to decide on priorities. They focused on changing literacy practices and moving from a search for the correct answer to active engagement with texts. They also sought to make the curriculum more responsive to the changing student population. Their focus on new curriculum resources and child-centred approaches to literacy was more easily adopted – and therefore made more of a difference – at the elementary level, where provincial guidelines were flexible and teachers worked with the same students for more time per day.

In the secondary system, structural issues of streaming and alternative programs rather than issues of pedagogy, were the focus of debate. The research on what difference it all made was rudimentary; reform was driven much more by belief systems than by data, although the TBE did marshall research evidence against streaming. There was considerably less success in changing secondary schools, largely because teachers did not support changing the practice of streaming.

A second critical choice was how much pressure to put on schools. Despite wanting to change teachers, most reformers viewed teachers as professionals who deserved respect and autonomy. Reformers recognized that active support from a large number of teachers was essential for change, and that coercing teachers into supporting change could not work. Both boards focused on improving relationships within schools as much as on increasing student achievement, because they assumed that good relationships would promote achievement. Both districts relied on strategies in which change was a matter of persuasion, volunteers, and multiple approaches in different contexts. The boards tended to work with schools and teachers who wanted change, rather than persisting in the struggle for system-wide reform. Moreover, they maintained those strategies, even through the 1980s and 1990s when the larger policy context shifted towards aggressive accountability.

Despite these relatively soft strategies, teachers and principals in both cities sometimes opposed – both publicly and, more often, quietly – the districts' pedagogical interventions, though progressive educators often sided with reformers. The opposition reinforced the boards' strategy of working selectively with cooperating schools, and maintained the status quo in areas that were not open to change. However, even in inner-city elementary schools with willing staff, change in classroom practice was partial, slow, fragile, and difficult to document.

Creating a Welcoming Classroom Environment

In both cities, the 1970s ushered in a new era of concern about how the system had been ignoring, or actively marginalizing, students from less advantaged backgrounds, particularly those from poor families, visible minorities, and Aboriginal communities. These concerns were not only about low achievement levels; in both cities, reformers recognized that respect for the diversity among students and their families needed to be a first and central concern of any change effort.

The late 1960s and early 1970s was a period of 'student power' and rebellion. Ideas about the hierarchical relationship between youth and adults were changing, and youth culture produced significant mainstream cultural change. The period was the high point of 'child-centred pedagogy' and non-hierarchical movements in counselling, including T-groups, Rogerian non-directive counselling, and other forms of self-development. These ideas were portrayed in Alan King's movie *Warrendale,* and were incorporated into pedagogy at alternative schools such as Everdale. Many educators and most inner-city advocates believed that strong personal relationships with students were essential to better outcomes.

These trends had a powerful presence in Toronto. Many reforming trustees had worked with marginalized young people as social workers or teachers in alternative schools, and brought that understanding to their work as elected officials. John Piper had 'hung out with the kids' as a long-haired community worker with the YMCA. George Martell started Point Blank, an alternative school, in his home, and was interested in Herbert Marcuse and psychoanalytic theory. Gord Cressey was a social worker living and working in a group home for kids in trouble with the law, and decided 'that the problem wasn't the kids, that the problem was the system.' Myra Novogrodsky started an alternative school called City School and taught there for years.

In Winnipeg, many of the reform leaders also had strong community development or social service backgrounds. Heather Hunter helped low-income families prepare tax returns. Mario Santos worked with Portuguese youth. Wayne Helgason was a child protection worker in the inner city. Myra Larammee was a poor single mother battling with schools when she decided to become a teacher. Another group was formed by their experience in alternative programs. One interviewee put it this way:

> I started teaching in the Winnipeg School Division in [the late 1970s] in the basement of a junior high school. I had what I now consider to be an impossible task – teaching an alternative program ... with kids kicked out of every school in the inner city. Although I have many reservations about alternative programs, [that program] did indicate a genuine interest on the part of the education system to reach out to kids who were not in school.

For people with alternative backgrounds, there was an urgent need to have students and parents view schools as friendly and approachable. Several interviewees told us that 'kids' lives were at stake,' 'mothers were afraid of schools,' and that 'we tried to reach out and understand why people were alienated from school. We tried silly little things like a colourful leaflet in laundromats. And a phone call to all the kids who hadn't been there.' The TBE's resolution to abolish the strap was not about improving achievement; it was about replacing a classroom based on coercion and fear with one based on respect and conversation. Later, the Board developed a policy promoting student involvement and student rights, and supported a significant effort to train student leaders (McCaskell, 2005).

In Winnipeg, concern about achievement in inner-city schools also grew. A number of our respondents spoke of their shock at entering inner-city schools and realizing that the instruction was inadequate for student success. The same points were made repeatedly: children were preoccupied with the struggle to survive, did not have the background teachers expected, and were not succeeding under traditional teaching practices. One senior Winnipeg administrator who worked as a principal in a high-poverty school in the early 1970s remarked:

> Within two or three months of my being at [this school] the primary teachers came and said that they were not happy with what they were doing.

Many of the children in the classroom did not seem to be accomplishing anything. The achievement level of the children was not very high.

Another described the school she taught in during the 1970s:

> [This particular school] had lots of issues. It was a fairly traditional school that coped with its challenging clientele by having many special programs. The school had tons of Aboriginal kids but still ran school teas and taught curriculum by the book unless you were in an alternative program. The school still used the strap! Some work was done in involving staff in decisions, but there was no role for parents or for students.

Many educators felt that stronger personal relationships with students were essential. A group of nuns who operated Rossbrook House, a drop-in centre for inner-city youth in Winnipeg, noticed the difference in how children related to adults in that setting:

> Kids would drop in to our house as they had nowhere else to go. These were kids who were doing very poorly in school. . . . I bought a pool table, and we put the pool table in the basement. The children in the neighbourhood used it. That is how we got to know the children . . .
>
> There was such a contrast between their behaviour in my house, where they were so respectful, and their behaviour at [school], where they would always be in trouble. I concluded that the difference in behaviour had to do with feeling comfortable in their environment. Students needed acceptance more than they needed counselling. If they do not experience racism or feel like they are stupid, or have someone yell at them, then they behave in a like manner.

The Rossbrook nuns lobbied the board to establish an elementary school, Wi-Wabigooni, in 1981, and a high school, Rising Sun, in 1982, that would operate from their centre as alternative schools with a small number of students and staff working together on an individual level. Similar programs were associated with quite a few inner-city schools, usually at the instigation of school principals. According to one interviewee:

> There were several off-campus programs that we started . . . for kids who simply would not come to school. Several inner-city principals . . . developed a program . . . using funds from Child and Family Services, our money

and other stakeholder's money for children who were really acting out. You could not have those children even in special education programs.

One Winnipeg elementary principal described the board's approach as:

> Embracing alternative ideas: schools without walls, as well as interactive and hands-on learning. In general, the pedagogy was child-centered. The staff wanted to create a school where children who were disadvantaged could be assisted by different pedagogical practices ... I integrated more personal and physical activities into the curriculum. I linked up to the physical education teacher, and we did camping in the spring, fall, and winter, for which we had to raise funds. Such activities did seem to make a difference in the lives of the students, enriching their personal lives ... The best times were more expressive and personal activities, such as the arts.

According to another principal, such activities helped to build beneficial personal relationships:

> The personal relationship, building that sense of trust and respect with the children really translated into the classroom. At [one school] it was a group of four children with whom a student teacher and I connected. We took them swimming every Sunday afternoon, and then for a bite to eat, and then back to their homes. Such activities made a big difference in how they were able to grab onto learning and in behavioural and social issues in the classroom as well.

Another school, largely at the principal's initiative, implemented a large volunteer program with students from a local post-secondary institution in order to increase the amount of instruction that took place. According to that principal:

> I had fifty volunteers from the college who came for half an afternoon every week in order to do direct service with children who needed extra reading or other help. I would create the plan that the volunteers would use with those children. Again, it was a time when classrooms were changing; there was not a lot direct teaching to the whole class. There was very much group instruction, and a lot of project work. It was more research oriented, and the mathematics programs were also changing so there

was the beginning of using more concrete and conceptual approaches to mathematics.

The range of ideas and strategies was enormous. Teachers could diverge from the formal curriculum in their efforts to engage students, and the desire to offer personal support could mean less focus on what students were learning. At the elementary level, the connection between engagement and a focus on learning was easier to achieve. At the secondary level, some felt that this lessened the focus on academic outcomes. In Winnipeg, several of our interviewees expressed concern about academic standards deteriorating. One remarked that:

> I cannot say that there was academic rigour or that we followed the cur-
> riculum guidelines. For example, we got a big art table. We put plastic all
> over it. We grew grass, and we made an Indian village. It motivated the
> fourteen male students to come running in to class primarily to check on
> how the grass was growing more each day. However, these students had
> very high needs and often engaged in destructive behaviour.
>
> Every school did its own thing. Some schools did not even have a copy
> of the provincial curriculum.

As other schools created new alternative programs in response to student interests, some began to express anxiety about the trade-off between academic success and relevant curriculum. Teachers and principals worried that if academic demands were too high, students would leave school. Yet if students did not develop reasonable skills in reading, writing, and other curriculum areas, they would not be successful in life. Alternative programs with a negotiable curriculum could become a form of streaming and special education placement, in other words, not a way to increase learning and literacy. As one interviewee remarked:

> Margaret really tried. She told me that all they did was watch movies.
> This was an alternative program, and she was sick of watching movies. I
> often wondered how really challenging, inviting, or effective such a pro-
> gram was, especially for the teenage group. The obvious streaming
> resulted in reduced expectations. I wondered how much that dynamic
> contributed to the drop-out rate. There would be two or three children in
> classes that in September had been full.

A mid-1980s research project at a Winnipeg secondary school examined teaching styles in a school that had a large number of students with high needs and low previous success (Riffel & Levin, 1986). The school focused on building strong personal relationships with students, and on making all students feel welcome and supported. In a report, the project found that while this was a very significant accomplishment, there also seemed to be low expectations for students' academic work. The school staff rejected this finding, and argued that the most important requirement was for students to come to school, and that too much pressure on performance would drive them away. Getting students to want to be in school in the first place was a major focus.

Another attempt to make schools more welcoming and relevant viewed schools as community hubs that would offer various social services to help with family, child, and youth development. Both cities experimented with linking a wide range of social services to schools over the years, and Winnipeg made this a major focus in the early 1970s. However, bringing social services into schools has always been difficult (Volpe, 2000). According to one interviewee:

> We worked with members of the community and certain organizations to lobby the board to keep the old building in place so that we could use it as the centre for many of the social services (child welfare, economic services, health services, safety [police] services) needed by the children. We already knew that the closer at hand the services needed by the children and the school were the better. The idea was excellent, and schools today are still struggling with the same issue. If this proposal – and others – had been implemented, we might have been in a different position than we are today. The agencies found such a proposal worthwhile.

A similar effort was made in the 1980s through the Core Area Initiative. Again, the challenges were significant. According to one interviewee:

> We worked a fair bit with school-linked services and tried to push that through the government, but there was no real willingness at the time to grab hold of that. We were really pushing the concept from the education community because we saw that as an inner-city solution ... There was a pilot project with social workers on site at an inner-city school. There was tremendous potential there for something to happen, but it never moved past the pilot stage.

Both boards, but especially that in Toronto, increased nutrition programs in schools in which students were given breakfast or snacks. As one interviewee put it:

We aimed first of all to get the kids in the schools, and then to begin to build whatever way we could. Nutrition programs we understood. Kids are the best messengers. So if they came home and asked for peanut butter and walnuts and celery sticks, the mothers would get together. They all had peanut butter, and celery wasn't too bad, and they could buy a package of walnuts in Regent Park.

In Toronto, childcare in schools also expanded considerably. John Davies, who became director of the TBE, initially found no support from the administration, which worried about the additional financial and management pressures of taking on these responsibilities. But he persisted:

I knew we could always win the politics around it. You can get away with a few things in a big bureaucracy, and we did. I was watching some young women in the school, going in and out of the women's washroom in the foyer. And I eventually asked them what they were doing. They were minding a child in the school washroom because the mother wanted to be in school and it was the only way she could think of to look after her kid. That was the first childcare centre in any secondary school in Toronto. When I moved to the next school I did the same thing, opened a childcare centre. It was in the same neighbourhood. We developed a major comprehensive adult education program, too.

Creating a welcoming environment was a priority for engaging marginalized students. They were the ones who were leaving, not learning, and who were feeling left out. In Toronto, there was considerable support; in Winnipeg, the resistance to local efforts, particularly on academic grounds, was stronger.

Changing the Curriculum

Making curriculum and textbooks more representative of student diversity was an early initiative in both cities. The curriculum defines essential knowledge for students and is a direct link between policy and the classroom. Even if many teachers ignore much of the mandated curriculum, the materials that are developed to help them implement it make some ideas and concepts more easily available than others. Between the late 1960s and late 1990s, both boards developed new materials that reflected the life experiences of students from different backgrounds and challenged discrimination based on race, gender, and sexual orientation. These changes came from a desire to make schools inclusive; to express respect for different cultures, experiences, and languages; and to keep students engaged and in class.

In Toronto, the board appointed consultants and equity advisors to examine and change the curriculum. Although provincial guidelines were in place, the TBE had a great deal of control over the curriculum. It organized committees that encouraged community activists to provide ideas, content, and political support for change. The result was a plethora of resource binders, curriculum units, and pamphlets that introduced new material into the classroom.

One example is the effort started by Dan Leckie to examine the way that workers were represented in the school curriculum. A committee consisting of board staff and representatives from the labour council was established, and unions provided some funding. One member explained that the committee was trying to create a more inclusive, integrated, and unbiased way of learning:

These kids learned 'the star system' in the history books. It's about [what] Champlain discovered – but no one's talking about who rowed the boat and who cooked the food, as though those people didn't exist. We started demanding that the children of workers be properly educated and not be taught that their fathers or their mothers were somehow not appropriate because they happened to work in low-paying job areas. We developed a K-to-thirteen curriculum, or aspects of the curriculum, that integrated subject areas and had students working cooperatively in groups. You could integrate not just history and geography but even music and math. We developed the class bias materials, which are available on DVD . . . We took the existing textbooks. We went through them, looked at them, and found blatant examples of bias, and just wrong information. They were including things that had been sent to them by the Board of Trade, where it talked about how Eaton's did more for improving workers' conditions than unions did.

This kind of curriculum development was done on a small budget. Not all teachers were aware of, or used, the resulting materials. Nevertheless, it created debate about the nature of important knowledge and changed what was taught in the classrooms of sympathetic teachers.

Curriculum to challenge gender bias and racial bias was also developed. Surveys of elementary textbooks, done by the Royal Commission on the Status of Women and many local teacher groups, showed that women and girls were portrayed in traditional roles as housewives, princesses, and teachers. Female characters were also less active and less positively described than male characters. To address this disparity, the Women's Kit and the women's history project were developed at OISE, with support from staff at the board office, as resources to help teachers change their classroom practices.

Trustees at the board successfully lobbied to create a position in women's studies and left-leaning trustees formed the hiring committee. They had political support, a women's liaison committee to connect to parents and a green light from supervisors. According to one trustee, 'we would go over to Myra Mather's house and drink wine and talk about how far we could really push this.' They organized conferences, developed curriculum materials, and ran workshops, but the effect on classrooms was less significant than they wished. Some of the principals and vice principals went through training and were good curriculum leaders; others were not. One Toronto advocate noted how much each school varied on these issues: 'We discussed all of the 157 schools and tried to identify key teachers and what was happening. And even in the best of times, things were very, very uneven. People gravitated to certain schools where there was leadership. There were pockets in the city, and people certainly knew where they were.'

Multiculturalism and racism were the focus of board reports and staff hiring. The resultant impact on curriculum was uneven, intense, and political. Emphasis was put on professional development. According to one interviewee: 'We ran a series of programs ... one called Challenging Racism. By the time that I left the board, I could look at a group of elementary school principals and vice principals and see dozens of them who'd been through that program.' A principal in one of those schools recounted:

> We spent many, many, many hours trying to put together what we call now the goals and visions for [our school] for the next five years. We argued over every word in here. And everyone who applied for a job here ... read this and had to respond to it in an interview as to whether or not this is the kind of place they wanted to be or not and if they didn't that's fine, but then [they shouldn't] come.

Heritage language programs were an attempt to redress curriculum bias through signalling respect for the many cultures of students in the city. According to one interviewee, introducing new languages into the curriculum meant 'that you are worth it, your culture's worth it, your language is worth it. What you do with it is another matter but, just in itself, it's a really valuable thing and so your kids ought to learn it.' At a contentious, crowded, media-packed board meeting, an opposing trustee 'demanded that the director provide a pedagogical rationale. And Duncan got up in his lovely, lovely way, and he started out by saying something like, "If you want to communicate with somebody, you first have to communicate in their language. And once you can establish that, then there's room to grow."'

The work around curriculum change was engaged with activists in social movements and legitimated by the board's commitment to equity. In the 1990s, analysis and activism around homophobia produced a new high school, and a new curriculum. Triangle, which serves gay and lesbian students, still exists and is well-regarded. According to one interviewee,

> The gay kids felt really uncomfortable at Jarvis Collegiate. So we rented the second floor and painted it. I'm not sure everyone thought that was a good use of inner-city money, but it was. There is no doubt that it was. We tried not to do things that weren't our job, but what we did try to do was pull other people into the action.

In Winnipeg, the early years of inner-city initiatives in the late 1960s and especially the early 1970s resulted in teachers experimentating with curriculum and program ideas, though in those years with less direction and strategic support from the board than in Toronto. According to two former principals:

> We [staff in a Winnipeg elementary school] developed a grade 4 reading curriculum with parents. We also developed a series of readers on people who lived in the community.
> ... We revamped all the grade 10 language arts programs. We started a remedial program for children who were really at the extreme end and thought we were at least addressing some of the educational problems of the inner city. Once we got the language arts under way, we turned to mathematics and did the same kind of things.

Initiatives by individual schools were significant, as were those from the Department of Education. Efforts were made to revise the curriculum and support documents, to change minority representation, and to pay more attention to areas such as labour history. Yet even though there was significant work in this area in the early 1970s, the same concerns about curriculum content and materials appeared again in the late 1980s as an important issue in the work of the Task Force on Race Relations in the WSD.

Lack of attention to the needs of Aboriginal students was a major theme for the early Winnipeg reformers in the same way that class and racism were in Toronto. By the early 1970s, some Winnipeg schools were made up almost entirely of Aboriginal students, a reality that the WSD had not yet addressed. New principals in inner-city schools discovered that 50 per cent to 80 per cent or more of their students were Aboriginal, yet there were no programs aimed at these students, no curriculum materials for them, and no Aboriginal staff.

The development of Aboriginal-focused schools was part of a larger rethinking of the curriculum in relation to Aboriginal people. Winnipeg struggled to provide more professional development and materials for teachers on Aboriginal issues for years. Aboriginal education was declared a priority in the 1980s, and has remained one since. As described in chapter 2, the board hired consultants and undertook, in the 1990s, an extensive process of developing its own materials. Still, Aboriginal leaders remained critical of the lack of attention and of the inadequate number of Aboriginal teachers and leaders in the WSD. According to one interviewee:

> We started to look at learning materials, and that was safe. When we asked them to start looking at their pedagogical practices, that was much more difficult.
>
> . . . In elementary schools it was really easy to deal with the curriculum; the curriculum is a soft thing in my view. It's soft stuff. The real divides came when kids were divided off into secondary schools.

Curriculum change was an intermediate step between provincial or district policy on one hand, and teaching and learning on the other. New materials and workshops could be developed, circulated, and funded centrally, or they could be created by entrepreneurial teachers with innovative ideas and access to resources. However, the impact of new resources and professional development opportunities depended on whether teachers and principals took advantage of them. As a result, they had a greater impact in elementary schools than in secondary schools, and were uneven across the system.

Rethinking Literacy

The way that these initiatives worked in practice is well-illustrated by looking at efforts in Toronto to change literacy instruction. Teaching reading and writing has always been the central issue for education. During the early period of this study, there was a great deal of debate about pedagogy and, in particular, the meaning and best ways of teaching literacy. Especially in elementary school, a child-centred approach to literacy was more widely accepted in both boards over this period. But the priority and approach to literacy was quite different in the two boards. Greg Selinger, then a Winnipeg activist and now the Manitoba premier, made the following remarks on school reform:

> The weakness of the community-school model was not to pay enough attention to pedagogy. Literacy, numeracy, and the community curriculum have to all be integrated. You cannot say either numeracy and literacy or community curriculum. All are required. The skills side is important, in particular literacy. You have to have it all.

Don Rutledge, a key person in Toronto's efforts, summed up his view of reform at the TBE as:

> Sustained effort at curriculum change lasting more than a quarter of a century, an effort only partly successful and by no means completed, but a real effort in a real place by ordinarily imperfect human beings ... What is unusual in Toronto is the unifying nature of its linguistic policy and the political and popular approval that policy has won. (1988, p. 220)

There was a more systematic attempt to change literacy practices in Toronto, although the debates about equity, community involvement, and multiculturalism sometimes overshadowed, rather than complemented, them. This kind of systematic effort only arrived in Winnipeg in the 1990s, when the trustees established an inner-city department under Pauline Clarke to build a sustained dialogue about effective teaching that combined a focus on achievement with community outreach.

The TBE, as Jim Cummins put it, 'opened up intellectual space' for debates about how language worked and should be taught. A trustee/staff workshop with Basil Bernstein and William Labov, described in chapter 4, was one expression of this, as was Cummins' ongoing discussion with the board about teaching languages other than English. Don Rutledge spearheaded it, accessing expertise and providing a coherent framework for change. Rutledge started as an English teacher who had studied with Northrop Frye at the University of Toronto. His doctoral work at the Institute of Education at the University of London 'got me interested in psycho-linguistics and the language of the child and the evolution of the nervous system, reading Vygotsky and Luria.' It also brought him into close contact with a group of teachers and academics associated with Jimmy Britton, whose 1970 book, *Language and Learning*, placed ideas about how children learn language at the centre of language teaching.

Literacy was taught in the 1960s mostly as a set of skills to be learned: spelling lists were memorized for weekly tests, grammar rules were learned to parse complex sentences, exemplary poems were learned by heart, and texts were read and correctly interpreted. Students were marked on their understanding of formal English. Rutledge, Britton, and a group of literary theorists at the time challenged the utility of this approach to language as a discrete subject area, and instead viewed it as a tool for learning across the curriculum. Britton's 1965 address to school inspectors in Toronto examined the way human beings used every day language to represent and come to terms with their experience. Language teaching, he argued, should help children actively use language to represent the world around them, because the social use of that symbolic system was what distinguished human beings as a species and allowed thought in every area of inquiry, from science to history to mathematics.

Britton's conception of language had profound implications for teaching (Britton, 1972). It meant that the language that children brought to the classroom was the starting point for learning, and that the teachers' role was to work interactively to make students' speech, reading, and writing more effective. The curriculum was to be negotiable, and was meant to take the stories, conversations, and understanding that children already had into account. To understand and adopt these methods, teachers needed a grounding in linguistic theory and child development. In order to get the support of parents, administrators, and the public, the board needed to carefully articulate and constantly share the 'system belief.' A formal literacy policy was adopted by the board in 1982, and was the result of fifteen years of learning and debate among trustees, teachers, and administrators.

Professional development was seen as important to change and as the main way to build teacher understanding and commitment, given a mostly voluntary approach. The new literacy teaching was intense in the places where it was welcome, but it was never compulsory. Marg Simmons worked in an inner-city elementary project school where teachers were eager to learn, and James Britton visited. She remarked:

> All of our [professional development] was inside the building and had direct connection to what we were doing in the classroom. It was us discussing the issues around education and literacy and so on. And we had wonderful access to people ... James Britton, he was a brilliant man and he was brought over every year from England to spend two or three weeks with us. So, he would come into the school he would go in and out of classrooms and spend time in them and not just walk in and walk out. He would talk about the staff that he saw and we could talk about them and really learn a great deal from each other. I had to articulate what I was doing and why. This was theory going into practice in a really true manner. And it profoundly affected the way I thought about what I was doing ... quite profoundly. There was a project officer in the school and she acted as an in-school consultant with the staff as well as resource tea-cher; she would do a lot of community liaison.

Later, Simmons led a project school herself, and the approach was similar and the resources plentiful: 'I had a project staff of four ... who worked in specific classrooms helping people, but then when we worked together they would go in and replace the teacher. It was a very rich resource.' She reported that the approach was clear, and mandated at the board level: 'I think the leadership had to have clarity. The people who I didn't consider good leaders weren't clear about what they really believed in ... pandered to the children and the community in a way that really wasn't very healthy ... it lacked respect.'

Nanci Goldman also described the way professional development in inner-city schools worked for teachers. A consultant was placed in the school for a period of several weeks. Goldman remarked:

> She was a wonderful and fabulous woman. If you wanted to come in and learn from her she was there for the whole two weeks. She would work

with kids, work with teachers, she did some PD, but she was there. And I just asked and asked and asked and she just gave and gave and gave.

She truly believed in equity ... She understood equitable access and outcomes. And she also understood how children learn to read. The many ways that one could get children to learn to read. She also understood the barriers and how to break down some of those barriers, and introduced me to a lot of different methods that I would have never considered. I can say that I used to be a guru of context and whole language and probably still am, but I explored many, many different options. She also introduced me to my program at OISE [in second language learning]. She was just a fine and very bright lady.

Rutledge is credited with a great deal of success in changing ideas about literacy and education. As one Toronto superintendent said, he succeeded in 'bringing Vygotsky to surface and making people understand the importance of learning inside the egg instead of outside the shell.' He invited the charismatic Britton to Toronto each year to do in-service work with teachers, to spend weeks in inner-city project schools, and to give lectures, seminars, and workshops. Britton also joined the faculty at the Ontario Institute for Studies in Education in 1977, ten years after it was founded.

As board staff, principals, and teachers adopted this new approach to literacy, a new orthodoxy emerged, even if it wasn't universally accepted. In the 1990s, the new board director, Joan Green, had done her graduate work in literacy and described it as the sine qua non of leadership in Toronto. In 1988, Rutledge concluded, 'The changes in teaching practice in Toronto have been uneven, but they have been substantial. It would not be too much to call them a revolution' (p. 224).

This new understanding of literacy had important implications for immigrant and non-English speaking students. The same ideas of starting with students' current knowledge and building on their interests also animated efforts to improve education for the burgeoning immigrant population in Toronto. There was significantly more attention given to producing new materials, providing materials in children's home languages, and translating school materials into multiple languages for parents.

However, improving English language learning required more than good literacy practices. Cummins' work on the performance of students who did not have English as a first language was influential. He discovered that many teachers were not aware of which students these were, because their conversational English was fluent, even if their under-standing of the language used across the curriculum was not. When they did not do well in school, they were classified as failures, rather than as new language learners. Cummins reanalysed the Every Student Survey data, and showed that length of residence, not age of immigra-tion, was crucial in predicting school success:

> People thought of learning English as ... one thing. The distinction between how rapidly students could catch up in conversational fluency and the much lengthier period of time required to catch up to grade norms in academic aspects had not been made. But it has all kinds of implica-tions in terms of how much and what kind of ESL (English as a second language) support is required – for example what a science teacher needs to know to teach high school science to kids who have been here for three years, who speak English fluently, but still have a big gap [in their acade-mic skills]. Particularly, it had implications for special education, where kids who were perceived to be experiencing difficulty were being referred for psychological assessment [when their real issue was language skills].

Winnipeg had no equivalent to Toronto's ongoing, determined focus on literacy. For most of the late 1960s to the early 1990s, the district worked on diverse curriculum areas in a sporadic way, with the excep-tion of the growing focus on Aboriginal education. However, in the 1990s, a more systematic and board-directed approach to pedagogy was adopted for inner-city schools in Winnipeg, as described in chapter 2. Over a period of many years, the principals and their staff developed a common approach to teaching and learning, with particular focus on key areas such as improved student assessment practices, increased awareness of Aboriginal issues, and stronger parent outreach. This approach was rooted in building of a common culture and set of val-ues among inner-city schools and staff, which developed gradually and was sustained over time. It mirrored much of what had been done in Toronto in terms of consistent and persistent work, but involved only a subset of the district's schools.

Streaming and Secondary School Change

Secondary education was a more difficult challenge in both districts. Elementary schools were smaller and less bureaucratic, curriculum could be adapted more easily to local circumstances, parental involve-ment was more widely accepted with young children, and the longer periods of time that elementary teachers spent with students allowed them to respond flexibly to a variety of pressures. One Toronto organizer remarked that 'you could always marshal parents to work on their kids' education in elementary schools. The same wasn't true of secondary schools. But the secondary schools were extremely conservative ... the people there were powerful, male dominated ... [and] very powerful within the system.'

Secondary schools were larger, more conservative, and had teachers who were less likely to agree on any new approach. Secondary schools competed for students and were less inclined to share good practices. They were, and remain, more focused on covering a prescribed curriculum in short and defined periods every day. Teachers interacted with large numbers of students and rarely came to know them on an individual level.

The secondary schools were also more independent and powerful, with weaker connections to central office and district policy. A former Toronto director remarked that 'the secondary school culture was much more independent. Principals saw their roles as much more autonomous than elementary teachers. And that is true of most boards, but more so in Toronto ... I know what I'm doing; don't bother me with the board stuff.'

In secondary schools in both cities, reform leaders started by addressing the disproportional representation of students from poor, immigrant, and racialized backgrounds in the lower curriculum streams. Toronto's secondary schools had long been organized based on students' academic destinations and capacity. The provincial curriculum guidelines determined different paths for academic, vocational, and basic students. Grade 13 in Ontario was strictly for academic students going to university. Secondary schools could be located very close together, but one served students intending to go to post-secondary education or specifically university, while a nearby school was attended by students headed to work, or without a specific destination. Dismantling this structure was an important goal of Toronto reforms in the 1970s (Nagle, 1975).

One effort involved setting up a secondary education review committee in the mid-1980s, but the issues were very thorny. One trustee described it:

There was incredible politics around the secondary educational review group ... because the NDP made a video, an anti-streaming video, and I was saying we didn't have a predetermined agenda. Anyway, we did an incredible consultation process. We had this wonderful document called What We Heard that juxtaposed the issues and responses in such a way that nobody could walk away without thinking that there weren't issues to deal with. And then we had the election and the right wing trustees, with the help of the director, scuttled it. They didn't want to proceed with it. That was the rawest politics I had seen. The director didn't support a look at secondary schools, we knew most of the principals didn't and we knew the superintendents didn't. So we had streamed secondary schools in Toronto. Toronto trustees think they closed down vocational schools, but vocational schools closed frankly because parents stopped sending their kids there.

The issue was taken up again later, after a provincial report urged de-streaming and a resolution to de-stream grade 9 passed by one vote in the 1990s. But Toronto's secondary schools remain streamed, and the city continues to support schools very close to each other with different programs and destinations, as well as different tracks within schools.

Winnipeg's high schools were never as explicitly streamed as Toronto's, and the distinctions in program are more a result of neighbourhood characteristics; the city does not have schools with very different programs intentionally near each other. Manitoba did not have the grade 13 requirement that separated university-bound students in Ontario. Despite this, schools reflected their neighbourhoods, and in disadvantaged communities the local secondary school would have more vocational programming and less post-secondary preparation. Winnipeg high schools also competed for enrolments, especially in the 1970s when enrolment began to decline, so that the impression of some of our respondents was that segregation of students by class and destination actually increased in Winnipeg secondary schools during the 1970s and 1980s.

In Winnipeg, the issue around secondary schools was streaming within schools; moving disadvantaged and minority children into special education or other alternative programs. As noted earlier, while these programs were started to re-engage students, as their numbers increased, they also moved students out of mainstream programs and the opportunities those provided for better outcomes. One interviewee who had been the principal of a junior high school put it this way:

A school could get more teachers and resources if it had more kids in special education or in alternative programs. So the system provided a strong incentive for schools to label kids as having problems. Most kids who went into these special programs were never reintegrated into the mainstream.

When I became principal of [a junior high] the school was largely seen by parents and the community as a special needs school, with perhaps half of the 230 students in some kind of special education program ... Under those circumstances the community stops seeing the school as a healthy environment for their kids and starts sending their kids to other schools.

We worked hard to turn that around. One strategy was to reduce the number of special programs and mainstream all the kids. A second strategy involved developing performing arts and in that way focusing on kids' talents instead of their deficits. We wanted the school to be an interesting, inviting place. We tried to reduce the number of times each day kids had to move around the school and to make it more like an elementary school in terms of building strong connections between teachers and students. We were very successful at holding our staff; turnover of staff dropped from 30 per cent a year when I arrived to having only two teachers change in three years.

Over time, concerns about streaming and alternative programs grew. A former senior administrator in Winnipeg described the problem:

We also looked at the prevalence of alternative classes. This really bothered me because in too many situations the bottom 10 per cent of the students in a school were being put into alternative classes ... The children in the alternative classes were those who were nonattenders and trouble makers in the classroom but generally there was nothing wrong with them intellectually. They were not special education students. It is just that they missed so much school; their attitude in the classroom was such that principals did not believe that they could contain them in a regular grade 7, 8, or 9 class.

The schools did have good intentions. They had a group of children who did not fit in anywhere and who were not particularly wanted. However, the programs often involved devoting a lot of time to floor hockey and going to activities in the community. The goal of them all was to reintegrate the students back into the classroom but this rarely happened.

When I discussed these programs with the principals of the schools that had the alternative programs, I asked them how the students were going to be integrated into the regular classroom. I pointed out that the students were getting very little in the way of any kind of academic upgrading. Consequently, they would never succeed in a regular classroom; they would be bounced back into the alternative class because they were not learning anything that would make them successful. They might have learned to have a better view of themselves, but the regular classroom teacher would want to know whether the student knew subject content.

The other thing that concerned me was that if the bottom 10 per cent were moved to an alternative classroom, there would still be a bottom 10 per cent in the regular classroom so that the possibility for the creation of another alternative classroom arose and so forth. In fact, in one school in the Division we had more alternative classrooms than regular classrooms.

When we sat down with very dedicated teachers and administrators, spent time with them, and had a philosophical discussion with them about the issue, they came to understand what had been the result of these classes. They had created another segregated class, whether special education, alternative LAC (students with behavioural disorders), or other alternative classrooms. They just kept creating a bottom 10 per cent without realizing what was happening in the school as a whole.

Like Toronto, Winnipeg was ultimately unsuccessful in addressing these issues at a district level, and both districts' secondary schools continue to have unequal curriculum streams that are highly related to socio-economic status.

Testing and Assessment

Both districts engaged in lively debates over student assessment and large-scale testing. School and pupil test results are one way to judge the degree of inequality in student outcomes. When there is no such data – as was the case for much of the late 1960s to late 1990s – it is difficult to know whether some groups of students are systematically underachieving, and the degree to which that underachievement is due to schools as opposed to students' backgrounds. Testing is a powerful way to steer classroom instruction, and can provide information to improve instruction if it is designed for that purpose. However, it can also reinforce a narrow curriculum and prevent the local involvement in teaching and learning that both boards were trying to promote.

In the 1970s, as today, most reformers felt that mandated tests had limited value, especially for the children most in need of assistance. Provincial examinations had just been abolished in both Manitoba and Ontario, allowing much more curriculum autonomy for the boards.

Although the research division in Toronto collected data on which students were in the higher academic streams and which students graduated, they did not collect data on student achievement. Nor was there such data in Winnipeg. Assessment remained the purview of classroom teachers, whose judgments were communicated in report cards to parents and administrators.

Winnipeg did have its own district-based testing program, but it had little impact on policy or program. According to one interviewee:

> At the time we used to do division-wide testing, which I discovered was generally meaningless for the schools ... When I pointed out to a secondary principal that the division-wide testing showed that there were some real deficiencies with the children, he criticized me severely, arguing that the tests were meaningless ...
>
> Division-wide testing was, ultimately, a waste of time since the results correlated so highly with the level of poverty of the community. The only focus for a solution that was accepted by many people was a concentration on self-esteem, frequently at the expense of the children learning anything at all.

Aboriginal educators were particularly critical of the tests. According to one:

> Another aspect of the problem with the division was the focus on standardized tests. Of course, standardized tests in the public schools presuppose that there are standardized people. Aboriginal children are not, however, standardized children.
>
> The ranking of schools on standardized tests correlates highly with family income; the bottom schools are also schools with high Aboriginal populations ... It is not therefore surprising that Aboriginal children are at the bottom of standardized tests.
>
> Rather than standardization, we do need to focus on strengths, not standards. Inner-city students have many strengths; surviving in the inner city is a strength in itself. The testing of inner-city students does the opposite. It negates their self-esteem. Students who fail these tests know that they are considered to be different in some way.

While the critique of testing was dominant among educators, it was not universal. Some Winnipeg leaders felt that the tests, whatever their faults, were useful because they revealed inequities in outcomes. One Winnipeg trustee said:

> Some of my colleagues in the NDP ... got this notion that examinations and testing were bad news. In my view, they were and still are an opportunity – not to fail children; examinations should never be used to fail children and, in fact, it is never the children who fail; someone else fails. Examinations and testing are means for taking a picture to see how children are doing relative to curriculum expectations. If expectations are not being met, then the child can receive help.

In Toronto, the literacy policy deemphasized testing and system wide norms. Students' work was not to be 'constantly evaluated and graded with reference to its comprehensiveness, accuracy and freedom from solecisms. Only on rare pre-arranged occasions was that to happen. It was, instead to be seen as part of an evolving thought process which would both influence and result from the students' linguistic growth. The cumulative writing folder became important' (Rutledge, 1988, p. 224). Classroom-based assessment, individual student growth, and the appreciation, rather than grading, of different kinds of academic performances was consistent with the ethic and policy of the board.

Over time, public sentiment changed, and provincial governments insisted more strongly on standardized testing, believing that public trust in teachers' assessments had diminished. In the late 1990s, Winnipeg implemented a program of every-student assessment, though it faced strong resistance from teachers who felt it was a workload increase and who worried that the results would be used to evaluate or compare teachers (though they never were used for that purpose).

In 1995, the Ontario Royal Commission on Learning, which was established by the NDP and reported to the Harris Conservative government, recommended provincial achievement tests for all Ontario students. There was some sympathy for the idea at the TBE, because of interest in how different groups of students were progressing, but also substantial wariness about the narrow outcomes and short time frame that the province was suggesting for implementation. While the Board initially resisted provincial testing, it helped structure it once such testing became inevitable. The provincial testing that was eventually mandated was curriculum- and classroom-based, and used a model based on benchmarks developed in the Toronto school board. When the Education Quality and Accountability Office (EQAO) was set up in 1995 to operate a provincial testing program, it was headed by Joan Green, who was a former TBE director, a Rutledge admirer, and a Britton student.

Relationships with Teachers and their Unions

Changing teaching and learning methods means changing the behavior of teachers and principals. They are the front-line educators with professional discretion, are members of powerful unions, and are board employees. Boards are organizations that are responsible for ensuring good outcomes for students, and this often involves wanting staff to adhere to board-mandated patterns. However, school board leaders also generally recognize that teachers' commitment and professional judgment are essential to student success. Boards are always caught between pushing staff to do more and be better, while also ensuring they feel appreciated and supported. This challenge is especially significant in high-poverty schools, where outcomes are typically worse and educators feel the most pressure from their daily work, in addition to pressure to improve results.

Over the course of this study, the relationships between boards and teachers waxed and waned. They were more difficult during times of scarce funding, unhelpful provincial government intervention, and when the political climate turned against public sector workers and poor people. Although there were many innovative teachers in both districts who supported board policies, this support was by no means unanimous, especially in secondary schools. A significant number of teachers felt change was lowering standards, and others simply did not want to change the way they worked. They were represented by powerful unions, and the result was ongoing tension.

Research was part of the argument about change in Toronto, and persuasion was the chosen tactic, but behind both stood the power of the Board over teachers. The inner-city school projects involved changes in staffing to ensure that teachers working in these schools shared the board's belief systems about literacy, community involvement, and multiculturalism. John Bates, Toronto's inner-city coordinator, describes his approach to staffing and pedagogical expertise:

> Some said, well, what's wrong with what we are doing? It was pretty obvious; none of the kids were going anywhere! One of the teachers stood up and said, 'Well, I guess what you want us to do next is go stand on the

street and if we want to come back here, we'll have to apply for a job.'
And I hadn't thought of that. And then I said, I hope you apply. But a lot
of people didn't apply.

The people out in the schools, the ones who were against this whole
thing, particularly the principals, could only slam on a personal level;
there was no intellectual argument! No principal would tackle the whole
idea of kids writing before they read, but they would tackle Rutledge and
they would certainly tackle me, and say, 'Who in the hell are you guys to
say that you know better than us?'

Teachers were allowed to unionize in Ontario in 1975 and were given
the right to strike. Ontario teachers were organized into five different
federations, and the TBE had to bargain with three of them: secondary teachers, female elementary teachers, and male elementary teachers
(the latter two organizations have since merged to form the Elementary
Teachers' Federation of Ontario). Principals were part of the teachers'
federations and provided considerable leadership for the period of
our study, though they were removed from union membership in the
late 1990s.

For the Toronto reformers, relations with unions were important because many reformers identified strongly with a pro-labour approach.
Marg Simmons was on the executive of the Toronto Teachers' Federation,
and remarked:

The majority of people on the executive at the time that I became friends
with and colleagues with ... we all taught in the inner city, we were all
dedicated to it and it was just part of our persona ... It was a time when
the teachers' federation and the board [trustees] worked together. People
knew each other. There was lots of backroom discussion, but things were
talked through and I think intelligent decisions were made. It wasn't so
top down.

At the same time, the focus on improving outcomes for students,
and the belief of many reform leaders that the school system was
at times complicit in creating negative outcomes for such students, inevitably brought them into conflict with teacher organizations. Internally,
the unions faced the same tensions. Many union activists agreed that
aspects of schooling, including the practices of some teachers, hurt
poor, working-class, and immigrant students. However, unions as
organizations were dedicated to protecting teachers, both individually

and collectively, including protecting them from too many demands to change their behaviour and teaching practices.

There were times when a shared commitment to improving schools for children from disadvantaged backgrounds provided enough common ground for an agreement. According to one interviewee:

> There was really a sense that you were allies in a bigger social cause, it wasn't just about group interest ... The Toronto teacher unions, both elementary and secondary, had been somewhat independent of their provincial affiliates. And they had strong relations with the NDP. So they were teacher leaders, they weren't simply followers. They would make deals with us and they would interpret them to the teachers in ways that they could get support. And that was the same on the caretakers side as well, the CUPE side.

Pat Case recounted a story of labour relations with the teachers from 1979 that also demonstrates a resolution based on the mutual desire to improve inner-city education:

> The board had been in negotiation with elementary school teachers for about a year and was getting nowhere in the contract negotiations. One of the things we ran on was putting an end to what the board had said, which was, 'we don't have the money,' 'we have to downsize,' 'we have to chop 108 teachers.' These 108 teachers became a cause for those who were running in that election. A week after the election, a few of us were involved with the negotiations directly with the teachers. Within about three or four weeks, we concluded a contract with the teachers that saved those 108 jobs. We put them all into inner-city schools. The idea was we would use them to reduce class size in the inner city, using the inner-city criteria ... It was the local levy that was used; that, plus a bit of a kick back from the teachers. The teachers said, 'OK, we'll go in with you on this. If our pay increase is going to be 5 per cent, we'll kick back half a per cent to help fund those 108 teachers.'

Agreement on flexible staffing procedures for inner-city schools in Toronto also benefitted from cooperation between the union and the board. As one interviewee put it:

> This is perhaps one of the best examples of union and management cooperation. Every principal in an inner-city school that was going to be a

project school had a chance to be the leader of that school. Any teacher that wanted to stay and make a commitment could do so, and they didn't have to go through a selection process. But more importantly, anyone who wanted out could leave. You ended up with some of the best teachers gravitating to the inner city.

However, such collaboration did not always succeed. Creating limited-term appointments for principals was discussed, but was not approved because of union opposition. One reform trustee described his disappointment:

The principals were in the federation at that time, and they supported their members in rejecting the idea. But it seemed to me that if you could bring about term appointments with principals then you would create incentives and competition among teachers, as well as attracting women and visible racial minorities. We ought to get people who are differently located into those jobs, for however long that might be. Term appointments for me was the absolute key and we lost it.

There were other, more significant disagreements. For instance, teachers in Toronto went on strike over salary issues several times. This put trustees in a quandary, as many were sympathetic, but other Metro Toronto boards did not want Toronto to increase salaries and pressure them to do the same.

In the mid-1970s, a debate about heritage languages displayed the TBE's sense of its power and distrust of existing school personnel. Unions opposed the proposal to implement heritage language programs during the school day because it would have extended teachers' hours in the classroom. The battle was impassioned and the unions filed court actions against the board. In the end, heritage languages were introduced, but on a more limited basis than many supporters wanted. One very committed staff member concluded, in a comment that shows the gap between the different positions in the district, 'We've got all this wonderful multicultural rhetoric ... there was still no real acceptance of multiculturalism as involving anything more than lip service.'

The resistance of schools to heritage language programs as well as the struggle over board authority is illustrated by this account of a staff meeting:

The principal says, 'I am not going to have this program at my school. I am in charge of my school and it will not happen in my school.' Charlie

[Novogrodsky, head of school-community relations] goes up to the mike, and it's now six o'clock or seven, and he says, 'Let me tell you something. It's sort of like the army. I'm the general, you're the private, and you are going to run this program. This meeting is adjourned.' Just like that, 'I'm the general, you're the private. This meeting is adjourned.' And finally, and of course, they did it in the school, they loved it, and they got huge community support. Every single kid was enrolled.

This example also illustrates why the school-community relations department reported to the board rather than working collaboratively with the teachers and principals, who were often resistant to their efforts to change schools from the outside. The department was disbanded when a more conservative slate took over the Board in 1985:

> These [twenty-five community organizers] were attached to fifty schools, and they had a two-year contract to build a parents organization and make changes to the curriculum or at least enrich the curriculum. The principals resisted it, thinking, 'now all these community workers are going to gate-keep and drive my teachers crazy and make life impossible.'

The board's distrust of principals and teachers became less pronounced as it realized how much it needed their support. Principals and teachers also learned to work within the system more amicably. Still, the left-wing orientation of a substantial number of trustees mattered. According to one, 'the nice thing was is that we had an NDP caucus and a staunch conservative board of education as far as the staff goes. So if anything went wrong, it was the damn NDP. But, the intellectual argument was just so strong!'

Many of the same tensions existed in Winnipeg. Teachers in Manitoba have long been unionized, but are legally prohibited from striking and settle contract disputes by arbitration, so bargaining was never as tense as it was in Toronto. However, the Winnipeg Teachers' Association was by far the largest local union in the Manitoba Teachers' Society, and they often disagreed with the school board on policy matters.

Quite a few Winnipeg school board members were teachers in other districts or former teachers. There was at least one teacher or former teacher on the board through most of the late 1960s to the early 1990s, including one long-serving trustee, Ed Kowalchuk, who was a former president of the Manitoba Teachers' Society. The WSD always had members sympathetic to the situation of teachers. As in Toronto, though, reformers also understood the need for change in how teachers worked. Community activists often found teachers to lack understanding of inner-city realities. A former social service worker who went on to be a community leader recounted his experience in the early 1970s:

> At the time, there was a real interest in the school to respond to the challenges posed by inner-city education, but from the make-up of the teaching staff, it was more like they were working in this battleground, trying to save kids from their families and community. Very few of the staff actually came from the community or were attached to the community, with the exception of those aides who worked in the before-and-after school program. There was relatively limited interaction. It was elitist and quite hierarchical.

Conflict is inherent in union-employer relationships, and Toronto and Winnipeg were no exceptions. Nevertheless, both the boards managed these tensions reasonably well, and were often able to maintain positive relationships with their employee groups. If anything, some reform advocates felt that professionals were given too much weight in discussions, in comparison with what they saw as the needs of parents and students:

> When I retired, the WTA chose not to even bother thanking me for my years in public service. Everybody else did except the WTA because, in their view, I cost them a lot of money through negotiations; I also cost them a lot of goodwill through the public, who saw that in a lot of instances we were not talking about the interests of children but rather about those of adults. Someone was using children to get what they wanted. I saw that as a betrayal of children. You negotiate; everybody is entitled to negotiate. However, I never tolerated [it] when someone claimed, during negotiations, that they were concerned about the children when in fact I knew that their concern was more money. I took exception to that. Some people did not like my attitude, but I called it the way I saw it.

Developing positive relationships between the districts and their staff, while still focusing on the changes needed to improve student outcomes, remained a challenge in both districts throughout the period of this study. The districts generally worked hard to create and maintain those relationships, but sometimes the price was less change, more slowly, than many of the reformers wanted.

Conclusions

Improving day-to-day teaching and learning in schools requires more than launching new programs but is the only way to change student experiences across a large number of classrooms. Both districts tried to improve instruction in the classroom, although the degree to which they focused on this varied over time.

Efforts to change school practices fall on a continuum from more centralized and prescriptive to more decentralized and voluntary. The decentralized approach provides resources for innovation, and allows initiatives to percolate from educators who find new ways to connect with students with the hope that successful models will spread. The National Literacy Strategy in England, or some school reform models in the United States, would be closer to the centralized approach, as they require all teachers to follow centrally determined practices. The charter school model is closer to the decentralized approach, as it assumes that talented educators will find better strategies and other schools will emulate them. Neither approach is followed in full, as the most prescriptive model has some degree of voluntarism and local adaptation, and even the most decentralized models still incorporate externally imposed regulations and constraints.

Education is biased towards voluntarism and school-by-school adaptation, partly because there is little sense of what form a common professional practice would take. The beliefs that each school must find its own way, and that each teacher should be an autonomous professional with a unique practice, are deeply embedded in the education psyche, even though common practices define most professions.

Both Toronto and Winnipeg used a variety of approaches to changing teaching and learning. Both districts worked with schools that wanted to try new approaches more often than they attempted to mandate or inculcate new practices across the entire district, or even among groups of schools facing similar problems. But this, too, was not a universal approach; for instance, improving literacy in Toronto had a systematic and sustained strategy, though it produced uneven and tenuous results.

For most of the period of this study, the WSD had a local approach that depended on the efforts of individual principals. As a result, initiatives often did not last as people moved on or short-term funding disappeared. At other times, the WSD focused on standardized policy and was even seen as anti-innovation. A number of our respondents discussed the division's lack of support for innovations proposed by schools, and the overall impression that the senior management was not supportive of many new ideas. The position of the Manitoba Department of Education on various issues, and its willingness to provide resources and intervene directly (sometimes without the agreement of district leaders), often influenced what the WSD did. The board was also often split politically, which made it difficult to sustain a consistent approach. It was only in the 1990s that Winnipeg slowly began to create a focused and consistent approach to education in all its inner-city schools.

In Toronto, throughout the period of this study, the TBE had a fairly consistent overall approach. Efforts to change literacy practice, engage parents, and reach out to ethnic communities were consistent over many years. The district supported those efforts, not only by working extensively with interested schools, but through board policies, resource allocation, principal appointments, and pressure on schools through central units such as school-community relations or equity. In elementary schools, Toronto also had more consistent common values that principals and teachers understood to be directive of their priorities and work. Despite this, not all schools were engaged. The TBE often relied on project schools where the right principal, staff, or determined group of parents tried to ensure that reforms were implemented and sustained. Such programs tended to work in poorer neighbourhoods where the appetite and need for change was stronger.

In both cities, reformers encountered both success and challenges. In Winnipeg, most of the main initiatives in the early 1970s were dismantled in the 1980s due to changed politics and budget restraints; it was only in the 1990s that the WSD developed a more comprehensive approach to teaching and learning in inner-city schools. At about the same time in Toronto, the amalgamation of the various boards into one very large board had an opposite effect on reform. There were certainly changes in many schools in both districts, and a heightened awareness of what was required to improve the situation for poor or marginalized populations. But both boards learned how hard it was to translate ideals into realities across large and complex systems, and how easy it can be to dismantle carefully-built programs and approaches.

7   Lessons from Canadian Urban School Reform

In this final chapter, we consider what can be learned from the experience in Toronto and Winnipeg over the last forty years about how to create real and lasting improvement in urban schools in Canada. We call these conclusions lessons, understanding that lessons are open-ended and should create discussion. We will draw on the evidence from our cases, and push the analysis further on the basis of what we have come to understand about the history and sociology of education more generally.

We consider first how much progress, if any, has taken place over the last forty years, and why creating and sustaining improvement seems so difficult. There are grounds for both optimism and pessimism about the state of urban schools. We then consider what we have learned about specific policy approaches, before arguing for the usefulness of the three lenses employed in this book – research and ideas, politics, and teaching and learning – in understanding how urban school systems can meet the needs of children from disadvantaged and culturally diverse families.

Have Things Improved over the Last Forty Years?

Enormous efforts were made in both cities over the period of this study to try to improve inner-city education. Many people gave large amounts of time and energy to this cause. Yet many of the people we interviewed were disappointed with what had been achieved, especially those who had maintained a strong community development focus. Pat Rowantree, a teacher and community worker in Winnipeg, felt that 'in many ways we are not much further ahead – if at all – now than in the 1970s, partly because we do not sustain our commitments. If we had parent-child centres in every school in the 1980s, for example, and kept them in operation, that would have made a profound difference. We are always reinventing the wheel.' Greg Selinger, who was also very involved in community work in Winnipeg, commented that:

> Comparing the present and the past, we are not today even at the level of support for the inner city that we had thirty years ago. The thinking now is much narrower ... The model at the time was a transformational model; it was a model that would change the essence of how a school ran. The school was to become an ally of inner-city communities to fight class oppression, to fight racism, and to fight socio-economic barriers.

George Martell, a community activist in Toronto, noted that 'the inner city crisis has expanded with little recognition of the concerted effort required to address it.' No interviewees in this study felt that the problems had largely been resolved or that successes had been substantial and lasting.

Evidence suggests that these beliefs are well-founded. Despite the efforts described in earlier chapters, inner-city students in Winnipeg continue to have educational outcomes that are significantly worse than city and provincial averages, not least because these areas continue to have high levels of poverty and deprivation, and are worse off in relative terms than they were in the past. In Toronto, poverty is more concentrated than it used to be, and the school system continues to struggle with achievement levels, graduation rates, and community support. Dropout rates remain unacceptably high, especially among certain minority groups and in poor neighbourhoods. Yet that is not the whole story either.

Reformers began with huge ambitions: to make society more egalitarian, to reduce or eliminate gaps in outcomes based on students' backgrounds, and to do so by making dramatic changes in policies and practices in large school systems. Such ambitions add up to an enormous undertaking, made even more difficult by the pressure to reduce taxes and public expenditures, and the increased inequality in incomes that Canada has experienced over the last twenty years.

These pessimistic comments should not obscure the accomplishments in urban education over the last forty years. In many ways, schools in urban Canada have progressed on a range of important issues. More educators agree that they should teach all children, and not just sort out the talented from the less talented in order to track them into the appropriate streams. Views of students, teaching, and learning are more respectful and informed. Respect for diversity, while still far from ideal, has improved dramatically. There is growing awareness of the importance of early development, helping students catch up in the primary grades, and working closely with parents and families. Perhaps most importantly, schools' sense of responsibility for student outcomes has changed. Educators understand the importance of high expectations for all students, and the dangers of stereotyping students' futures based on their backgrounds. While the degree to which schools can improve results on their own remains controversial, few educators would now argue that everything is decided by the child's background and home and that the school has no impact on social disparities and graduation rates.

There have also been improvements in programs and practices. Programs for English language learners are widespread and more engaging, as are early literacy practices, engagement with parents, and community outreach. Teaching literacy incorporates many more approaches and engages a wider range of students and learning styles. Targeted programs for Aboriginal learners, black students, boys, and other underachieving groups are in place in many school boards, including in Winnipeg and Toronto. Practices that were accepted and commonplace, such as streaming, retention in grade, and corporal punishment of students, are now controversial and have been curtailed.

These changes have produced improved results. More students are reaching higher levels of attainment in Canada today than in the past – even if current levels are still too low to meet the requirements of a changing world. Fifty years ago, it would have been unthinkable that nearly all students would graduate from high school, or that half or more would participate in post-secondary education. In 1941, 20 per cent of Canadian eighteen year olds were in school; in 1996 it was 80 per cent (Clark, 2000). In 1951, more than half of Canadians had less than a grade 9 education and about 2 per cent had been to university. By 1996, there were more Canadians with a university degree than there were with less than grade 9. Similarly, Canada consistently ranks highly on international measures such as the PISA assessment of skills of fifteen year olds, or PIRLS, an assessment of elementary school reading, which is evidence of the successes of its schools, especially given that other social factors have become more unequal. Canada is an international example of a country with high student achievement and relatively low outcome inequality.

Still, nobody could be complacent about education in our cities, and especially in neighbourhoods characterized by high levels of poverty or marginalization. The outcome gaps that provoked reforms forty years ago still exist. Overall achievement is higher, but there are still large disparities in outcomes related to factors such as income or ethnicity that would, in a fairer world, have no independent impact on outcomes.

There continue to be serious concerns about the governance and operation of urban schools in Canada. School boards in large cities are often fractious, and election turnouts remain dismally low. Boards struggle with finances, with multiple demands, and with a lack of consensus on priorities. Every issue, from a school closing to the location of a new program, can be a source of political conflict. Several urban boards in Canada have been taken over, if only for short periods of time, by provincial governments. While there have been significant accomplishments, Canada's city school systems, like those in other countries, are far from ideal. The cup is half full and half empty.

The Toronto District School Board now has a budget of approximately $2.5 billion per year, the Toronto Catholic District School Board has one of $1 billion, and the Winnipeg School Division has one of $300 million. These districts enrol about 15 per cent of the students in each province. They are large organizations with significant responsibilities and large amounts of public money. Their success is important to all Canadians. While money does matter, and the budget of each district grew in real terms between the late 1960s and late 1990s, better funding alone is insufficient for improvement. New initiatives increased the most during the times of the greatest funding increases, in the early 1970s. After that, board discussions focused on how to implement cuts, but it was at that point that the priorities of the districts were most evident. In Toronto, the focus on the schools in the most disadvantaged areas was consistent; in Winnipeg, it was less so until the inner-city department was set up. Increasing evidence (Grubb, 2008) shows that how money is used and what people actually do in their work matters more than the amount of money available. Per pupil expenditure in real terms has risen significantly in Canada. This increase is a necessary – but not sufficient – reason for improved practice. The question is how to ensure that resources are used optimally.

Policy Proposals and Their Limits

The search for a policy prescription that will solve the problems of inner-city schools is ongoing. In chapter 1, we discussed many of the proposals that are popular today, particularly in the United States: school choice, an emphasis on the quality of teaching, increased testing, and new governance models. Interestingly, the districts we studied considered, discussed, and adopted several of these initiatives, although the focus was not single minded and the language used to describe them was different from that used today. Experiments with these directions were important and changed schooling for the better. But the boards did not treat a single policy direction as the answer and did not push the reforms in the radical directions that are being proposed today in the United States and, to some extent, in Canada.

Both districts moved in the direction of providing more alternative programs, responding to some of same pressures and beliefs involved in the current enthusiasm for greater parental choice, voucher-like systems, and charter schools. Alternative schools developed a substantial following, particularly in Toronto, where they continue to provide choice within the public system. Concerned liberal, middle, or upper middle class parents looking for a more flexible, creative approach to education started alternatives. One, ALPHA (A Lot of People Hoping for Alternatives) elementary school, still exists today and is one of many Toronto alternative schools that, as the district describes it, 'offer something different from mainstream schooling. Each alternative school, whether elementary or secondary, has a distinct identity and approach to curriculum delivery along with a strong volunteer commitment from parents and other community members.' Alternatives today increasingly cater not just to the children of the middle class, but to poor, inner-city, Aboriginal, homeless, gay, and racialized youth (Zwarenstein, 2002). In Winnipeg, Aboriginal-focused schools have been accepted, after working through substantial opposition. The involvement of parents in local school governance has improved, especially in schools where parents in the past had little input. Parent councils, parent involvement in the selection of administrators, and parent representation on board committees all increased.

Despite these improvements, the reforms stopped short of the current proposals for charter school systems, school vouchers, and local autonomy. The board debated the value of all the alternative proposals and oversaw their operations. Parents had to convince district administrators and trustees of the value of their views. While there is a role for innovation, variation, and competition in developing effective schooling, our evidence demonstrates that increased alternatives and parent voice are not a policy panacea for school improvement (Levin, 2010). Real gains come from having widespread – not selective – use of better practices, and from local democracy, which entails public discussion and accountability.

Improving teacher quality by providing better initial teacher education and professional development is another approach that these districts emphasized, and maintain today. Winnipeg developed an initial teacher education program to increase the supply of Aboriginal teachers; Toronto, because of its reputation as an innovator, managed to attract some of the most progressive teachers and principals in Ontario. In both districts, systematic professional development was a major focus, and it was consolidated in Toronto through a district-wide focus on curriculum reform. The curriculum leadership of Don Rutledge in Toronto, the resources he had available, and his awareness of the importance of institutionalizing change transformed literacy teaching in many Toronto schools. Changing the curriculum to reflect the new realities of students' lives and the languages they spoke at home was part of the initiative, which was supported by equity working groups of many kinds. The focus on systematic instructional and curriculum change came later in Winnipeg, but a shared approach to instruction in inner-city schools was developed and implemented under Pauline Clarke's leadership of the inner-city division.

Teacher unions became stronger between the late 1960s and late 1990s. They provided more security for teachers in both districts, and often offered political support for initiatives for disadvantaged students. The partnerships between a left-leaning union and progressive trustees on inner-city education helped in taking other new initiatives forward. Union contracts were not easily resolved; strikes took place; and seniority provisions, working conditions, and salaries were fought over. But the ability to fire teachers did not become a major concern at either district, and neither did the idea of merit pay or paying for performance. The primary concern was professional development for teachers, so they could work together to enhance students' learning.

Canada has approximately 500,000 teachers. Education must be able to operate effectively with a considerable number of people who are relatively ordinary, but who receive excellent preparation and support. Teachers, like anyone else, can get better at their work, and facilitating this improvement should be a major focus. Actively engaging teachers in reform is essential, and depends on treating teachers as professionals whose views merit respect. However, professionalism does not mean unrestricted individual autonomy. Professions are based on a body of common knowledge and practice to which all members are expected to conform. It is within those guidelines that members of a profession exercise their judgment. The literature suggests that professional autonomy must co-exist with collaboration among teachers and principals, that any evaluation should lead to improvement, and that unions can work with districts to improve professional development and equity programs.

The districts also increased their use of data and testing, another policy issue that is currently the centre of discussions on accountability and improvement. The districts moved gradually to standardized and consistent testing as the technology for carrying it out improved and the political demands for accountability increased. Data on the discrepancies in student outcomes and the marginalization of some students and families was important in Toronto in 1970, when the Trefann Court mothers wrote their brief (discussed in chapter 3). The districts developed local data systems, most notably Toronto's Every Student Survey, that monitored district-wide graduation rates and credit accumulation, and related them to student demographics. The purpose was not to evaluate teachers, but to evaluate and justify policy and its implementation. Both districts progressed slowly on standardized testing and believed that excessive testing and unwise use of test results could distort education practice. Both districts wanted to avoid a system in which higher test scores were more important than improvements in student outcomes. The TBE was a pioneer in the new testing regime in Ontario, as district administrators worked with the province to ensure that the curriculum-based tests the district developed to reflect its literacy goals were adopted at the provincial level.

Today, an increasingly well-educated public will not put its faith in professional expertise that does not examine its performance openly and critically; testing has become part of that process. Schools must communicate effectively about what they do and why they do it; the accumulation of sophisticated data is part of that communication, although there is no reason to limit public reporting to any single outcome measure.

The new governance models being proposed for big cities today, notably mayoral control and privatized management systems, were not part of the debate in Winnipeg and Toronto at the end of the last century. School board politics had connections with municipal and provincial politics. The shifting opinion climate affected politics at all levels, and friendships along party and ideological lines carried issues from one arena to the other. The reform school board trustees elected in the early 1970s in Toronto moved in the same circles as the reforming mayor, David Crombie, and the more activist mayor, John Sewell. Similarly, the provincial NDP in Manitoba had close connections with the NDP school trustees at the board, but jurisdictional separation was insisted on. Debate about governance continued as the roles of the province, the city, and the districts were discussed and adjusted, and the role of Metro in the rapidly growing city of Toronto changed with amalgamation. Nevertheless, school governance remained the purview of the school boards, even as their responsibilities were restricted by provincial decisions about curriculum, funding, and testing. Gradual change rather than structural reorganization was the approach until the provincial government amalgamated the TBE with its suburban neighbours, causing a major rethinking of policy, staffing, and budget priorities. There is no evidence that this was an improvement, and discussions about finding a new, more decentralized model continue today.

There are no simple answers to the challenges of urban education. Our examination of Toronto and Winnipeg shows the complexity of improvement in urban schools. Substantive institutional improvement across a large and diverse community requires multiple initiatives and ongoing learning over a considerable amount of time. Given the degree to which the education challenges of urban areas are rooted in broader social conditions, an education strategy must also involve a social change strategy. The latter should go beyond integrated services to address other issues that have implications for the ability of schools to succeed. Some of these, such as early childhood development and adult education, are closely linked to education, while others, such as housing, maternity leave, and employment policies, are more removed but are still equally important. Additionally, all of the above must be grounded in local data and broader research evidence, so that efforts are not wasted on policies or programs known to be less effective.

Creating the consensus and common purpose described by Stone (1998) as necessary for sustained progress in urban education is very difficult and therefore unusual. But that consensus is what will ultimately lead to change. Educational improvement is more than policy implementation; it is the outcome of a complex, historically-situated political process that creates social, economic, and political capital for use in schools. This process must combine ideas about education, the political mechanisms for debating those disparate ideas, and the practicalities of translating them into teaching and learning conditions. If the politics cohere, the process results in agreement to move forward. If they do not, polarized disagreement prevents progress (Gaskell 2001, 2002).

Ideas and Research

Ideas matter to how the public engages with schools. Developments in Toronto and Winnipeg were significantly influenced by changing beliefs, understanding, and values on least at two levels. First, the beliefs and understanding of people in key leadership roles matter a great deal. Sometimes those leaders are elected; the core commitments of many trustees we interviewed influenced not only their own positions, but also those of their colleagues on the boards and in the larger organizational and political landscape. Public speeches and writings from trustees such as Gordon Cressey, Fiona Nelson, and George Martell created and consolidated new engagement with education in Toronto. Passionate, articulate, and committed spokespeople for ideas of equity, of parent engagement, and of community building can have far more influence than their single vote on a board, whether that board has nine members or twenty-two.

The same was true of the educational leaders in these cities. The beliefs of directors and superintendents often had a very large impact on the work of these districts, whether one considers Duncan Green's commitments to flexibility, research, and public involvement, or Jack Smyth's twenty years of work on Aboriginal education and inner-city schools to inculcate shared principles of learning and student assessment. When a leader in an important role works steadily over time on a particular issue, there is overall improvement.

Parent and community advocates outside the system can have a similar effect. The nuns at Rossbrook House or the parents who led advisory committees also helped shape decisions, policies, and programs in these districts. The brief put together by mothers in Trefann Court articulated an agenda for reform that animated the Toronto Board of Education for many years.

At the same time, school districts' work exists in a larger context which contains dominant ideas – what Donald Schon (1973) described as 'ideas in good currency.' Many of our interviewees had unconventional worldviews, and had to face the challenge of trying to change a system in ways that did not correspond to common assumptions, whether by staff, parents, or other voters. There is also no requirement that citizens be knowledgeable, reasonable, or consistent in their views. There is nothing to prevent people from wanting several contradictory things at once. Most people are not well-informed on most public issues, nor could they be, given the volume of issues in the public domain at any given time, and how little time most people devote to the public sphere.

Disagreeing with current thinking is a challenge, but ideas do change over time, and part of that change is the result of careful, sustained efforts by advocates who bring evidence to bear on public debate. Wilkinson and Pickett (2009) point out that, in historical terms, ideas such as human rights, children's rights, and labour laws are recent developments. Social inequities, while large, are smaller than they were a century ago. In the spheres in which public thinking has changed, those changes often came about due to hard work by many people using political processes, media, or the legal system. There are examples in education, such as the elimination of corporal punishment, changes in the way children with disabilities are treated, or understanding the importance of very early childhood to long-term development and success.

Research often plays an important role in shifting public or professional thinking. Strong evidence and argumentation about the purposes of schooling, the development of language, or the positive or negative effects of various practices can be an important element of change. Research alone is not enough. Its results have an effect through larger social and political processes, and not always in ways that researchers think are accurate. Still, it is affirming to see that evidence does matter, and was one of the main tools used by the reformers in Toronto and Winnipeg. The TBE and several community groups used the Every Student Survey to reinforce the argument that social class and ethnic background affected outcomes. Advocates made this point repeatedly, using data over many years in an attempt to change attitudes and practices in the system and in the public. In some cases, there was change in attitudes, policies, and programs, such as in regard to English language learning, Aboriginal education, parent engagement, or student assessment. In other areas, such as vocational schools, it was harder to overcome the entrenched interests supporting the status quo. Change was never solely dependent on evidence, but evidence did play an important role.

Educators should embrace research and data as a key part of their practice. Research not only provides data on the current situation, but also is part of the process of informing debate and changing opinions. Every urban school district should have a significant research capacity and strategy, and research should be seen not just as a technical resource to analyse test results or student backgrounds, but as a central element in generating public and professional dialogue about issues and possible solutions. School districts need to be concerned with influencing attitudes and ideas in their staff and, even more, in the broader community.

From this perspective, research by a school district – or a provincial government – should not only focus on evidence from that district or province. As the field of education research matures and there is increasing evidence on which practices are effective, it is increasingly important to communicate that evidence to educators and the public. That is especially so where the evidence seems counterintuitive, such as in the current debate over 'failing' students, where strong evidence showing the long-term negative effects of failure (e.g., Hattie, 2008) refutes the widespread belief that failure teaches people to work harder. Communicating knowledge or reasonable claims based on research is as important as having the results in the first place; knowledge that does not enter the public domain cannot have its due influence.

It is naïve to believe that evidence alone will trump everything, and that simply sharing research results will change minds and alter behaviour. There is significant evidence to the contrary. Social practices are just that – social – and are unlikely to change just because people are told to believe something different. Practices with compelling evidence behind them, such as regular exercise, proper hand washing, or not smoking, are still far from universal, indicating how hard it is to get people to change their behaviour (Gawande, 2007).

Nevertheless, research and its communication are necessary first steps. In education systems around the world today, research still tends to be weak (Levin, 2010). There is not enough research, and the results are poorly communicated, whether by researchers or by school systems. Where school systems do have research capacity, it is often used for low-level tasks and strong public engagement with ideas is rarely on the agenda. School systems could do a lot to raise the profile of their research, and much of it would require little effort. However, the role of research must be not only a concern for school districts and provincial governments, but a central concern for researchers and universities – which in Canada remain the prime source for education research. Unless the researchers and their institutions do more to share their work, its potential value will never be actualized. Stronger partnerships between school systems and researchers are important to this agenda.

A compelling example of the power of intelligently-used research is Ontario's People for Education (P4E), a grass-roots parents' organization. Concerned about education funding cuts in the 1990s, P4E organized to gather information on those cuts, and regularly shared that information with media. Within a few years, it became the most widely-cited source of information on the situation in schools, more so than the Ministry of Education itself. The numbers released by P4E were widely used, including in the public debate over education policy and funding. This example is particularly instructive as P4E was run by a volunteer group of parents.

The same processes are now widely used by various think tanks and interest groups, who gather data or commission research and spend time getting their conclusions into the public domain in order to influence public policy. While some may see this as the politicization of research, we agree with Lindblom and Cohen's (1979) argument that new thinking and new practices are produced through social interaction around ideas, and not just by the ideas themselves.

Politics

Many educators view politics as interfering with their work, and wish it would go away, so they could get on with professional practice. The same sentiments are expressed by professionals in other fields, such as doctors and nurses in regard to health care, or the police in regard to criminal justice. As a public activity, though, education will always be in the public and political domain. People will continue to disagree about what schools are for, what should be taught in them, and how they should be operated. Such disagreements get resolved through political processes which, despite their flaws, are still the most effective means of resolving differences.

Whether defined as the determination of 'who gets what, when and how' (Laswell, 1950), or more formally defined as 'the authoritative allocation of values for a society' (Easton, 1953), politics operates at every level of human interaction through both formal and informal mechanisms. We may typically think of politics as involving governments, political parties, and elections, but the determination of what will be done, by whom, and how, takes place in every organization at every level.

The fundamental importance and influence of politics is clear throughout the stories of Toronto and Winnipeg. At every stage, political considerations were important to elected officials, senior managers, and school principals. Every actor had to review the range and depth of opinion on various issues. Principals had to consider the views of their staff and community; superintendents had to consider the politics of their trustees and of their organization; trustees had to consider what their voters and parents would accept, and so on. However, this is not a distasteful state of affairs. In a democratic and open society, progress requires discussing, arguing, convincing, and compromising with others. This process may feel cumbersome or even impossible, but it is nonetheless necessary. The respondents in this study, even those with formal political roles such as school board members, did not always like the politics associated with their jobs. However, they all recognized that they were important to achieving their goals.

Since the world is a political place, and human action is inherently political, the next step is to pay attention to the politics around one's goals, to see them as important, and to organize to manage them. This means engaging people in debate, discovering and challenging their views, and providing the mechanisms through which a community can express a collective will regarding education. It means finding ways to express differences, yet also looking for consensus wherever possible.

Multiple interviewees in this study, particularly those who worked on community engagement or organizing in the 1970s and thereafter, discussed the politics of engagement. These reformers were explicitly committed to involving people in political discussion, particularly those they regarded as previously marginalized or excluded. They accepted the inherent messiness of the process. When the districts engaged in policy debates with public hearings, task forces on key issues, or creating citizen advisory groups, they were trying to build community understanding and, where possible, agreement on how schools should address some of the challenges they faced.

The everyday state of schooling, like that of other public institutions, does not always embody these approaches. Large organizations tend to avoid public debate in favour of attention to operations. Most school districts have few or weak mechanisms for public engagement and political action. Where mechanisms such as parent councils do exist, they may easily become complacent, be co-opted by staff, or engage only a small number of parents. Public engagement requires time and energy, whereas most school districts are consumed with trying to make the current system function reasonably well. One of Levin's formative experiences as a school trustee was having his board colleagues reject the idea of holding board meetings in venues other than the board office, because, as one trustee put it, 'if people want us, they know where to find us.' Given the size, financial requirements, and long-term importance of public education, the need is exactly the opposite: to reach out to engage citizens, and not just parents, in the challenges and issues of public education, especially when they require disrupting the status quo.

Urban school systems face particular political problems. They are large organizations, and so citizens may feel removed from their elected representatives. Each trustee in Toronto or Winnipeg represents more people than a member of the provincial legislature. Yet trustees have none of the structure that provincial or federal politicians have to stay connected and communicate their views. Political parties are not significantly involved. School boards get little media coverage and elections have low voter turnout, so people are not likely to know who their trustee is. There is no public election financing or tax credits for school board elections; a trustee campaign must be paid for by the candidate or her supporters, which means campaigns are often low key.

At the same time, the politics of urban education can be very fractious. Canada's cities are diverse in almost every way, from income to ethnicity to language to other lifestyle elements. Not surprisingly, people often disagree on issues related to education. The debates described above around heritage languages in Toronto or Aboriginal schools in Winnipeg show how sharp and divisive discussions can be. Urban school districts face many competing views and interests with a weak political infrastructure. It's no wonder that school board politics can be difficult.

There have been many suggestions for changing governance systems in urban school systems. A number of cities in the United States have replaced elected school boards with mayor-appointed boards. England took most authority away from its school districts and gave it to individual schools, which are now largely self-governing, as they are in New Zealand. Many countries run schools through municipal governments, while others run them as national enterprises controlled by the national government. All of these approaches are alternatives to the current Canadian system of elected boards in cities. However, their desirability is questionable. Mayoral control of school boards in United States cities does not seem to have yielded better results for students (Cuban & Usdan, 2003; Henig & Rich, 2004). Countries with self-governing schools, such as England or New Zealand, find it difficult to get coordinated action across their systems, which limits improvement. Local school governing bodies were seen as a solution in some places, but interest in serving often dries up and many schools in countries using this approach cannot find enough people to serve on their governing bodies. In Canada and the United States, some school districts operate with wards and others with election at large, but each system has its problems as well as its advantages. Neither centralization nor decentralization of power in school districts seems to be a solution. The truth, however unpalatable, is that the problems of politics cannot be evaded with an alternative governance structure – what Plank and Boyd (1994) called 'the flight from democracy.'

There are steps that could be taken to improve politics and governance in Canada's urban districts, though our suggestions are more modest than some of the proposals already mentioned. One possibility is to make education politics more like provincial or national politics, to recognize that education is a political activity, and to organize so that the political positions of those running for office are evident. Though possibly controversial, such a move could bring public financing into school board elections to make it more feasible for new candidates to run in school board elections. Political parties would, as they do at other levels, look for attractive candidates, including from various minority groups, and then support them in running. Parties would also have programs to present to voters instead of making vague promises to benefit children. If existing political parties had no interest in school board elections, local coalitions of civic-minded citizens could endorse and support a slate of candidates with a similar approach. Such an approach led to the election of the first reform slate in Toronto; it also led to a more conservative group being elected in 1985.

Another option is a closer link between school governance and municipal governance. In many countries, municipal authorities are responsible for education in addition to other local services, while in North America there are separate elected school boards. If education were an arm of municipal government, with the same elected official responsible for both, there might be more public interest in municipal elections and politics, as well as stronger connections between schools and other local government-provided social services.

A second area of potential improvement relates to public communication. School districts, like other organizations, are loath to communicate anything that does not portray them in a positive light. When they bother at all, most school districts are involved in public relations rather than communications. From the standpoint of creating political engagement, districts should be seeking a richer dialogue with their constituents. Some districts or provinces have moved in this direction. British Columbia and Alberta require that districts survey and publicly report on parent satisfaction with schools. While that is a good policy, it could be supplemented with additional requirements for school districts to report publicly on various aspects of their work. Student achievement would be one area, which would also allow districts to broaden their indicators of achievement beyond provincial tests or exams. Data for suspensions and expulsions, special education placement rates, staff turnover and absenteeism, the condition of facilities, and expenditures by category in relation to provincial averages could also be publicly reported. Parent and student attitudes and satisfaction levels should also be important public indicators. The goal would be to give citizens more information about what their schools were doing, including struggles as well as successes. Since citizens are already aware that public schools are imperfect, there seems to be little risk and a lot of potential benefit in using data to encourage discussions of what might be improved.

A third possibility for improvement – and the three are not mutually exclusive – that has not been discussed extensively involves third party accountability mechanisms. Currently when a school district runs into trouble, provincial ministries of education decide whether and how to intervene. They are often reluctant to do so, but if the problems are too egregious, they will step in. Typically, they have only blunt tools for doing so, such as directly appointing directly to take over the powers and functions of the school board. That step has been used several times in Canada, including in North Vancouver, Calgary, Hamilton, Toronto, Ottawa, Halifax, and several suburban Ontario boards. Provincial takeover is a clumsy mechanism at best. Official trustees or supervisors are in a difficult position, and generally provinces want to end supervision as soon as possible but sometimes find it hard to do so.

Under current legislation across Canada, provinces maintain the final responsibility for a school district that is failing in its basic responsibilities. But there could be other, less punitive mechanisms that might achieve similar results. For example, large urban districts could be monitored by an independent organization without any decision-making power but with the ability to comment publicly on the actions and achievements or failures of the districts, similar to what auditors do for companies' finances, or to what public advocates do in areas such as children's care. These bodies, composed of unpaid citizens and some staff, would give independent views on the state of education. Their views would have to be taken seriously by elected boards, but a board would be entitled to disagree and give reasons for doing so. While the result might create more conflict, it, or similar alternatives, could also generate a more informed citizenry, and that can only benefit public education.

Teaching and Learning

Governance that successfully manages the fundamental conflicts about urban education will focus educational debate on the improvement of teaching and learning, since that is what schools are for. In chapter 6, we noted that issues of teaching and learning were often not at the centre of the struggles with which Winnipeg and Toronto school systems were grappling. That seems a very odd admission, given that the ostensible purpose of schools is to teach and enable learning.

In one way, this departure from the core task is not surprising. Organization theory suggests that it is a struggle to keep any organization focused on its core mission. As Herndon (1971) argues, 'an institution is a place to do things where those things won't be done.' Within all organizations, the achievement of material goals is only one driving force behind internal activities; individual interests and needs of the organization's members often end up being more important than its stated goals and purposes. As any manager knows, reallocating office space usually generates more excitement in an organization than changing its goals; allocating parking space can eclipse strategic planning. Yet as research findings on effective teaching and learning accumulate, the benefits of greater focus on those issues in schools increase. There is simply more knowledge today about good and bad practice in many areas of schooling (e.g., Hattie, 2008; Marzano, 2003). We know that appropriate teaching techniques make a difference. We know that generating more student engagement results in more learning. We know that failure does not typically lead to greater future effort, but to less. We know that one-time professional development sessions have little or no impact on what teachers do. We know that principals need to build trust and support with their staff, and not rule by coercion, if they are to have effective schools. The list could go on indefinitely.

Moreover, there are more grounds than ever before to be optimistic about what schools can achieve. Objective evidence suggests that the limits of human capacity to learn and to achieve have not yet been reached (Levin, 2008). Levels of educational accomplishment that were regarded as the preserve of a small minority only two generations ago are now regarded as a universal entitlement, if not a requirement. People who were considered at one time to be uneducable – women, minorities, those with physical restrictions, and children with Down Syndrome – have much greater capacity than was previously believed. If one assumes that talent is roughly equally distributed among, for example, ethnic groups, then the lower achievement of some groups means that their talents have not yet been developed (Livingstone, 2004). Everything suggests that potential remains to be tapped, as the Trefann Court mothers so powerfully articulated in Toronto, or as Brian O'Leary, a former Winnipeg principal, remarked:

> I remember Sister Lesley Sacouman from Rossbrook House reminding me that 'these kids are bright kids.' We need to remind ourselves of that all the time in the inner city, but we lose sight of kids' abilities due to their problems and their families' problems. Our tendency is unfortunately to give in to the pressures and lower our expectations for what students can achieve.

The challenge is to translate the growing knowledge about effective education into widespread practice. How do we build policy around that knowledge, and also help educators do what we know to be more effective and, equally, cease to do what we know to be less effective?

Much of the effort in these two districts consisted of projects of various kinds – experiments in which one or several schools would undertake a new practice. Such whole school reform certainly has its merits; it is a way of testing ideas to see what their practical implications and problems are. Many good ideas in education have come from such experiments, from Summerhill to dual credit programs to inclusive education, and so on. There continues to be a need for experimentation in education.

However, education systems also suffer from many experiments that were never pursued or generalized. Organization theorist James March (1991) points out that organizations need both 'exploration' and 'exploitation' to be successful. They need to learn about new ideas and practices, but the real benefits are only reaped when those practices become norms for the organization as a whole. That has too rarely been the case in public education. Important things were learned in both cities, but only sometimes was that learning applied across an entire system on a sustained basis. In some areas, such as literacy in elementary schools in Toronto or Aboriginal education in Winnipeg, there was enough sustained effort and support to ingrain new practices. In other areas, such as community engagement, new practices were more difficult to sustain, and in still others, such as some of the special programs launched in both cities, once the money or individuals supporting an initiative were no longer there, the programs and ideas ended.

Experiments that begin but do not last occur because it is much easier to get the political support to launch a new pilot program in one supportive context than it is to change system-wide practices (Levin, 2008). Pilot projects tend to rely on enthusiastic volunteers who work in an environment where their objectives are appreciated. That is not, however, a sustainable way to run a large system, which must perform with the assumption that it will be staffed by ordinary people making an ordinary effort. If an improvement strategy requires having the top 5 per cent of all teachers in a school then, by definition, it can only apply to 5 per cent of schools. Therefore, the goal should be helping 100 per cent of the people working in our school systems improve in their work. In practice, however, this strategy has rarely been attempted because it requires a very high level of commitment, infrastructure, and effort. Toronto, for example, built departments for parent engagement and equity, something almost unheard of among school districts. It also built experimental inner-city schools that used different methods of teaching. These units had an impact on the system as a whole, yet even at their peak, they were small relative to the system they were trying to change, and the process of implementing system-wide change was often less carefully and strategically managed than the initial innovative models. Few school systems, or provincial governments, have been willing or have had perceived public support to make and sustain that investment.

Several factors must be in place in order to improve teaching and learning practices in dozens of schools and hundreds, if not thousands, of classrooms. Large numbers of teachers and principals have to understand what practices they are being asked to change, agree that the changes make sense, and comprehend them well enough to follow them. Equally important, educators have to be motivated to try. Experience in education in many places shows that you cannot force teachers to improve any more than you can force students to learn. Significant effort has to be invested in addressing not only educators' skills, but also their motivation. Mundane but important matters, such as working conditions or collective agreements, can become stumbling blocks. As always, there are multiple interests at work, not all of which are centred around students. It is easy to bemoan this state of affairs, but the real task is to manage it.

It would be fair to say that there is very little evidence about how to create system improvement at scale (Levin & Fullan, 2008), though there has been some progress (Barber, 2007). This work will require new leadership skills in schools and districts, because the leadership must be able to sustain political support for action. Educational change takes the kind of political commitment that many of the reformers discussed in this book possessed: the unrelenting drive to create change for the better by working together and overcoming obstacles.

There are instances of such effort in these two cases. The TBE's efforts around literacy, parent engagement, and equity are examples, as is the ten-year effort in Winnipeg's inner-city schools to develop and implement evidence-informed common practices. However, these efforts remain the exceptions. Too often, there are pilot projects, short-term efforts, or programs that rely on exceptional individuals or additional money, all of which are insufficient to generate sustained, system-wide change.

What Should Be Done?

We conclude with suggestions for improving urban education, whether in Winnipeg or Toronto, in other Canadian cities, or internationally. The problems are formidable, yet improvement is not only possible but necessary. The cost of having large numbers of students who do not enjoy school or benefit from it, or who do not acquire the knowledge and qualifications to live reasonable lives, is unacceptably high. Canadian urban education systems are much better than the 50 or

60 per cent high school graduation rates in large cities in the United States, but it is unacceptable and even dangerous to have 20 or 25 per cent of young people without a high school diploma or the ability to get a job, earn a decent living, and support a family (Picot, Saunders, & Sweetman, 2007). Moreover, these students are disproportionately from poor and minority families. That failure belongs not only to those directly affected but to all of us who also bear some of the costs through more crime, less public revenue, weaker families, poorer public health, lower productivity, and a less vibrant democracy.

The Winnipeg and Toronto cases show that there are many elements important to the ability of urban districts to provide good education. Their evidence, as well as the broader literature, suggests that any serious effort to improve urban schools would need to consider at least eight areas:

1. School districts with clear, well-founded, plans;
2. Productive links between large urban districts and provincial governments;
3. More public debate based on data on the political controversies inherent in urban public education;
4. Urban schools as good places to work and learn, so as to attract and retain skilled and dedicated educators;
5. A central and sustained focus on improved teaching and learning;
6. Strong and consistent community engagement;
7. Better use of research and evidence; and
8. The necessary infrastructure to support all of the above.

School Districts Need Thoughtful Strategic Plans

School districts must play a critical role in any urban school improvement. Despite their complexities, described in this book, school boards remain the primary governance mechanism for schools in Canadian cities and there is no serious alternative to them.

However, school districts, especially large urban districts, need a more strategic approach to their work. Given their size, complexity, and internal and external pressures, it is vital that they implement long-term strategies, clearly linked to budget and resource allocations, that show how they will use the best available evidence to improve results. Effective planning also requires effective working relationships between elected trustees and senior staff, which need to be developed carefully. Plans need to go beyond declaring priorities, and show how those priorities will translate to sustained new system-wide practices. They need to link not only to budget, but to hiring, leadership development, staff development, recruitment, evaluation, community engagement, communications, and all other important district functions, since without a comprehensive effort, goals are only statements of intention. Where Winnipeg and Toronto were successful in reaching their goals, they had clearly articulated plans and strategies that were backed with resources.

Stronger Links between Urban Districts
and Provincial Governments

While school boards are the most important actors in urban education, they cannot be successful unless they can work effectively with provincial governments. The lack of cooperation, or outright conflict, between the two levels in both Toronto and Winnipeg often undermined improvement efforts.

Cooperation between political levels will always be difficult. The attraction of having another level of government to blame prevents effective collaboration. But provincial governments have more resources and greater ability to coordinate a range of services in related areas, such as health. Where relationships are productive, as they were during several periods in both Toronto and Winnipeg, all parties are more effective. Both school boards and provincial governments should aim to develop formal accords signed by leaders at both levels for working together to improve urban schools. Such agreements would allow the better mobilization of the necessary resources to make sustainable and substantial progress. The Core Area Initiatives in Winnipeg in the 1980s and 1990s provide one model for how this can be done.

More Public Debate Based on Data on the Political
Controversies Inherent in Urban Public Education

Education systems can only do what the public, which provides both children and funding, is prepared to accept. But rather than seeing public acceptance as a problem, districts need to see public dialogue as an important part of what they do. Especially in diverse urban settings, supporting informed debate and the exchange of views is essential to sustaining good public education. Many school districts still see the goal of communications as convincing people they are doing a great job and that they could do more if they only had more money. Vibrant democracy cannot be built on public relations, but can only be sustained through the real, often arduous work of hearing from people and asking them to consider their beliefs in light of other beliefs and evidence.

School boards can play a central role in enabling public dialogue and debate. Both the Toronto and Winnipeg districts did this at times – for example, by creating task forces and working groups to gather input on important policy issues. Yet these processes were mostly ad hoc, even though they often produced good results, both in participation and in changing public and professional thinking. We suggest that urban districts should have standing processes for public engagement on the larger issues facing them. For example, urban districts might have at least one task force or public engagement process each year on an important issue. They might establish regular processes for gathering opinion and evidence from students, staff, parents, and other community members. Public debate built on evidence would then become a standard part of urban districts' work, and over time, they could build greater public understanding of and commitment to urban education.

Urban Schools Must Be Good Places to Work and Learn
so as to Attract and Retain Qualified and Dedicated Educators

One of the most important findings of recent education research is the difference that effective teaching practice makes (Darling-Hammond, 2010; Hattie, 2008). In urban schools it is especially important to recruit, develop, and retain good people, even though the nature of the communities makes teaching conditions more difficult.

Succeeding in this effort is not primarily a matter of pay. The focus on pay based on student outcomes, or 'merit pay,' for teachers is misguided for many reasons – not least because it misunderstands the nature of teaching and works against promoting good practice among teachers. Other professions are not paid on merit. Equally importantly, recent research by Leithwood (2006) on behalf of the Elementary Teachers' Federation of Ontario shows that many of the working conditions that are most important to teachers are also crucial to building effective schools. These include a clear and sustained focus on improvement, effective leadership, good opportunities for collegial learning,

reasonable physical facilities and supplies, and respect for effort coupled with feedback on performance. (These conditions are very similar
to those that motivate students, as noted earlier.) Putting these elements
in place is possible and would be more productive than giving individual teachers bonuses for working in challenging schools.

At the same time, school systems must make a real effort to try to
have their best educators teaching where they are most needed. If the
district culture places the most experienced teachers in the most advantaged schools or with the most capable students, the results will not be
good. Very few districts, including those in this study, have been consistently able to place teachers and principals where they can make the
most difference. This issue should be openly discussed, both in and out
of collective bargaining settings.

A Central and Sustained Focus on Improved Teaching and Learning

Many education reforms do not last because they are not adequately
supported. They are either small-scale projects that never spread to
most schools, or large-scale changes in practice that are presumed to be
brought about by a few professional development workshops, a policy
document, and a resource manual. The Toronto and Winnipeg cases
demonstrate that neither of these strategies work.

Improving everyday teaching and learning in thousands of classrooms is a large task that requires that large numbers of people to
change their habits, which can be a difficult proposition even if they
are willing. A recent analysis of research on teacher development and
learning (Timperley et al., 2007) concludes that change requires much
more than time. It requires challenging existing ideas and practices
(usually through external expertise), active leadership, and opportunities to explore and extend new habits in practice. Of course, this is no
different from learning anything else; any worthwhile skill takes hours
of practice and feedback. Teaching, as a complex act, is the same.

Very few jurisdictions ever put in place the scale and scope of support needed for this kind of change. It means committing to years of
ongoing focus on a small number of issues or tasks. It means having a
network of experts and supports to ensure that the focus is real, substantive, and ongoing, and leads to changes. It might also mean changing other activities and policies to support the new practices. Unless
change is recognized as a major undertaking, schools will continue to
have short-term initiatives with no lasting impact.

Strong and Consistent Community Engagement

Many of the challenges and inequities that affect student performance fall primarily outside of school: in poverty, low wages, unemployment, housing, inadequate social services, or racial discrimination. These are not the responsibility of schools, yet they cannot be ignored.

Urban school districts and their allies walk a fine line between an external focus that implies that schools have no ability to affect students' outcomes, and a false assertion that a school can achieve any results if it has enough willpower. Neither is correct. Schools cannot do everything, but this does not mean they can do nothing, which is why a strong focus on changing teaching and learning practices is essential.

At the same time, one of the most exciting parts of the reforms described in this book was the attempt to connect schools with their local communities. Such engagement means more than inviting parent participation on school councils. It means connecting with and supporting the elements of local neighbourhoods that sustain families and hence schools, such as youth groups, faith organizations, community services, ethnic associations, sports and recreation groups, and so on. In cities, building stronger local communities is fundamental to schools' success. The ideas of community development that animated many of the reforms noted earlier remain valid. Nor can building such relationships simply be added to the existing duties of school principals. It must be planned, and someone must be responsible for it. Winnipeg and Toronto both had organizations dedicated to this work that had some good results. Community engagement should remain a core function of urban districts, which includes active lobbying of other levels of government to address the broader issues that so deeply affect urban students and schools.

Better Use of Research and Evidence

Research has a significant potential role in improving urban education. These cases show the impact that research, ideas, and data had over time in each city. There has been growing interest in education in both research and data analysis. Professional educators no longer have the disdain for research that was widespread several decades ago, and data on schooling are both more available and more likely to be used.

Yet, as we noted earlier, the capacity to produce and use research effectively is not well-developed in education. Districts lack research capacity, and even where they have it, they do not have a strategy to build on research and data with the goal of improvement. Toronto's powerful use of research in the 1970s has rarely been replicated elsewhere. Relationships between school districts and university researchers are largely a matter of happenstance, and depend on individuals. The growing interest among educators in using evidence effectively has not yet been matched by concomitant support processes and systems.

The Necessary Supporting Infrastructure

Both money and other resources are necessary to support the previous seven elements of effective education. But simply increasing funding for school or district budgets will not produce better outcomes. Research suggests that after a basic level, spending has a tenuous relationship with educational outcomes (Grubb, 2009). On the other hand, good education does require money. If we want talented people to be teachers, we must pay them decently and provide decent working conditions. Schools with high levels of disadvantage will need additional resources to compensate – not just for smaller classes, but for individualized support to students, community outreach, or enrichment activities such as music or travel that many other students take for granted. Similarly, as noted earlier, having the best educators working in the most challenging schools and communities gives them the opportunity to make the most difference. Currently, very few systems provide more than a small amount – perhaps 5 per cent – of additional funds to high-need schools, when, given the scale of the problems poor urban families face, that number should be closer to 50 or 100 per cent – provided that the money is used towards evidence-supported initiatives and practices.

Organizational supports are as important as funding. Principals in urban schools need support because they have more critical tasks to perform. Teachers may need more time to work on improved practices. Staff or volunteers are needed to liaise with parents, to translate materials into various languages, and to support struggling families. These factors all require organization and infrastructure. It is a cliché to say that a task worth doing is worth doing well, but it is also a cliché that is often ignored in the world of education.

Leadership also plays an important role. Even in the difficult conditions of the late 1980s and early 1990s, certain individuals in the school systems, whether educators, elected board members, or other community leaders, played vital roles in creating and sustaining support for important initiatives. Dedicated people can make a difference.

Conclusions

While all these factors matter, we return to the importance of a politics that engages the public in public education, focuses on the key issues of teaching and learning, and sustains the support necessary for respectful and informed debate about directions and compromises. In a changing world, where cities are becoming more diverse, more economically divided, and more geographically segregated, these challenges will be harder to meet.

The status of inner-city education is largely shaped by broader social, economic, and political developments. The most dynamic period of activity in both Toronto and Winnipeg occurred from the late 1960s through the 1970s, when there was a high level of social optimism and activism, and governments had, and were prepared to spend, money for inner-city issues. As this climate changed in the late 1970s and 1980s, there was less support for inner-city education and the situation worsened in many respects, even though people in inner-city schools and communities were still working hard to address issues. The growth of political activism by ethnic minorities and Aboriginal people brought a local politics into play that demanded action and led to some positive developments. Although external advocacy can make things difficult for school system officials, political pressure on all public services is vital to keeping equity issues on the agenda and encouraging progress. A degree of conflict is necessary; the task of leadership is to manage conflict for productive purposes.

There is no magic policy that can make schools perform while the rest of the world ignores them. Much of the recent attention to eliminating poverty and educational disadvantage appears to be rhetorical, such as the Parliamentary resolution of 1989 to end child poverty in Canada by the year 2000. Nevertheless, progress has been made over the years, and several areas have seen significant improvement. At a time when Canadian society is more unequal, schools have been able to reduce inequities. The problems in schools mirror the problems of society, and there is no technical, management, or policy shortcut to good schooling. Sustained social and educational policies require active, engaged citizenship; wise, pragmatic leadership; and widely shared democratic commitments that sustain respect for all learners and teachers alike. It is only through such efforts that will we truly be able to make a difference in urban schools.

Appendix on Methodology

This book arose from a research study supported by a general research grant from the Social Sciences and Humanities Research Council of Canada in 2003. The bulk of the data collection was carried out in 2004 and 2005, but most of the analysis took place from 2007 on. As noted in the introduction, work on the project was delayed by job changes for both principal investigators.

The research includes document analysis and interviews. The document analysis includes a review of the minutes of both the Toronto and Winnipeg school boards, as well as key documents such as annual reports and policy statements. The archives of the Toronto Board of Education are both more complete and more accessible, but we did review many documents in Winnipeg. We also reviewed a range of related documents in both cities, such as reports of social planning councils and other anti-poverty and social welfare groups. We read books, articles, and journals of the day to understand the mindset of the times, especially in the early years covered by the study. By the end of our research, we had amassed thousands of pages of documents and put together an extensive chronology of events in each city, not just in the school districts, but in the cities, provinces, nation, and world, as these all related to urban education, poverty, and diversity.

Our main data source was interviews with key participants. We interviewed twenty-two people in Winnipeg and twenty-eight people in Toronto. Our interviewees included:

- In Winnipeg: three trustees, twelve principals and superintendents (a number of whom held both roles), and seven others, including various community leaders.

- In Toronto: eight trustees, ten principals and superintendents, six other board staff (teachers and equity leaders), and four community leaders.

Given a forty-year period of interest, and our concern both for political and educational leaders, we could have interviewed hundreds of people. The WSD board, for example, had fifty different members between 1970 and 2000, and Toronto's had more than twice that number. If we include senior administrators and community leaders, thousands of people have had a significant role in the political and educational histories of these two organizations.

We attempted to interview a cross-section of key actors, including trustees, senior administrators, and other important leaders, over the span of the study. Inevitably, our ability to do so was affected by accessibility. A few key people had died or had serious health problems, while others had moved and were difficult or impossible to locate. Still, we believe that our fifty interviews gave us a good overview of events and developments in both organizations, especially when paired with documented evidence.

We interviewed each of our respondents at length, and a typical interview ran an hour or longer. Interviews were tape-recorded. We then produced detailed written records of the interviews, which were returned to our respondents for their review and editing. We could not promise confidentiality due to the public nature of the positions many of our interviewees held, but we assured them that we would only use a version of the interview that they approved. This allowed respondents, some of whom still have public roles, to feel confident that they expressed their views accurately. Some respondents made quite a few changes, while others made few or none. In our view, an edited transcript of this kind is the best record of what respondents wish to communicate, especially given the limitations of oral language, and was therefore an appropriate research approach.

In addition to these standard research techniques, we interacted with interviewees and others in a variety of ways. Some of the earlier papers written from this project were presented at conferences and were shared with some of the key actors involved, such as Pauline Clarke of the WSD. We contacted almost all of those we interviewed, gave them access to the website on which we posted papers emerging from the study, and invited their feedback. One of our Winnipeg research assistants, Jennifer Lawson, was an inner-city principal in

Winnipeg for several years and provided further feedback on some of our findings and conclusions. Together with WSD colleagues, we ran an interactive session at an inner-city education conference in Toronto in 2007 that also brought comment from people in both cities. We ran similar sessions in other settings. In 2008, Levin organized a seminar in Winnipeg for our interviewees, and several of them discussed our interpretations and conclusions. In all these ways we sought to involve our partners.

Finally, as noted in the introduction, Levin was an active participant in some of the events described in this book and an interested observer of many of them. He was a school trustee in Seven Oaks School Division from 1971 to 1974, and knew and worked with the early reform trustees in Winnipeg. He was actively involved in NDP politics and interacted extensively with ministers and senior officials in the Schreyer government. He served as a senior official in the Department of Education through much of the Pawley government and the early stages of the Filmon government in the 1980s, during which he had responsibility for the Core Area Initiative. His recollections of these events are also woven into this account.

References

Ainley, J. (2000). *Outcomes and funding in the Commonwealth Literacy and Numeracy Programme*. Melbourne: Australian Council for Educational Research.

Alinsky, S. (1969). *Reveille for radicals*. New York: Vintage Books.

Anyon, J. (1997). *Ghetto schooling*. New York: Teachers College Press.

Audit Commission (England). (2002). *A force for change*. London: Audit Commission.

Axelrod, P. (2005). Beyond the progressive education debate: A profile of Toronto schooling in the 1950s. *Historical Studies in Education, 17*(2), 227–41.

Barber, J. (20 February 1988). Different colours, changing city. *Globe and Mail*.

Barber, M. (2007). *Instruction to deliver*. London: Methuen.

Barber, M., & Dann, R. (Eds.). (1996). *Raising educational standards in inner cities*. London: Cassell.

Berkman, M., & Plutzer, E. (2005). *Ten thousand democracies: Politics and public opinion in American school districts*. Washington, DC: Georgetown University Press.

Boyd, W.L., Kerchner, C.T., & Blyth, M. (2008). *The transformation of great American school districts: How big cities are reshaping public education*. Cambridge: Harvard University Press.

Bracey, G. (2003). PIRLS before the press. *Phi Delta Kappan, 84*(10), 795.

Bradley, R., & Whiteside-Mansell, L. (1997). Children in poverty. In R.T. Ammerman & M. Hersen (Eds.), *Handbook of prevention and treatment with children and adolescents: Intervention in the real world context* (pp. 13–58). New York: John Wiley & Sons.

Bremer, J., & von Moschzisker, M. (1971). *The school without walls: Philadelphia's parkway program*. New York: Holt, Rinehart and Winston.

Britton, J. (1972). *Language and learning*. Harmondsworth, England: Penguin Books.

Brownell, M., Roos, N., Fransoo, R., Guevremont, A., MacWilliams, L., Derksen, S., et al. (2004). *How do educational outcomes vary with socioeconomic status?* Winnipeg: University of Manitoba Centre for Health Policy.

Bryk, A.S., Sebring, P.B., Allenswroth, E., Luppescu, S., & Easton, J.Q. (1998). *Organizing schools for improvement: Lessons from Chicago.* Chicago: University of Chicago Press.

Bryk, A.S., Sebring, P.B., Kerbow, D., Rollow, S., & Easton, J.Q. (1998). *Charting Chicago school reform: Democratic localism as a lever for change.* Boulder: Westview Press.

Bumstead, J.M. (1994). *The Winnipeg General Strike of 1919: An illustrated history.* Winnipeg: Watson and Dwyer.

Campaign 2000. (2009). National report card on child and family poverty in Canada 2008. Toronto: Author. Retrieved 13 May 2009 at http://www.campaign2000.ca/reportcards.html

Campbell, C., Evans, J., Askew, S., Hughes, M., & McCallum, B. (2004). *Evaluation of education partnership boards: Final report.* London: Department for Education and Skills.

Canadian Council on Social Development. (n.d.). *A profile of economic security in Canada.* Ottawa: Author. Retrieved 1 March 2010 from http://www.ccsd.ca/factsheets/economic_security/poverty/index.htm

Canadian Council on Social Development. (n.d.). *Economic security fact sheet #2: Poverty.* Retrieved from http://www.ccsd.ca/factsheets/economic_security/poverty/index.htm

Canadian Teachers' Federation. (1989). *Children, schools and poverty.* Ottawa: CTF.

Canadian School Boards Association. (2001). *Action against poverty: School boards making a difference.* Ottawa: Canadian School Boards Association.

Carter, S.C. (2000). *No excuses: Lessons from 21 high-performing, high-poverty schools.* Washington, DC: The Heritage Foundation.

Chafe, J. (1967). *An apple for the teacher: A centennial history of the Winnipeg School Division.* Winnipeg: Winnipeg School Division.

Clark, W. (2000). 100 years of education. *Canadian Social Trends, 59,* 3–7.

Clarke, F. (2002). 'Keep communism out of our schools': Cold war anti-communism at the Toronto Board of Education, 1948–1951. *Labour/Le Travail, 49*(spring), 93–119.

Cochrane, H. (Ed.). (1950). *Centennial story: The board of education for the city of Toronto 1850–1950.* Toronto: Thomas Nelson and Sons.

Cohen, M.D., March, J.G., & Olsen, J.P. (1972). A garbage can model of organisational choice. *Administrative Science Quarterly, 17*(2), 1–25.

Coleman, J. (1966). *Equal educational opportunity.* Washington, DC: United States Department of Health, Education and Welfare Office of Education.

Committee on the Aims and Objectives of Education in the Schools of Ontario. (1968). *Living and learning ('Hall-Dennis report')*. Toronto: The Newton Publishing Company.

Connell, R., White, V., & Johnston, K. (1991). *Running twice as hard: The disadvantaged schools program in Australia*. Geelong: Deakin University Press.

Cuban, L., & Usdan, M. (Eds.). (2003). *Powerful reforms with shallow roots: Improving America's urban schools*. New York: Teachers College Press.

Cuban, L. (2010). *As good as it gets: What school reform brought to Austin*. Cambridge: Harvard University Press.

Curtis, L. (2007). Socio-economic status and human capital: Recent Canadian evidence. In G. Picot, R. Saunders, & A. Sweetman (Eds.), *Fulfilling potential, creating success: Perspectives on human capital development* (pp. 37–54). Kingston: Queen's University School of Policy Studies.

Darling-Hammond, L. (2010). *The flat world and education: How America's commitment to equity will determine our future*. New York: Teachers College Press.

Delhi, K. (1996). Travelling tales: Education reform and parental choice in postmodern times. *Journal of Education Policy, 1*, 75–88.

Deosaran, R., & Wright, E.N. (n.d.). *The 1975 Every Student Survey: Students' background and its relationship to program placement*. Toronto: Research Department, the Board of Education for the City of Toronto.

Department for Children, Families and Schools, England. (2009). *Deprivation and education: The evidence on pupils in England, foundation stage to key stage 4*. London: HMSO.

Easton, D. (1953). *The political system: An inquiry into the state of political science*. New York: Knopf.

Edelman, M. (1988). *Constructing the political spectacle*. Chicago: University of Chicago Press.

Elmore, R. (2004). *School reform from the inside out*. Cambridge: Harvard Educational Press.

European Commission. (2006). *Efficiency and equity in European education and training systems*. COM(2006) 481 Final.

Field, S., Kuczera, M., & Pont, B. (2007). *No more failures: Ten steps to equity in education*. Paris: OECD.

Food Banks Canada. (2009). *Hunger count 2008: A comprehensive report on hunger and food bank use in Canada*. Toronto: Author. Retrieved 13 May 2009 at http://www.foodbankscanada.ca/getmedia/35265e3e-e325-472e-925b-595ef1732206/hunger-count-2008.pdf.aspx?ext=.pdf

Fruchter, N. (2008). Mayoral control in New York City. In W.L. Boyd, C.T. Kerchner, & M. Blyth (Eds.), *The transformation of great American school districts: How big cities are reshaping public education*. Cambridge: Harvard Education Press.

Fullan, M. (2007). *The new meaning of educational change* (4th ed.). New York: Teachers College Press.

Galabuzi, G-E. (2005). Factors affecting the social economic status of Canadian immigrants in the new millennium. *Canadian Issues* (Spring 2005), 53–7.

Gallagher, K. (2007). *The theatre of urban youth and schooling in dangerous times.* Toronto: University of Toronto Press.

Gaskell, J. (1988). Policy research and politics. *Alberta Journal of Educational Research, 34*(4), 403–17.

Gaskell, J. (1995). *Secondary schools in Canada: The national report of the exemplary schools project.* Toronto: Canadian Education Association.

Gaskell, J. (2001). Constructing the 'public' in public schools: A school board debate. *Canadian Journal of Education, 26*(1), 19–37.

Gaskell, J. (2002). Creating school choice: The politics of curriculum, equity and teachers' work. *Canadian Public Policy/Analyse de Politiques, 28*(1) 39–50.

Gaskell, J. (2010). Changing urban education in Canada. *LEARNingLandscapes Journal, 3*(2), 29–35. Retrieved from http://www.learninglandscapes.ca/images/documents/LL-no6-june2010-low-res.pdf

Gawande, A. (2007). *Better.* New York: Metropolitan.

Gerin-Lajoie, D. (2008). *Educators' discourses on student diversity in Canada: Context, policy and practice.* Toronto: Canadian Scholars Press.

Gidney, R. (1999). *From Hope to Harris: The reshaping of Ontario's schools.* Toronto: University of Toronto Press.

Gorard, S., Fitz, J., & Taylor, C. (2001). School choice impacts: What do we know? *Educational Researcher, 30*(7), 18–23.

Grant, G. (2009). *Hope and despair in the American city: Why there are no bad schools in Raleigh.* Cambridge: Harvard University Press.

Green, A., Preston, J., & Janmaat, J. (2006). *Education, equality and social cohesion: A comparative analysis.* Basingstoke: Palgrave MacMillan.

Green, D., & Rutledge, D. (February 1980). *Recommendations from the Dundas project.* Report to the chairman and members of the Inner City Committee, Toronto Board of Education.

Grubb, W.N. (2009). *The money myth: School resources, outcomes, and equity.* New York: Russell Sage.

Halpin, D., Dickson, M., Power, S., Whitty, G., & Gewirtz, S. (2004). Area-based approaches to educational regeneration: The case of the English education action zone. *Policy Studies [London], 25*(2), 75–85.

Hannaway J., & Usdan, M. (2008). Mayoral takeover in the District of Columbia: The need for a shake up. In W.L. Boyd, C.T. Kerchner, & M. Blyth (Eds.),

The transformation of great American school districts: How big cities are reshaping public education. Cambridge: Harvard Education Press.

Hattie, J. (2008). *Visible learning.* New York: Routledge.

Henig, J., Hula, R., Orr, M., & Pedescleaux, D. (1999). *The color of school reform: Race, politics and the challenge of urban education.* Princeton: Princeton University Press.

Henig, R., & Rich, C. (Eds.). (2004). *Mayors in the middle: politics, race, and mayor control of urban schools.* Princeton: Princeton University Press.

Herndon, J. (1971). *How to survive in your native land.* New York: Bantam.

Hess, F.M. (2005). *Urban school reform: Lessons from San Diego.* Cambridge: Harvard University Press.

Hess, G.A. Jr. (1995). *Restructuring urban schools: A Chicago perspective.* New York: Teachers College Press.

Hightower, A. (2002). San Diego's big boom: Systemic instructional change in the central office and schools. In A. Hightower et al. (Eds.), *School districts and instructional renewal* (pp. 76–93). New York: Teachers College Press.

Hulchanski, J.D. (December 2007). The three cities within Toronto: Income polarization among Toronto's neighbourhoods 1970–2000. *Centre for Urban and Community Studies. Research Bulletin* (41), 1–12.

Hunter, H. (2000). In the face of poverty: What a community school can do. In J. Silver (Ed.), *Solutions that work: Fighting poverty in Winnipeg* (pp. 111–25). Toronto: Fernwood Books.

Illich, I. (1970). *Deschooling society.* New York: Harper & Row.

Jantzen, L. (2004). Top seven Aboriginal census metropolitan areas: Similar issues and different circumstances. *Our Diverse Cities, 1,* 76–86.

Jencks, C. (1972). *Inequality: A reassessment of the effect of family and schooling in America.* New York: Basic Books.

Jenson, H. (1998). *Mapping social cohesion: The state of Canadian research.* Canadian Policy Research Networks Study, F-03.

Joshee, R. (2004). Citizenship and multicultural education in Canada: From assimilation to social cohesion. In J.A. Banks (Ed.), *Diversity and citizenship education: Global perspectives* (pp. 127–56). San Francisco: Jossey-Bass.

Justus, M. (2004). Immigrants in Canada's cities. *Our Diverse Cities, 1,* 41–7.

Kotlowitz, A. (1992). *There are no children here: The story of two boys growing up in the other America.* New York: Anchor Books.

Laswell, H. (1950). *Politics: Who gets what, when, how.* New York: P. Smith.

Leithwood, K. (2006). *Teacher working conditions that matter: Evidence for change.* Toronto: Elementary Teachers' Federation of Ontario.

Lemon, J. (1985). *Toronto since 1918. An illustrated history.* Toronto: James Lorimer and Company.

Lenskyj, H. (2005). *A lot to learn: Girls, women and education in the 20th century.* Toronto: Women's Press.

Levin, B. (1973). Reform and school trustees. In T. Morrison & A. Burton (Eds.), *Options: Reforms and alternatives for Canadian education* (pp. 302–7). Toronto: Holt, Rinehart & Winston.

Levin, B. (1998). An epidemic of education policy: (What) can we learn from each other? *Comparative Education, 34*(2), 131–41.

Levin, B. (2001). *Reforming education: From origins to outcomes.* London: RoutledgeFlamer.

Levin, B. (2003). *Approaches to equity in policy for lifelong learning.* Paper prepared for the OECD, Paris.

Levin, B. (2005). *Governing education.* Toronto: University of Toronto Press.

Levin, B. (2008). *How to change 5000 schools.* Cambridge: Harvard Education Press.

Levin, B. (2010). Leadership for evidence-informed education. *School Leadership & Management, 30*(4), 303–15.

Levin, B. (2010b). Governments and education reform: Some lessons from the last fifty years. *Journal of Education Policy, 25*(6), 739–47.

Levin, B., & Alcorn, W. (2000). Post-secondary education for indigenous peoples. *Adult Learning, 11*(1), 20–5.

Levin, B., & Fullan, M. (2008). Learning about system renewal. *Educational Management, Administration and Leadership, 36*(2), 289–303.

Levin, B., & Riffel, J. (2000). Current and potential school system responses to poverty. *Canadian Public Policy, 26*(2), 188–96.

Levin, B., & Ungerleider, C. (2007). Accountability, funding and school improvement in Canada. In T. Townsend (Ed.), *International handbook of school effectiveness and improvement* (pp. 411–24). Dordrecht: Springer.

Ley, D., & Smith, H.A. (1997). Immigration and poverty in Canadian cities, 1971–1991. *Canadian Journal of Regional Science, 20*(1, 2), 29–48.

Lind, L. (1974). *The learning machine: A hard look at Toronto schools.* Toronto: Anansi Press.

Lindblom, C.E. (1990). *Inquiry and change: The troubled attempt to understand and shape society.* New Haven: Yale University Press.

Lindblom, C.E., & Cohen, D.K. (1979). *Usable knowledge: Social science and social problem solving.* New Haven: Yale University Press.

Lipman, P. (2004). *High stakes education: Inequality, globalization and urban school reform.* New York: RoutledgeFalmer.

Livingstone, D. (2004). *The education-jobs gap: Underemployment or economic democracy.* Toronto: Garamond Press.

Llewellyn, K. (2006). Gendered democracy: Women teachers in post-war Toronto. *Historical Studies in Education, 18,* 11–25.

Lloyd-Ellis, H. (2003). On the impact of inequality on productivity growth in the short and long term: A synthesis. *Canadian Public Policy, 29,* S65–86.

Marchak, P. (1975). *The ideological foundations of Canada.* Toronto: McGraw-Hill Ryerson.

Marlyn, J. (1990). *Under the ribs of death.* Toronto: McClelland & Stewart New Canadian Library.

March, J.G. (1991). Exploration and exploitation in organizational learning. *Organizational Science, 2*(1), 71–87.

Martell, G. (Ed.). (1974). *The politics of the Canadian public school.* Toronto: James, Lewis and Samuel.

Marzano, R. (2003). *What works in schools: Translating research into action.* Alexandria: Association for Supervision and Curriculum Development.

Marzano, R.J. (2007). Leadership and school reform factors. *International Handbook of School Effectiveness and Improvement, 17*(5), 597–614.

Masten, A. (2001). Ordinary magic: Resilience processes in development. *American Psychologist, 56*(3), 227–38.

Mayer, S. (1997). *What money can't buy: Family income and children's life chances.* Cambridge: Harvard University Press.

Mayer, S. (2002). *The influence of parental income on children's outcomes.* Wellington: New Zealand Ministry of Social Development. Retrieved from http://www.msd.govt.nz

Maynes, W. (1993). Child poverty in Canada: Challenges for educational policymakers. *Canadian Review of Social Policy, 32*(1), 1–15.

Maynes, B., & Foster, R. (2000). Educating Canada's urban poor children. *Canadian Journal of Education, 25*(1), 56–61.

McCaskell, T. (2005). *Race to equity: Disrupting educational inequality.* Toronto: Between the Lines.

McLaren, P. (1980). *Cries from the corridor: The new suburban ghettos.* Toronto: Methuen.

McMurtry, R., & Curling, A. (2008). The roots of youth violence (Vol. 2). *Executive summary.* Toronto: Queen's Printer.

Melucci, A. (1989). *Nomads of the present: Social movements and individual needs in contemporary culture.* London: Hutchison Radius.

Micklewright, J. (2003). *Child poverty in English-speaking countries.* Innocenti working paper #94. Florence: UNICEF Innocenti Research Centre. Retrieved from http://www.unicef-icdc.org/cgi-bin/unicef/Lunga.sql?ProductID=354

Mirel, J. (1999). *The rise and fall of an urban school system: Detroit, 1907–1981* (2nd ed.). Ann Arbor: University of Michigan Press.

Morone, J. (1998). *The democratic wish: Popular participation and the limits of American government* (Rev. ed.). New Haven: Yale University Press.

Mortimore, P., & Whitty, G. (2000). Can school improvement overcome the effects of disadvantage? In T. Cox (Ed.), *Combating educational disadvantage* (pp. 156–76). London: Falmer.

Nagle, F. (1975). There's some hope yet. *Interchange, 6*(2), 36–8.

National Council on Welfare. (2006). *Poverty profile, 2002–03*. Ottawa: Author. Retrieved 13 May 2009 from http://www.ncwcnbes.net/documents/researchpublications/ResearchProjects/PovertyProfile/2002-03Report_Summer2006/ReportENG.pdf

Neill, A.S. (1968). *Summerhill*. England: Penguin.

Nelson, F. (1973). Community schools in Toronto: A sign of hope. In T. Morrison & A. Burton (Eds.), *Options: Reforms and alternatives for Canadian education* (pp. 353–60). Toronto: Holt, Rinehart & Winston.

Novgorodsky, M. (2006). The struggle against educational inequality at the Toronto board of education. *Our Schools/Ourselves*, October, 153–8.

O'Connor, A. (2001). *Poverty knowledge: Social science, social policy and the poor in twentieth-century US history*. Princeton: Princeton University Press.

OECD. (1996). *Lifelong learning for all*. Paris: OECD.

OECD. (2000). *From initial education to working life: Making transitions work*. Paris: OECD.

OECD. (2001a). *Knowledge and skills for life: First results from the OECD Programme for International Student Assessment (PISA)*. Paris: OECD.

OECD. (2001b). *Starting strong: Early childhood education and care*. Paris: OECD.

OECD. (2003). *Beyond rhetoric: Adult learning policies and practices*. Paris: OECD.

OECD. (2006). Measures of material deprivation in OECD countries. *OECD Social, employment and migration working papers, 37*, DELSA/ELSA/WD/SEM (2006)6. Paris: OECD.

OECD. (2007a). *Programme for International Student Assessment 2006: Science competencies for tomorrow's world: Vol. 1*. Paris: OECD.

OECD. (2007b). *No more failures: Ten steps to equity in education*. Paris: OECD.

OECD. (2008). *Growing unequal: Income distribution and poverty in OECD countries*. Paris: OECD. Retrieved 13 May 2009 from http://www.oecd.org/dataoecd/44/48/41525292.pdf

OECD. (2009). *Education at a glance*. Paris: OECD.

Office for Standards in Education (OfSTED). (2001). *Education action zones: Commentary on the first six zone inspections, February 2001*. London: HMPO.

Office for Standards in Education (OfSTED). (2003a). *Education action zones: Tackling difficult issues in round 2 zones.* London: OfSTED.

Office for Standards in Education (OfSTED). (2003b). *Excellence in cities and education action zones: Management and impact.* London: Author.

Omidvar, R., & Richmond, T. (2005). Immigrant settlement and social inclusion in Canada. *Working Papers Series,* 1–23.

Ontario Human Rights Commission. (2004). *The Ontario Safe Schools Act: School discipline and discrimination.* Toronto: Author.

Orlikow, L. (1988). The politics of caution: Education in Manitoba NDP government 1981–88. *Our Schools/Ourselves,* 134–41.

Ornstein M. (2006). *Ethno-racial groups in Toronto, 1971–2001: A demographic and socio-economic profile.* Toronto: York University Institute for Social Research. Retrieved from http://www.yorku.ca/isr/download/Ornstein-Ethno-Racial_Groups_in_Toronto_1971-2001.pdf

Osberg, L. (1981). *Economic inequality in Canada.* Toronto: Butterworths.

Osberg, L. (1995, April). *The equity/efficiency trade-off in retrospect.* Working paper 95-04. Dalhousie University, Department of Economics. Retrieved from http://myweb.dal.ca/osberg/classification/articles/academic%20journals/EQUITYEFFICIENCY/EQUITY%20EFFICIENCY.pdf

Osberg, L. (2008). *A quarter century of economic inequality in Canada: 1981–2006.* Ottawa: Canadian Centre for Policy Alternatives.

Payne, C.M. (2008). *So much reform, so little change: The persistence of failure in urban schools.* Cambridge: Harvard Education Press.

Phipps, S., & Lethbridge, L. (2006). *Income and the outcomes of children.* Ottawa: Statistics Canada Analytical Studies Branch Research Paper Series.

Plank, D.N., & Boyd, W. (1994). Anti-politics, education and institutional choice: The flight from democracy. *American Educational Research Journal,* 31(2), 263–81.

Podair, J. (2002). *The strike that changed New York: Blacks, whites and the Ocean Hill-Brownsville crisis.* New Haven: Yale University Press.

Policy Research Initiative. (2005). *Social capital in action: Thematic policy studies.* Ottawa: PRI PH4-26/2005E.

Porter, J. (1965). *The vertical mosaic: An analysis of social class and power in Canada.* Toronto: University of Toronto Press.

Portz, J., Stein, L., & Jones, R. (1999). *City schools and city politics: Institutions and leadership in Pittsburgh, Boston, and St. Louis.* Lawrence: University Press of Kansas.

Putnam, R. (2000). *Bowling alone: The collapse and revival of American community.* New York: Simon & Schuster.

Radwanski, G. (1987). *Ontario study of the relevance of education, and issue of dropouts.* Toronto: Ministry of Education.

Raffo, C., Dyson, A., Gunter, H., Hall, D., Jones, L., & Kalmbouka, A. (2009). *Education and poverty in affluent countries.* New York: Routledge.

Ravitch, D. (2000). *Left back: A century of failed school reforms.* New York: Simon & Schuster.

Ravitch, D. (2010). *The death and life of the great American school system.* New York: Basic Books.

Reville, P. (Ed.). (2007). *A decade of urban school reform: Persistence and progress in the Boston public schools.* Cambridge: Harvard Education Press.

Riffel, J., & Levin, B. (1986). Unsuccessful encounters: Teachers meet researchers in schools. *McGill Journal of Education, 12*(2), 110–18.

Rogers, D. (1968). *110 Livingstone street: Politics and bureaucracy in the New York City school system.* New York: Random House.

Roos, N., Brownell, M., Guevremont, A., Fransoo, R., Levin, B., MacWilliam, L., & Roos, L. (2006). The true story: a population-based perspective on school performance and educational testing. *Canadian Journal of Education, 29*(3), 684–705.

Rothman, L. (2007). Oh Canada! Too many children in poverty for too long. *Education Canada, 47*(4), 49–53.

Rothstein, R. (2004). *Class and schools: Using social, economic and educational reform to close the black-white achievement gap.* New York: Teachers College Press.

Royal Commission on Learning. (1995). *For the love of learning.* Toronto: Government of Ontario.

Rutledge, D. (1988). Institutionalizing change: The problem of a system belief. In M. Lightfoot & N. Martin (Eds.), *The word for teaching is learning: Essays for James Britton.* Oxford: Heineman.

Ryan, B., & Adams, G. (1999). A model of family-school relationships. *Bulletin of the applied research branch, Human Resources Development Canada* (Special edition, Fall, 1999).

Sahlberg, P. (2006). Education reform for raising economic competitiveness. *Journal of Educational Change, 7*(4), 1389–2843.

Schon, D. (1973). *Beyond the stable state: Public and private learning in a changing society.* Harmondsworth: Penguin.

Shipps, D. (1998). Corporate influence on Chicago school reform. In C. Stone (Ed.), *Changing urban education* (pp. 161–83). Lawrence: University Press of Kansas.

Siemiatycki, M., & Isin, E.F. (1997). Immigration, diversity and urban citizenship in Toronto. *Canadian Journal of Regional Science, 20*(1–2), 73–102.

Silver, H., & Silver, P. (1991). *An educational war on poverty.* Cambridge: Cambridge University Press.

Sirin, S. (2005). Socioeconomic status and academic achievement: A meta-analytic review of research. *Review of Educational Research, 75*(3), 417–53.

Sloane-Seale, A., Wallace, L., & Levin, B. (2004). The post-secondary education of disadvantaged adults. In J. Gaskell & K. Rubenson (Eds.), *Educational outcomes for the Canadian workplace: New frameworks for policy and research* (pp. 118–37). Toronto: University of Toronto Press.

Solnicki, J. (1992). *The real me is going to be a shock: A year in the life of a classroom teacher.* Toronto: Lester.

Stanford, J. (2001). The economic consequences of financial inequality. In E. Broadbent (Ed.), *Democratic equality: What went wrong?* (pp. 224–44). Toronto: University of Toronto Press.

Stone, C. (Ed.). (1998). *Changing urban education.* Lawrence: University Press of Kansas.

Stone, C., Henig, J., Jones, B., & Pierannunzi, C. (2001). *Building civic capacity: The politics of reforming urban schools.* Lawrence: University Press of Kansas.

Stone, D. (2002). *The policy paradox: The art of political decision-making* (Rev. Ed.). New York: W.W. Norton & Co.

Thiessen, V. (2007). *The impact of factors on trajectories that lead to a high school diploma and to participation in post-secondary education among those with low reading competencies at age 15.* Ottawa: Human Resources and Skills Development Canada.

Thomson, P. (2002). *Schooling the rustbelt kids: Making the difference in changing times.* Sydney: Allen & Unwin.

Thomson, P. (2007). Making education more equitable: What can policy-makers learn from the Australian disadvantaged schools program? In R. Teese, S. Lamb, & M. Durubellat (Eds.), *International studies in educational inequality, theory and public policy: Vol. 3* (pp. 239–56). Dordrecht: Springer.

Thrupp, M. (1999). *Schools making a difference: Let's be realistic.* Buckingham: Open University Press.

Timperley, H., Wilson, A., Barrar, H., & Fung, I. (2007). *Teacher professional learning and development: Best evidence synthesis iteration.* New Zealand Ministry of Education. Retrieved 13 September 2010 from http://www.education counts.govt.nz/data/assets/pdf_file/0017/16901/TPLandDBESentire.pdf

Troper, H. (2003). Becoming an immigrant city: A history of immigration into Toronto since the Second World War. In P. Anisef & M. Lamphier (Eds.), *The world in a city* (pp. 19–62). Toronto: University of Toronto Press.

Tyack, D. (1974). *One best system: A history of American urban education.* Cambridge: Harvard University Press.

Ungar, M. (2007). The beginnings of resilience: A view across cultures. *Education Canada, 47*(3), 28–32.

Ungerleider, C. (2003). *Failing our kids: How we are ruining our public schools.* Toronto: McClelland and Stewart.

UNICEF. (2007). *Child poverty in perspective: An overview of child well-being in rich countries.* Innocenti Report Card 7. Florence: UNICEF Innocenti Research Centre, Florence.

Volpe, R. (2000). *What have we learned documenting and evaluating school-linked services for children and youth at risk?* Paper presented to the Pan-Canadian Education Research Agenda, Ottawa.

Wilkinson, R., & Pickett, K. (2009). *The spirit level.* London: Allen Lane.

Willms, D. (2003). *Ten hypotheses about socioeconomic gradients and community differences in children's developmental outcomes.* ARB report SP-560-01-03E.

Willms, D. (Ed.). (2002). *Vulnerable children.* Edmonton: University of Alberta Press.

Woolcock, M. (1998). Social capital and economic development: Toward a theoretical synthesis and policy framework. *Theory and Society, 27*(2), 151–208.

Wright, E.N. (1970). *Student's background and its relationship to class and program in school.* Toronto: Board of Education, Research Department.

Yeo, D. (2008). *School division/amalgamation in Manitoba: A case study of public policy decision.* Unpublished doctoral dissertation, University of Manitoba.

Zwarenstein, C. (2002). Toronto alternative schools: Survivors of the common sense revolution. *Canadian Dimension, 36*(1), 20–3.

Index of Names and Organizations